Proceedings of the Third British National Conference on Databases (BNCOD 3)

THE BRITISH COMPUTER SOCIETY WORKSHOP SERIES

EDITOR: P. HAMMERSLEY

The BCS Workshop Series aims to report developments of an advanced technical standard undertaken by members of The British Computer Society through the Society's study groups and conference organisation. The Series should be compulsive reading for all whose work or interest involves computing technology and for both undergraduate and post-graduate students. Volumes in this Series will mirror the quality of papers published in the BSC's technical periodical *The Computer Journal* and range widely across topics in computer hardware, software, applications and management.

Some current titles:

Data Bases: Proceedings of the International Conference 1980
Ed. S. M. Deen and P. Hammersley

Minis, Micros and Terminals for Libraries and Information Services
Ed. Alan Gilchrist

Information Technology for the Eighties BCS '81
Ed. R. D. Parslow

Second International Conference on Databases 1983
Ed. S. M. Deen and P. Hammersley

Research and Development in Information Retrieval
Ed. C. J. van Rijsbergen

Proceedings of the Third British National Conference on Databases (BNCOD 3)
Ed. J. Longstaff

Proceedings of the Third British National Conference on Databases (BNCOD3)

Leeds, 11–13 July 1984

Edited by J. LONGSTAFF
School of Mathematics and Computing, Leeds Polytechnic

Published by
CAMBRIDGE UNIVERSITY PRESS
on behalf of
THE BRITISH COMPUTER SOCIETY
Cambridge
London   New York   New Rochelle
Melbourn   Sydney

Published by the Press Syndicate of the University of Cambridge
The Pitt Building, Trumpington Street, Cambridge CB2 1RP
32 East 57th Street, New York, NY 10022, USA
10 Stamford Road, Oakleigh, Melbourne 3166, Australia

© British Informatics Society Ltd

First published 1984

Printed in Great Britain by the
University Press, Cambridge

Library of Congress catalogue card number: 84–45250

British Library cataloguing in publication data
British National Conference on Databases
(*3rd: 1984: Leeds*)
Proceedings of the Third British National Conference on Databases (BNCOD 3). – (The British Computer Society workshop series)

1. Data base management 2. File organization (Computer science)
I. Title II. Longstaff, J. III. Series
001.64'42   QA76.9.D3

ISBN 0 521 26841 9

Contents

	Organising committees	*page* vi
	Preface	vii
1	Application of relational database and graphics to the molecular sciences *S. J. P. Todd, A. Morffew and J. Burridge*	1
2	Occurrence dependencies, linkages and the structure of a relational database *H. Noble*	15
3	Integrating data and metadata to enhance the user interface *R. G. Johnson*	29
4	Do embedded dependencies always lead to a wild goose chase? *G. Loizou and P. Thanisch*	41
5	A diagrammer for the automatic production of entity type models *P. Feldman*	57
6	An analysis of certain data models with respect to their handling of selected integrity constraints *D. J. Flynn*	71
7	New IDMS design and documentation tools produced for the FEDOS database *G. Loizou and El-S. N. O. El-Shebini*	91
8	Logic as a database language *R. Kowalski*	103
9	HERCULES: database query using natural language fragments *R. N. Cuff*	133

10	The construction of interfaces to triple based databases N. J. Martin	151
11	An approach to interactive definition of database views A. Laender	173
12	A design for an implementation of a runtime system to support dynamic incremented foreground reorganisation of a network database systems A. L. Zorner	187
13	An architecture and language syntax for distributed databases for the network model H. H. Alexander et al.	207
14	The Proteus distributed database system M. P. Atkinson et al.	225
15	The design and implementation of an analyst/programmer training scheme for a large IMS DB/DC user A. T. Wakefield	247

Organising committees

Steering committee

S. M. Dean, University of Aberdeen
M. J. R. Shave, University of Liverpool
P. Hammersley, Middlesex Polytechnic

Programme committee

J. Longstaff, Leeds Polytechnic
M. J. R. Shave, University of Liverpool
P. M. Stocker, University of East Anglia
J. K. Moody, University of Cambridge
J. Roper, University of Durham
P. J. H. King, Birbeck College
T. Brurne, CACS Inc. International
G. Baker, BCS Database Specialist Group
E. Tozer, DMW

Preface

This conference forms part of the BNCOD series of conferences, with the previous conferences being held at the Universities of Cambridge and Bristol in 1981 and 1982 respectively. The BNCOD conferences are mainly concerned with implementation oriented research work in Britain. However the theme of BNCOD3 has been extended in that papers and panel discussions have been included which focus on commercial experience with database software and concepts, in addition to research contributions. The objectives of BNCOD3 are twofold: to encourage database research in the UK by facilitating the dissemination and exchange of new ideas, and to provide a forum in which researchers and users can debate the latest directions in databases. The conference is being organised by Leeds Polytechnic in association with BCS.

The papers for the conference were selected in two stages. An initial selection was made on the basis of submitted abstracts, and then the full papers which had passed the initial selection were each reviewed by at least three members of the Programme Committee. Thirteen papers were finally selected for presentation, and a further five papers were selected for the poster session. There are two invited papers, by Robert Kowalski (Imperial College, University of London), and Stephen Todd (IBM UK Scientific Centre). Two panel discussions have been arranged on the themes of the commercial application of new and emerging database technologies, and education and training of database users. The thirteen selected papers and two invited papers appear in the proceedings in the order of their scheduled presentation.

Among the topics covered in the papers are

Invited Papers
Relational Database/Graphics application (S. Todd, chapter 1)
Aspects of Database language Theory (R. Kowalski, chapter 8)

Selected Paper Sessions
Relational Database (*chapters* 2,3,4)
Application Modelling (*chapters* 5,6,7)
User Friendly Languages (*chapters* 9,10,11)
Distributed Database and Implementation (*chapters* 12,13,14)
User Training (*chapter* 15)

To conclude, I wish to thank all the people who have worked on the organisation of the conference, especially colleagues and research assistants at Leeds Polytechnic. Particular thanks are due to Dr. S.M. Deen, the originater of the BNCOD conferences, for his invaluable help and advice; and also to Mr P. Hammersley and his staff for the considerable work involved in the preparation of the Proceedings. The Programme Committee are to be congratulated for meeting the refereeing deadlines. The sponsorship given to the conference by Honeywell Information Systems is gratefully acknowledged.

Finally, I wish to thank the BCS for giving publicity to the conference.

J. Longstaff
Conference Chairman

Application of Relational Database and Graphics to the Molecular Sciences

Stephen Todd, Andy Morffew and Jane Burridge
IBM United Kingdom Scientific Centre, Athelstan House, St Clement St, Winchester, Hants SO23 9DR

We discuss in this paper the application of database and graphics technology to molecular sciences. We do not survey the whole subject, but take two particular areas, the display of large molecules, and solving problems about large molecules.

We describe the structure of large polypeptide molecules, and how we represent this structure in the database. We give a background to the Winchester Graphics system: with graphics and database subsystems; a bridge for simple display of relational data; and an interactive driver to control system functions and user extensions.

We use the database in the preparation of displays. Simple displays require no more programming than database manipulation and calls to the bridge. More complex displays require user code for fitting and smoothing of idealized shapes to the coordinate data.

We use the database for problem solving. We look at the study of subtilisin for certain features called salt bridges, of interest in genetic engineering. The application relies on the interaction of database, graphics, and an expert genetic engineer.

Our experience of database for this application has been good. Some problems are: exception data; over complex programming needed in the definition of secondary structure pictures; and the problem of saving the work of expert users. We think rule based systems will assist with these problems.

1. Introduction

This paper discusses the role of the database in applications in the molecular sciences. Computer applications in molecular sciences have long been associated with graphics; we also discuss the relationship between graphics and the database. Thus this paper highlights relationships of the database to molecular applications and to graphics. It is not intended to present new results in any of the three areas, nor to give a complete survey of any of them.

Computing has traditionally been used in molecular sciences for discovering the structure of molecules. This involves:

- massive computations in X-ray crystallography to produce a three-dimensional electron density map from X-ray data.
- interactive graphics to create a model of a molecule to fit the electron density map [1].
- optimization computations to improve the results of the interactive graphics.

The results of this work are then presented using a variety of graphical display techniques [2]. This work results in a large volume of data about each molecule. The data is stored in one of two international databanks, the Brookhaven databank [3] for large molecules, and the Cambridge database [4] for small ones. Though these store a large amount of mostly well structured data, they are stored in simple file formats, and are used mainly for collection and dissemination of data rather than analysis of that data. Thus molecular sciences use advanced computation and graphics techniques, but have not used databases as understood by this conference.

Database and graphics have long been accepted as powerful complementary techniques [5,6]. We have combined a powerful problem-solving relational database PRTV (Peterlee Relational Test Vehicle) [7] with three dimensional interactive graphics to produce an interactive system called the Winchester Graphics System (WGS) [8]. The first application of this system has been in the molecular sciences [9]. This is the subject of the rest of this paper, in which we concentrate on large molecules, especially polypeptides.

Section 2 discusses the background: subsection 2.1 is about the structure of molecules, subsection 2.2 is about the structure of WGS. Section 3 discusses how WGS is used to produce a wide variety of pictures from data in the database, and how the database itself simplifies the code for producing these pictures. Section 4 shows how the database is used for more complex problem solving, with the graphics displaying database results. We see section 3 as database support for graphics, and section 4 as graphics assisting in a database problem. Section 5 discusses some of the problems we have had, and suggests rule based extensions to databases as a future requirement. We end with a summary.

2. Background

This section gives background to the paper in two subsections: a discussion of the structure of large molecules, and of the structure of the Winchester Graphics System.

2.1. Structure of large molecules

Molecules may be broadly grouped into small and large. There are many interesting graphics and database aspects of small molecules, for example the use of low cost graphics [10], and information retrieval on structure as opposed to string patterns [11]. These are especially important in the drug industry. To avoid confusion by covering too wide a topic in a single paper, we concentrate on large molecules, especially polypeptides. What we say is easily generalized to most large molecules. Thus in this subsection we discuss the structure of polypeptides, and how this structure is represented in a relational database. For more details on the chemistry, see a standard textbook [12].

Polypeptides consist of chains of standard building blocks, called amino acid residues: residues for short. There are twenty commonly occurring residue types. They all have a similar structure:

```
            O           N    Nitrogen
            !           Ca   alpha Carbon
   -- N -- Ca -- C --   C    Carbon
            !           O    Oxygen
            x           x    a sidechain
```

where the sidechain is a set of connected atoms that varies between residue types. A polypeptide chain is made by connecting the C of one residue to the N of the next: this is called a peptide bond.

As well as peptide bonds, there are other connections between two residues. For example, a disulphide bridge is made where there is a bond between a sulphur atom in the sidechain of one residue and a sulphur atom in the sidechain of another. These disulphide bridges are important because they help a polypeptide keep a stable three dimensional shape.

To understand the structure of a polypeptide, we must know two things.

- The configuration (connectivity, topology) tells us the residue types, and how they are connected.
- The conformation (geometry) tells us the positions of the atoms in space.

Polypeptides also have a higher level of structure, called secondary structure. Successive residues in a polypeptide chain often wrap themselves into a helical shape; or separate sections of chain form into parallel strands to form sheet structures. These secondary structures are more important than the individual atoms and residues for a gross understanding of the way a molecule works. Molecular scientists are beginning to recognize yet higher level features, the supersecondary structure.

We show how we represent the primary structure of a polypeptide by relations. There are two kinds of relations involved, so called dictionary relations that hold information generally true about all polypeptides, and molecule relations that hold information specific to a given polypeptide. The underlying sets are:

- resnum, unique number for each residue in a molecule.
- restype, name for each of the twenty residue types.
- atid, unique identifier for each atom within a residue or residue type. (resnum,atid) identifies any atom.
- atcl, the atom class (element) of an atom. For example both atid 'C' and atid 'Ca' are carbon atoms, atcl 'C'.
- linkdef, defines the circumstances under which a link may be made. There are two kinds of links. Links within a residue (intra-residue links, such as N-Ca) are identified by a linkdef of the name of the residue type. Links between residues (inter-residue links, such as the peptide bond C-N) are given a name of their own. Note especially how these two kinds of linkdef are used in the examples below.
- linktype, defines the type of link, such as a valence bond.
- (x, y, z), spatial coordinate.
- others that vary with the application.

The dictionary relations include:

- LINKS(linkdef, atid1, atid2, linktype, length)
- ATOMDATA(restype, atid, atcl, charge)
- ATOMTYPE(atid, radius, colour)

Molecule relations for a molecule 'XX' are

- XXATOMS(resnum, atid, x, y, z)
- XXRESID(resnum, restype)
- XXLINKS(resnum1, resnum2, linkdef)

LINKS tells which atom types may be joined by a particular link type, and the typical interatomic distance. ATOMDATA tells which atoms are expected in each residue type, and their charge. ATOMTYPE gives the Van der Waals radius and conventional display colour for each atom type. XXATOMS defines the position of each atom, the conformation. XXRESID defines the residue types of which the polypeptide is constructed, and XXLINKS how they are connected.

From these basic relations, we define others in the normal way. For example, a defined relation (view) XXBONDS gives all bonds within molecule XX. It may be defined by the Query By Example queries [13] below: we show the definition of XXINTER and XXINTRA, inter- and intra-residue bonds. XXBONDS is defined by a union of XXINTER with XXINTRA. ' ' is used to denote constants, other names are examples (variables).

```
Define inter-residue links:
    LINKS   | linkdef | atid1   | atid2   | linktype
    --------------------------------------------------
            | PEPTIDE |   C     |   N     | 'BOND'

    XXLINKS | linkdef | resnum1 | resnum2
    -----------------------------------------
            | PEPTIDE |   101   |   102

    XXATOMS | resnum  | atid | x | y | z
    -----------------------------------------
            |  101    |  C   | 1 | 2 | 3
            |  102    |  N   | 4 | 5 | 6

    XXINTER | res1 | atid1 | x1 | y1 | z1 | res2 | atid2 | X2 | y2 | z2
    --------------------------------------------------------------------
            | 101  |   C   |  1 |  2 |  3 | 102  |   N   |  4 |  5 |  6

Derive intra-residue links:
    LINKS   | linkdef | atid1   | atid2   | linktype
    --------------------------------------------------
            |  ALA    |   C     |   O     | 'BOND'

    XXATOMS | resnum  | atid | x | y | z
    -----------------------------------------
            |  101    |  C   | 1 | 2 | 3
            |  101    |  O   | 7 | 8 | 9

    XXRESID | resnum  | restype
    ----------------------------
            |  101    |  ALA

    XXINTRA | res1 | atid1 | x1 | y1 | z1 | res2 | atid2 | X2 | y2 | z2
    --------------------------------------------------------------------
            | 101  |   C   |  1 |  2 |  3 | 101  |   O   |  7 |  8 |  9


                        O
                        |
          -- N -- Ca -- C -- N (of next residue)
                  |
                  x



                        O
                        |
          -- N -- Ca -- C -- OXT
                  |
                  x
```

In this section we have sketched the structure of polypeptides, and shown how this structure is held in a relational database.

2.2.   *Structure of the Winchester Graphics System.*

The Winchester Graphics System (WGS) [8] consists of four major parts: Driver, Database, Graphics Subsystem and Bridge. The user may also write extensions, typically in the interpretive executor (CMS System Product Interpreter REXX) [14] or PL/I. These extensions may perform calculations and call on any of the services of WGS.

The driver accepts user commands, performs prescan, and calls the appropriate routines. The driver may call both system routines and user extensions, and is responsible for interface conventions such as parsing and conversion of parameters to PL/I programs.

The database is the Peterlee Relational Test Vehicle (PRTV) [7]. It holds user relations, and manipulates them by an extended relational algebra.

The graphics subsystem accepts definitions of pictures in three-dimensions by low level calls such as move to (x1,y1,z1), draw a line to (x2,y2,z2). It also allows the user to change his viewpoint for such a picture, and perform manipulations such as rotating one part of the picture relative to the rest. The graphics subsystem provides device independence for a wide range of graphics devices. In some cases three-dimensional viewpoint and manipulation control is implemented in the graphics terminal itself, in other cases within the software of the graphics subsystem.

The graphics subsystem directly supports conventional vector graphics, where a picture is made up of lines, points and text. It also supports, indirectly, solid graphics where objects such as spheres and helices are displayed with full hidden surface and shading.

The bridge supports high level display of data held in relations, by transferring data from a relation to the graphics subsystem. A line drawing is made from a relation with columns (x1,y1,z1,x2,y2,z2). Text annotations may be made from a relation with columns (x,y,z,text). An optional colour column may be included on any relation, and so on. The bridge uses default column names, but alternative column names or constant values may be used as required.

A set of calls to the bridge may be used to superimpose pictures. Thus by suitable preparation of relations in the database and a few calls to the bridge we may set up a very wide variety of pictures. For example, we display a conventional bond picture of molecule XX by using relation XXBONDS defined in the previous section. We superimpose on this a picture derived from a join of XXATOMS with ATOMDATA and ATOMTYPE; this join gives us the positions of the atoms together with their conventional colours that may be used to annotate the bond picture with coloured markers.

The bridge and graphics also have special support for time data [15]. Animations may be made to represent molecular vibrations and other time phenomena by representing model time data stored in the database by display time. Alternatively we may represent model time data by a fourth display space dimension: display on the real screen is implemented by a four to two dimensional projection.

WGS consists of powerful database and graphics facilities, linked into a system by an interactive driver which supports user written extensions. A bridge permits graphical display of relational data without writing special code.

3. Display of molecular pictures

In this section we show how the database supports the graphics in the production of a variety of pictures of molecules. This section and examples will form a major part of the presentation of this paper, but is fairly short in the written version. We consider two types of pictures: those derived from the data in a simple way, and more complex pictures. The simple ones may be implemented by operations within PRTV, followed by one or more calls to the bridge. These are the graphical analog of the typical trivial queries so common in relational database literature. The more complex pictures use the database to prepare the basic data, but then require further processing before graphical presentation.

Most of the simple pictures rely on representation of various links by lines, and atoms or residues by some symbol sited at their positions. These are the geometric pictures. We also may produce more conventional abstract graphs, where the data is not directly derived from the coordinate data but from various properties. We do not discuss these in detail here, as this would require too much description of the underlying chemistry.

Lines may be drawn using

- All bonds, as defined in XXBONDS in section 2.1.
- Just those bonds which lie on the main peptide chain, but not those on the sidechains.
- Virtual bonds, lines between the Ca atoms of residues linked by a peptide bond. Virtual bond displays give less cluttered pictures emphasizing the overall structure rather than the details of each residue.

The point oriented data may be using

- Atoms.
- Residues, using a representative atom such as Ca.
- Residues, using the average atom position.

Point oriented data may have one of several forms

- Single point.
- Marker such as a cross, square or small circle.
- Filled or empty disk, with the size derived from the atom size.
- Text, such as atom or residue type.

We may use combinations of the above.

- Display most of the molecule as a virtual bond display, but with the active site (the 'interesting' part) represented by full bonds.
- Highlight particular atoms: atoms in a given residue; or atoms in a particular class.
- Colour atoms according to conventional colours, or according to their charge.
- Colour bonds according to whether their length is close to the typical length saved in the database.

The variety is endless, and for each display the programming of the database and the bridge is very simple.

All the pictures we have discussed above may be displayed instead using solid graphics rather than vector graphics. The results are more realistic, but processing and display much slower. With thin white cylinders to represent bonds and small coloured spheres to represent atoms, we make a realistic representation of a plastic model of a molecule. In principle, the role of the database is the same regardless of the style of graphics in use: though in WGS the interface to solid graphics is currently less clean than the bridge to vector graphics.

More complicated pictures cannot be produced simply by preparation in the database and calls to the bridge. They are typically pictures used to represent the higher level secondary structure of a molecule [16,17]. Where a helix is formed, we wish to represent it graphically by a helix or cylinder. The atoms do not precisely lie on a helix, so a program is required to fit a helix that is a close match. Similar fitting and smoothing is required for representation of sheets by ruled surfaces, or normal sections of polypeptide chain by splined curves.

A secondary structure picture may well contain a mixture of helices, sheets and splined curves, with atoms displayed by coloured spheres in important parts of the molecule such as the active site. The user program and the database have to collate:

- information about the fine structure on the data (as stored in the relations discussed in section 2.1);
- information about the secondary structure, which parts of the molecule form helices and so on;
- user requirements for the particular picture, which parts are to be displayed how, manner, what colouring is to be used for both secondary and primary features, and so on;
- procedures for fitting graphical objects to coordinates collected above.

In practice the database helps with the storage of the basic data, the better structured data about secondary structure, and its appropriate recovery as required by the user program. We believe that in principle a database should be able to give more assistance by a better understanding of the structure of such problems (see section 6).

We have shown the use of database to support graphics for display of molecular pictures. For simple pictures, a simple bridge routine permits the user easily to define a wide variety of pictures, but for more complex pictures the database provides only basic support. However, the general reaction to people working in the molecular sciences to this use of database is 'So what?'. The pictures we have produced can all be fairly easily produced using special purpose programs. Most of these programs already existed in at least one other system, and often ran faster than our more general programs. We need to look at more complex problems before we gain large benefits from the database approach.

4. Database problem solving

The main advantage we have derived from the application of database to molecular sciences is in the problem solving area. This section describes a single example, the design of a more stable washing powder.

We mentioned in section 2.1 the disulphide bridge, which forms a valence bond between one part of a polypeptide chain and another, thus providing a strong reinforcing brace to the overall structure. There are also weaker cross links, one example is called a salt bridge. Genetic engineers are interested in the possibility of replacing peptide pairs in a molecule that form a salt bridge with an alternative peptide pair that forms a disulphide bridge. If the alternative molecule is feasible, it is likely to be more stable at high temperatures owing to the stronger bridge. One example is the protein subtilisin that may one day be used in biological washing powders.

The rest of this section describes work performed with Prof Hartley FRS of Imperial College, London. He wished to identify potential salt bridges in subtilisin. The basic subtilisin data was already in our database.

A salt bridge may be formed when a positively charged residue lies close in space to a negatively charged one. The first step was the production from the basic subtilisin data of relations of the important atoms in positively and negatively charged residues. This is effectively a simple select. However we needed several attempts at it; it is not universally agreed which atoms are important; at first we got only one atom from each positive residue as required, but several atoms from each negative residue. As soon as we displayed each trial on the graphics, displaying the representative atoms by red and blue markers, it was clear if there was a problem, and fairly clear what alternative to try.

Having prepared these two relations, we viewed them on the display to look for close pairs. We immediately saw that this was better done in the database: we prepared a relation of all complementary pairs closer than a certain distance, and represented that by white lines. We now saw that some residues came close to many of opposite polarity. We thus found for each positive residue the closest negative, and vice versa. There were still cases where one positive had only one closest negative, but several negatives for which it was the closest positive. We had thus three kinds of pairs, which we colour coded:

- mutually closest, white.
- pair where the negative was the closest negative to the positive, but not vice versa, red.
- pair where the positive was the closest positive to the negative, but not vice versa, blue.

Thus the white lines displayed likely salt bridges suitable for replacement by disulphide bonds, and the red and blue lines possible but less likely alternatives.

The next step of this application is the generation in the database of models of the alternative structures. This requires energy calculation programs to find the positions the substituted residues would take up, and the effect this would have on the overall structure. Once the new version of the molecule is created in the database, the problem of probing its properties continues. We have not performed these last steps on WGS.

The final code that builds our pictures contains only 21 lines of calls to the database and the bridge. The important point is that the result was obtained in under half a day with no prior programming for the specific problem. We made many tests that were subsequently rejected. The key is interaction between

- the expert scientist
- the database
- the graphics subsystem.

We have shown in this section a classical application of interactive relational database in problem solving. An important feature is the close link between the database and the graphics. Scientists who were cynical after seeing the use of database for the production of pictures as discussed in section 3, very quickly became converted by this type of application.

5. Problems and future

We have discussed in the previous sections the overall use of the Winchester Graphics System in the support of picture generation and problem solving. We now describe a few of the problems we are facing, and show how we feel that they are leading us to the fashionable requirement for a rule based system integrated with our database.

The first problem is in the basic storage of data. The last residue in a peptide chain is an exception. A typical residue has the structure

For the last residue, the extra bond is made to a terminal oxygen, conventionally named OXT.

However, under these circumstances, both O and OXT have the same properties of charge and so on, but these properties are different from those normally associated with an O. Our current solution is to name them OXT1 and OXT2. This has two disadvantages: the database contains no information that states exactly the consistency rules of when O, OXT1 and OXT2 should be present, and users have to get used to the unconventional names for the terminal atoms.

The correct rules for terminals are easily stated formally. They can be converted to relational algebra definitions, but these are awkward and would probably be inefficient. This is our first example where we would like a rule based system.

Our second example is in the setting up of secondary structure pictures (see the later part of section 3). Again, there is much basic data stored in the database. However, the rules to define what colouring and style should be used in a particular picture are complicated, interconnected by priorities. 'Colour this atom red in this picture' is a high priority rule. 'Carbons are coloured grey' or 'Negatively charged atoms are coloured blue' are lower priority rules, and only one of them can apply to a given atom, though we may require both in different parts of a picture. We currently implement all this with a set of options coded into a fairly complex and limiting program. Again, a rule based system linked with the database should assist in the solution.

The last example comes from the traditional area of expert systems. The washing powder example of section 4 showed how an expert solved one particular problem. Part of the work he did is now encapsulated in programs we have saved, and defined relations we have created. The work could thus easily be repeated for other molecules. However, every time the work is repeated, further exceptions will be found, and changes needed. An expert system is intended to do just that.

6. Summary

We discussed in this paper the application of database and graphics technology in molecular sciences. We did not survey the whole subject, but took two particular areas: the display of large molecules, and solving problems about large molecules.

We began by describing the structure of polypeptides, and how this structure can be represented in a relational database. We gave a background to the Winchester Graphics system: with graphics and database subsystems; a bridge for simple display of relational data; and an interactive driver to control all system functions and to call user extensions.

We described the use of the database in the preparation of displays. Simple displays require no more programming than database manipulation and calls to the bridge. More complex displays require user code for fitting and smoothing idealized shapes to the coordinate data.

The real benefit of the database comes in problem solving. We looked at the study of subtilisin for certain features called salt bridges, where genetic engineering could be used to make more stable alternatives to subtilisin. The application relied on the power of the database, connected with the interaction, the graphics, and most of all relied on the expert genetic engineer.

Our experience using the database for this application has been very good. We still have some problems, exception data, over complex programming needed in the definition of secondary structure pictures, and the problem of saving the work of our expert genetic engineer. We think that rule based expert systems will assist with these types of problems.

References

[1] RJ Feldmann, The design of computer systems for molecular modeling, Annual Review of Biophysics and Bioengineering, Vol 5, pp 477–509, 1977.

[2] NL Max, Computer Representation of Molecular Surfaces, Journal of Molecular Graphics, Vol 2 No 1, pp 8–13, 1984.

[3] FC Bernstein, TF Koetzle, GJB Williams, EF Meyer Jr and M Tasumi, The Brookhaven Protein Databank, Journal of Molecular Biology, Vol 112, pp 535–542, 1977.

[4] FH Allen, SH Bellard, MD Brice, BA Cartwright, A Doubleway, H Higgs, T Hummelink, BG Hummelink-Peters, O Kennard, WDS Motherwell, JA Rodgers and DG Watson, The Cambridge Crystallographic Data Centre: computer based search, retrieval, analysis and display of information, Acta Crystallographica, Vol B35, p 2331, 1979.

[5] D Weller and R Williams, Graphic and relational database support for problem solving, Computer Graphics, Vol 10 No 2, pp 183–189, 1976.

[6] MT Garrett and JD Foley, Graphics Programming using a database system with dependency declarations, ACM Transactions on Graphics, Vol 1 No 2, pp 109–128, 1982.

[7] SJP Todd, The Peterlee Relational Test Vehicle: a technical overview, IBM System Journal, Vol 15 No 4, pp 285–308, 1976.
[8] T Heywood, B Galton, J Gillett, A Morffew, P Quarendon, S Todd and W Wright, The Winchester Graphics System: a technical overview, Proceedings of Eurographics UK 84, in press.
[9] AJ Morffew, SJP Todd and MJ Snelgrove, The use of a relational database for holding molecule data in a molecular graphics system, Computers and Chemistry, Vol 7 No 1, pp 9–16, 1983.
[10] AJ Morffew, SJP Todd, A Low-cost Graphics System for use in the pharmaceutical and related industries, Proceedings of Computer Graphics 84, Anaheim, in press.
[11] J Becker, D Jung, W Kalbfleisch and G Ohnacker, CBF – computer handling of chemical and biological facts, Journal of Chemical Information and Computing Science, Vol 21, pp 111–117, 1981.
[12] RE Dickerson and I Geiss, The Structure and Action of Proteins, Benjamin/Cummings Publishing Company, 1969.
[13] MM Zloof, Query by Example, Proceedings of the National Computer Conference, AFIPS Conference Proceedings, Vol 44, pp 431–438, 1975.
[14] VM/SP System Product Interpreter User's Guide, IBM Manual SC24-5238, 1984.
[15] SJP Todd, Time and Display Style for Applications in Scientific Graphics, in preparation.
[16] AM Lesk and KD Hardman, Computer-Generated Schematic Diagrams of Protein Structures, Science, Vol 216, pp 539–540, 1982.
[17] JM Burridge and SJP Todd, An Interactive Interface for Protein and Secondary Structure Representation, Journal of Molecular Graphics, Vol 2 No 2, to appear, 1984.

Occurrence Dependencies, Linkages and the Structure of a Relational Database

Hugh Noble
School of Mathematical Sciences and Computer Studies,
Robert Gordon's Institute of Technology, St. Andrew's Street,
Aberdeen, AB1 1HG

Occurrence dependencies, or referential integrity constraints, are concerned with the way in which attribute values in a given relation are constrained by the occurrence, or otherwise, of the same attribute values in other relations. These dependencies can be defined conveniently as the properties of a data structure, called here a LINKAGE, which is super-ordinate to relations. In addition, the linkage provides means of implementing functions which process linkages in the same way as the functions of the relational algebra process relations. These new functions therefore process iteratively, groups of tuples which are associated logically. A system is described which embodies these ideas.

1. Introduction

The ideas described here had their origin in an interest in prototyping systems. That is, systems which permit the designers of commercial data prossessing systems to realise their designs quickly and inexpensively in order to check the system logic, the data model and to demonstrate a working system to potential users to obtain approval. The relational model and the relational algebra are a good starting point for the development of such a system [1], and so a small relational database facility has been implemented and runs on our DEC20/50 at RGIT. It is called QIKSYS.

To make it easy for the user of QIKSYS to implement and run tests on a DP system design, it was necessary to provide facilities for the automatic generation of test data. This requirement resulted in QIKSYS having some novel features related to its ability to ensure consistency in the data being generated. In particular it was necessary to control the generation of inter-relation cross-reference codes or OCCURRENCE DEPENDENCIES (ODs). The structures which make this possible have interesting properties and have wider implications.

In Section 2 of this paper the definition of the conceptual schema of a database in QIKSYS is described, with particular reference to the LINKAGE structure which is used to hold information about the occurrence dependencies. A more detailed description of the QIKSYS schema structure has been published elsewhere. [5].

In Section 3 a notation for occurrence dependencies is introduced and this is used to enumerate 20 possible ODs, within the scope of the notation, which can exist between two relations.

Section 4 is a description of how QIKSYS uses the information held in the linkage definition to generate a set of database test data.

In Section 5 we describe briefly how DP application systems can be specified in QIKSYS using an extended relational algebra. We note the existence of applications which cannot be specified in this way.

Section 6 describes current research which aims to exploit the properties of the linkage structure.

2. Conceptual Schemas in QIKSYS

QIKSYS has the common structural elements of the relational model, *attribute*, *tuple* and *relation*.

2.1 Attributes

In QIKSYS an attribute definition is contained in a data structure which stores information about the attribute. This information includes a unique name and a specification of the domain. The domain is specified as a pair of functions, a generator function and a verifier function (a GENVER pair). The generator function will, when called, generate a single valid value (or instance) and the verifier function will verify or validate a potential attribute value (supplied as an argument) and yields a truth value as result. The GENVER pair allows QIKSYS to generate data automatically and also to validate data entered by the keyboard.

2.2 Tuples

A tuple definition is also contained in a data structure. It has a unique name and a list of attribute names which identify the subordinate elements of the tuple. The definition also uses a GENVER pair but in this case these control the inter-relationships on the attribute values within the context of the tuple. For example:

```
ATTRIBUTES-
----------------------------------------------------------------
JOURNEY_CODE = a unique identifier for individual
               train journeys. (J1,J2,J3,...)

STATION      = a unique name which identifies
               railway stations. (S1,S2,...)

ARRIVAL_TIME = a time in 24 hour clock notation.

DEPARTURE_TIME = a time in 24 hour clock notation.
----------------------------------------------------------------
```

```
TUPLE-
-----------------------------------------------------
JOURNEY-CODE  STATION  ARRIVAL_TIME  DEPARTURE_TIME
-----------------------------------------------------
     J1         S1        08.32         08.49
-----------------------------------------------------
```

Viewed as isolated attributes the domains of ARRIVAL–TIME and DEPARTURE–TIME are identical, but within the context of this tuple and its semantic interpretation, we require the additional constraint that

DEPARTURE–TIME < ARRIVAL–TIME.

This constraint is a property of the tuple rather than a property of the attributes, or of the relation or of the database as a whole.

2.3 Relations

A relation definition provides the unique name for the relation and the name of the tuple structure which is subordinate to the relation. There will be only one such tuple structure but there will normally be many tuple values or instances. A relation definition contains a GENVER pair which defines the inter-relationships between data values within the context of the relation (as distinct from the tuple). For example, the same train time-table information could be presented in a complete table of tuples with these additional constraints.

(a) The key-value given by (JOURNEY–CODE,STATION) must be unique within the relation.
(b) The time interval bracketed by arrival and departure times in a given tuple must be disjoint with respect to the time intervals in other tuples associated with the same journey code, (within the relation).

These are examples of constraints which can only be validated with respect to a whole relation.

```
-----------------------------------------------------
JOURNEY_CODE  STATION  ARRIVAL_TIME  DEPARTURE_TIME
-----------------------------------------------------
     J1         S0        -----         08.10
     J1         S1        08.32         08.49
     J1         S2        09.20         09.35
     J1         S3        10.05         -----
-----------------------------------------------------
```

This example also illustrates an interesting requirement for null values and a constraint based on these. (There must be one null arrival and one null departure at the beginning and ending of each journey).

NOTE:
So far we have used only the conventional relational data types. We have introduced the notion of a tuple schema which is distinct from a relation

schema because we wish to distinguish between the contexts of two types of constraint. We note that the data types form a hierarchy and that at each level the constraints defined refer to the data types in the subordinate level. This observation leads directly to the idea that to define the inter-relationships between relations, we need to extend the hierarchy upwards to a level above relation. This level we call the LINKAGE.

2.4 Linkage

A linkage has a unique name and a list of its subordinate relations. It also defines the relationships between these subordinate relations.

The syntax of a linkage definition in QIKSYS is:

NEWLD(<name>,<relation-list>,<constraint-list>);.

Consider for example, the record structure for sales orders shown below:

CUST–CODE = a customers identifier code
ORD–NO = an order number
ORD–DATE = the date of an order
ITEM–CODE = the identifying code of a sock item
QTY = the quantity on order

Record structure

```
------------------------------------------------------------
    CUST_CODE  ORD_DATE  ORD_NO                ITEMS
                                 ITEM_CODE QTY ITEM_CODE QTY
------------------------------------------------------------


------------------------------------------------------------
```

The pair of attributes (ITEM–CODE,QTY) are repeated as often as required.

In a relational database we would normalise this record structure to form two relations

```
         R1                                R2
    ------------------------------     ------------------------
    CUST_CODE  ORD_DATE  ORD_NO        ORD_NO  ITEM_CODE  QTY
    ------------------------------     ------------------------
    .........................          ord-1................
    ....................ord-1          ord-1................
    .........................          ord-1................
    ------------------------------     ------------------------
```

The logical connection between these two relations is maintained by the cross reference ORD–NO and there should exist a 1:N relationship between the two relations with respect to ORD–NO. In QIKSYS we can define this by means of the expression

ONE2N(ORD–NO,R1,R2)

declared as a property of the linkage in which R1 and R2 are both subordinate members.

To define such a linkage the user would type:

NEWLD('LINK1',[R1 R2],[ONE2N(ORD–NO,R1,R2)]);.

The user must then define an example or instance of this linkage with the statement:

NEWLE('FRED',LINK1);.

FRED is now an instance of the LINK1 definition and an appropriate set of files have been created to correspond to the relations which are the constituents of the LINK1 definition.

To summarise, within QIKSYS we have a hierarchy of data structures arranged as shown below

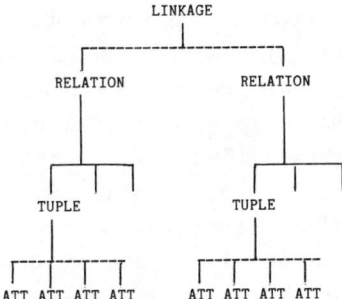

At each level the data structure holds a definition of the inter-relationships between the structural units which are subordinate to it.

3. Occurence Dependencies

Consider two relations R1 and R2 with a common attribute 'A'. Let there be an occurrence dependency such that there is a one:one relationship between the values of A in R1 and the values of A in R2. We denote this relationship thus:

$$A \begin{pmatrix} 1 & 1 \\ 0 & 0 \end{pmatrix} R1, R2$$

This is in fact a small truth table. The left hand column refers to the occurrence of A in R1 (1=occurs, 0=does not occur). The right hand column refers to R2 and indicates that when a value of A occurs in R1 it must occur in R2 (1 1) and when it does not occur in R1 it must not occur in R2 (0 0).

We can extend this notation to allow multiple occurrences

$$A \begin{pmatrix} 1 & N \\ 0 & 0 \end{pmatrix} R1, R2$$

denotes a 1:N relationship. We can also denote 'possible' occurrence thus:

$$A \begin{pmatrix} 1 & 01 \\ 0 & 0 \end{pmatrix}_{R1,R2} \text{ (each A-value in R1 may occur in R2)}$$

or

$$A \begin{pmatrix} 1 & 0N \\ 0 & 0 \end{pmatrix}_{R1,R2} \text{ (each A-value in R1 may occur one or more times in R2)}$$

The notation also suggests that we may have inverse, or negative, occurrence dependencies such as

$$A \begin{pmatrix} 1 & 0 \\ 0 & 1 \end{pmatrix}_{R1,R2}$$

which indicates that if a value occurs in R1 it must not occur in R2 and vice-versa. This looks a little alarming because it seems to give an open-ended committment to the occurrence of all values of A which do not occur in R1 (possibly an infinite set). However, while the domain of an attribute is defined, in the first instance, by its original attribute definition, the actual domain of an attribute when constrained by an occurrence dependency, is redefined by the first relation generated which has that attribute within its schema. In a well structured relational database, the cross referencing attributes will normally be unique codes which form the key of at least one relation. This relation we call the BASE relation for that attribute. If the user defines occurrence dependencies in such a way that all other relations are dependent upon the base relations, QIKSYS will ensure that the base relations are generated first and that all subsequent relations are constrained by the occurrence of values in that base relation. Therefore, the expression

$$A \begin{pmatrix} 1 & 0 \\ 0 & 1 \end{pmatrix}_{R1,R2}$$

should be interpreted in the context of the domain of A being constrained by the existence of a base relation (say R0) so that any values of A not occurring in R1 are still constrained to occur in R0.

The expression above could therefore be re-written as two ODs

$$A \begin{pmatrix} 1 & 01 \\ 0 & 0 \end{pmatrix}_{R0,R1} \quad \text{and} \quad A \begin{pmatrix} 1 & 0 \\ 0 & 1 \end{pmatrix}_{R1,R2}$$

or as one three relation OD

$$A \begin{pmatrix} 1 & \begin{pmatrix} 1 & 0 \\ 0 & 1 \end{pmatrix} \\ 0 & 0 & 0 \end{pmatrix}_{R0,R1,R2}$$

which indicates that any A value which occurs in R0 but does not occur in R1 must occur in R2 while those which occur in R0 and occur in R1 must not occur in R2.

There are 20 possible occurrence dependencies. This can be seen by writing down all permutations allowed by the notation in a matrix. Since only the right hand column varies we can dispense with the left hand column for these purposes and write

lower row	upper row				
	0	1	N	0 1	O N
0	0 0	1 0	N 0	0 1 0	O N 0
1	0 1	1 1	N 1	0 1 1	O N 1
N	0 N	1 N	N N	0 1 N	O N N
0 1	0 0 1	1 0 1	N 0 1	0 1 0 1	O N 0 1
O N	0 O N	1 O N	N O N	0 1 O N	O N O N

There are 25 possibilities here but the diagonal elements do not represent true dependencies because the occurrence in the right hand column is fixed and therefore not dependent upon the value in the left hand column (not shown, but always

$$\binom{1}{0}$$

In its present form QIKSYS provides facilities for defining only the most common of these occurrence dependencies. Of the full set of 20, a few represent conditions which are unlikely to arise in practice, but most correspond to conditions which can arise in the real world and may require representation. For example consider the database consisting of three relations

(EMP) = EMPLOYEES
(SAL) = SALARIED–STAFF
(NON) = NON–SALARIED–STAFF

with a single common attribute E which is a unique employee number. We then have the occurrence dependencies

$$E\begin{pmatrix}1 & 0\,1\\0 & 0\end{pmatrix}_{EMP,SAL}$$

and

$$E\begin{pmatrix}1 & 0\\0 & 1\end{pmatrix}_{SAL,NON}$$

where EMP is the base relation for E.

It is important that a test data generator should be able to create data which conforms to these constraints and it would also be desirable that a database could invalidate any data typed in from a keyboard which did not conform to these dependencies.

4. Data Generation

QIKSYS in its present form does not provide for all of the occurrence dependencies analysed in Section 3. It does provide three of the most commonly required occurrence dependencies:

ONE2N (1:N), ONE2ONE (1:1) and EXISTS.

To create a database and fill it with test data, the user defines:

(a) an appropriate set of attributes and their domains;
(b) a set of tuple-structures which group the attributes and define the constraints upon them;
(c) a set of relations which utilise the tuple-structures and place upon the data values within them particular constraints (such as uniqueness)
(d) a linkage (or linkages) which group the relations and define occurrence dependencies between them.

The user then defines an instance or instances of the linkages definition, thus

NEWLE(<linkage-instance-name>,<linkage-definition-name>);

each linkage instance is identified by its unique name.

Next the user sets a global maximum for the number of tuples to be generated in any file (the relations are implemented as files).

Finally the user types

GENLINK(<linkage-instance-name>,N);

N is an integer which determines the number of tuples to be generated for base relations.

A base relation is one which is not dependent upon any other (with respect to occurrence dependencies) and which can therefore be generated immediately. The occurrence dependencies ONE2N, ONE2ONE and EXISTS indicate clearly the sequence of generation for any pair of relations although the ONE2ONE dependency is reversable. The system scans the list of relations within the linkage and finds the base relations. Data is generated for these. When this is completed the system examines the data in these relations and constructs lists of data values to be used during the generation of dependent relations. These lists are added as additional constraints to the existing constraints for individual relations.

Generation of test data then continues and the process is repeated until all files are filled with test data or until a deadlock is encountered. In a well designed data model such a deadlock should not occur but if it does the user is advised and must modify the occurrence dependency definitions as described in Section 3.

Where a ONE2N occurrence dependency is involved the system will generate between 1 and J tuples for every tuple in the controlling relation. J is a user defined integer. Starting with a base relation size of N this multiplier effect can quickly fill some relations with a large amount of data. For most test purposes very large amounts of data are not required but the global maximum set earlier acts as a safety control.

Having created the test data the system will then examine each file in turn and build an index file for each with respect to the attributes identified in the occurrence dependency definitions. The index files names are stored within the linkage-instance. The linkage-instance structure therefore holds information which assists with the formation of JOINs and other operations to be described later.

5. Specifying Application Prototypes

As was remarked earlier, the relational algebra is a good starting point for the implementation of a prototyping system. Many common data processing requirements can be specified as a sequence of expressions in the relational algebra defined by Codd [2]. In many relational database systems the algebra has been extended to include aggregation functions [3,4], we have done the same in QIKSYS.

QIKSYS includes several additional functions which some of which are shown below. In this list the following notation is used:

Files/relations – R,R1,R2,R3,....
Attribute names – A,A1,A2,A3,....
Sets of one or more attribute names – X,X1,X2,X3,...
Function name – F (LEAST,GREATEST)

The functions are:

INPUT(R) invokes an online dialogue which accepts and validates data for R.

ADDATA(R) is the same as INPUT but the new data is added to the end of the file R.

AMEND(A,R1,X,R2) amends or updates the values of A in R1 using the values of A in R2, having matched the tuples of R1 and R2 with respect to X.

BSELECT(F,X1,X2,R) is a function in which F is a function name (LEAST,GREATEST,..). The function selects one tuple from each batch of tuples in R as determined by the key-breaks in X2 and by applying the function to the values of X1. eg select the supplier with least delivery time for any given part

DBENTRY(R,A1,A2,A3) takes the signed numeric values of A1 in R and creates a new relation with attributes A2 and A3 such that A2 receives the positive values of A1 and A3 receives the negative values. This is useful for double entry accounting reports.

SENTRY(R,A1,A2,A3) the inverse of DBENTRY.

..and many others which generate reports, calculate data values and distribute data values to new attributes. Most of these have been described in one form or another for other systems.

To specify an application prototype, the user must

(a) specify a database model,
(b) generate data to fill the database,
(c) specify a sequence of operations to be carried out on the data, including INPUT and REPORT generation.

The sequence of operations can either be carried out step by step with examination of the result relations at each step, or it can be defined as the function body of a POP2 function which then called. For example, the definition of a BILL of Materials process carried out using a file of orders for ASSEMBLY–UNITS and a file which indicates the numbers of each PART involved in the manufacture of each ASSEMBLY–UNIT requires one natural-join, two projections, two sorts, an EXTEND operation which calculates the value of an attribute given the value of others and two aggregation operations which calculate sub-totals. At each step of the process only simple tuple-by-tuple processing is required.

Most of the traditional batch processing systems can be handled in this way. Where the data to be processed is distributed over several relations, these can often be assembled into a single target relation by means of joins. It should be noted, however that not all applications fall into this simple mould. Those which require the specification of complicated conditional statements, as in payroll applications are not suitable for this treatment because of the variability of processing required. Applications which are concerned with the allocation of some shared resource are also not suitable. The development of techniques for dealing with such applications is the subject of current work.

Occurrence dependencies, linkages and database structure 25

6. Research on the Linkage Structure

6.1 *Current Work*

Consider a small database which contains data about applications by potential students to a college or university.

```
STUDENTS                      QUALIFICATIONS
------------------            ------------------
SNO  NAME   ADDRESS           SNO  SUBJ     GRADE
------------------            ------------------
..................            ..................
S1   smith  dundee            S1   english    a
..................            S1   maths      b
..................            S1   physics    c
..................            ..................
------------------            ------------------

APPLICATIONS                  COURSES
------------------            ------------------
SNO  CRS  OFFER               CRS  CNAME  MAX  CNT
------------------            ------------------
..................            ..................
S1   C1                       C1   BSc    40   10
S1   C2                       C2   BA     50   12
..................            ..................
S2   C1                       ..................
S2   C2
------------------            ------------------
```

where

SNO = student id number
SUBJ = is a school subject
GRADE = the grade achieved
OFFER = the decision concerning an offer of a place
CRS = a course id number
CNAME = the course name
MAX = the maximum number of places on offer
CNT = the count of the number of places currently offered.

In processing this database in order to make offers to students with suitable qualifications, it would be appropriate to process the APPLICATIONs relation tuple-by-tuple. But in doing so it would be necessary to have access to all of the related tuples for a given student and course (to which a given application refers). The tuples which are required are indicated by the occurrence dependencies involving SNO and CRS.

A join operation would create the relation shown below

```
SNO  NAME   ADDRESS  SUBJ      GRADE  CRS  OFFER  CNAME  MAX  CNT
-----------------------------------------------------------------
S1   smith  dundee   english     a    C1   .....  BSc    40   10
S1   smith  dundee   maths       b    C1   .....  BSc    40   10
S1   smith  dundee   physics     c    C1   .....  BSc    40   10
S2   brown  perth    english     b    C1   .....  BSc    40   10
S2   brown  perth    maths       b    C1   .....  BSc    40   10
-----------------------------------------------------------------
```

We could then apply some aggregation function which would produce a composite measure of suitability for the course called SCORE, based on the several qualifications held by each applicant. This would give the relation shown below.

```
SNO NAME  ADDRESS SCORE CRS OFFER CNAME MAX CNT
-----------------------------------------------
S1  smith dundee  5     C1  ..... BSc   40  10
S2  brown perth   3     C1  ..... BSc   40  10
-----------------------------------------------
```

If such a relation is processed tuple-by-tuple each offer of a place on the course C1 will be made in isolation without reference to the fact that other offers may have been made. What is actually required is that every application for course C1 must share a single copy of the COURSE tuple for C1.

```
SNO NAME ADDRESS SCORE OFFER CRS CNAME MAX CNT
-----------------------------------------------
S1  smith dundee  5     .....
                              C1  BSc   40  10
S2  brown perth   3     .....
-----------------------------------------------
```

In this way the COURSE data becomes global to the multiple tuples representing multiple applications. The target data-set must, therefore, consist of collections of tuples which are related logically but are distinct. This requires that the individual files which represent the relation-instances should be indexed with respect to the attributes involved in the occurrence dependencies. A linkage-instance holds exactly this information. What we are then able to implement is a set of functions which accept a linkage-instance name as an argument and which process the set of files iteratively not tuple-by-tuple but linked-tuple-structure by linked-tuple-structure.

The position is complicated, however, by the fact that it is possible to extract from a linkage several different groups of inter-related tuples (which we term LINKED–TUPLES). It is necessary for the user to specify the particular relation within the linkage which is to act as the CONTROL relation. In the example above the control relation is the APPLICATIONS relation. That is, it is the APPLICATIONS relation which must be processed tuple-by-tuple in an iterative fashion, but along with each APPLICATION tuple will be extracted all associated tuples from all other relations in the linkage.

6.2 *Implementation in QIKSYS*

In QIKSYS the physical structure or structures which correspond to a linkage definition is a set of indexed files. Indexing is automatic and the choice of key is determined by the attribute names mentioned in the occurrence dependency definitions. Each file carries its own index tables based on those attributes with which it is cross-referenced to other files in the linkage. In the example above the files corresponding to the relations STUDENTS and QUALIFICATIONS would be indexed on SNO, the COURSES file would be indexed on CRS and the APPLICATIONS file would be indexed on both SNO and CRS. The extraction of a linked tuple is governed by these index tables and by the choice of control relation. Current work is concerned with the indexing arrangements and with a natural language interface to the system which allows users to specify their processing requirements without recourse to a programming language. The natural language input is converted to a set of rules which are then stored as a rule-base within the database (as an additional relation). These rules are then applied to named relations and linkages by means of an APPLYRULE function [6].

Acknowledgements

I would like to thank the governers of RGIT for provision of the computing facilities on which this work was carried out and the Department of Artificial Intelligence, University of Edinburgh, for the POP2 compiler which greatly eased the development work.

References

[1] Codd E.F. Relational Database: a practical foundation for productivity. Comm ACM 25, No 2, pp 109–117 (1982)
[2] Codd E.F. Extending the relational model to capture more meaning. ACM Trans DB Sys. 4, No 4, pp 397–434 (1979)
[3] Gray P.M.D and Bell R. The Use of Boolean Grouping Functions in Relational Algebra. Research report, Dept of Computing Science, University of Aberdeen (1978).
[4] Klug A. Equivalence of Relational Algebra and Relational Calculus query languages having aggregation functions. J.ACM. 29, pp 699–717 (1982).
[5] Noble H. The automatic generation of test data for a relational database. Information Systems 8, No 2, pp 79–86 (1983).
[6] Noble H. On using production rule systems within a relational database. University Computing 6 (1984) (in press).

Integrating Data and Metadata to Enhance the User Interface

Roger G Johnson
Birkbeck College, London University, Malet Street, London
WC1E 7HX

BIDS (Birkbeck Intelligent Database System) is a software system which provides its users with a fuller understanding of the semantics of their data, and so enables them to make more informed use of the data. BIDS provides access to the data, the metadata and rules linking the data and metadata. These components provide the user with a detailed view of his application. This contrasts with conventional systems in which the metadata and validation rules are not normally accessible. BIDS, therefore, offers a significant advance over the facilities offered by existing query language interfaces. In addition to operation in a stand-alone mode, a BIDS database has been installed as the Birkbeck College node of the inter-university Proteus Distributed Database project.

1. Introduction

A fundamental requirement for any database system is that the user can find out easily the contents of the database, and the meaning associated with the stored data. Without this ability a user is unlikely to be able to formulate meaningful queries. This paper describes a software system, BIDS (Birkbeck Intelligent Database System), which provides the user with access through a single integrated interface to data, metadata and rules concerning data and metadata items. BIDS enables the user to obtain an integrated view of all aspects of the semantics of his data. A prototype BIDS database has been used since January 1984 as the Birkbeck College node of the SERC-supported Proteus Distributed Database project. The aim of this project is to build a heterogeneous database system linking seven British universities. The use of the database in this way should provide useful information on the problems experienced by users. This, it is believed, leads to the user formulating more accurate queries, as well as being able to make queries in the previously inaccessible areas of metadata. A number of recent papers have sought to assist with query formulation and processing. Two recent papers have proposed explanatory dialogues with the user [3, 11]. A Prolog database has been used by Futo et al [6] to increase the sophistication of the processing of queries in the complex domain of knowledge of pharmaceutics. However, the system does not assist the user to understand the semantics of the data.

The FACT system at the University of Strathclyde shares a number of features with the system described in this paper [10]. In particular, FACT can store rules about data, 'generic information'. It does not, however, appear to make explicit use of inference. It also concentrates on the problems of query processing and data manipulation rather than those of describing the database structure and semantics to the user. Section 2 of this paper discusses the shortcomings of the information retrieval facilities offered by existing systems. A description of the facilities of BIDS is given in section 3. Its current implementation and some initial conclusions based on its use are described in section 4.

2. Using current systems

2.1 Information content of systems

The traditional DBMS is usually described in two parts. Firstly there are record occurrences containing data and secondly there is metadata describing the organisation of the data in logical and physical formats. However, other valuable information is held elsewhere in systems.

Semantic information about the application is present in most computer programs. A particularly rich source is validation programs. In these programs there are sometimes hundreds of rules concerning the properties, occurrences and interdependence of fields in the database. This information is recorded in the program specifications, but is not otherwise available to users. Further information is held in system documentation. This paper does not consider the integration of system documentation into the online user interface, although the use of dynamic rather than passive data dictionaries, (or information resource managers), may ultimately make that information accessible online [4].

2.2 Query interfaces

The objective of a query interface is to enable 'casual users' to retrieve data in a simple to understand manner. Since the first DBMS appeared in the late 1960's, much work has been carried out on query processing. This has recently been reviewed in [12]. Current database query processors provide very little assistance to the user in understanding the data held in the system. A few, particularly relational systems, provide some simple information about the data, for example a description of the attributes in each relation which can be accessed via the query language. However, this is far short of what the casual user needs.

2.3 Data dictionary interfaces

To give some assistance to users in understanding the data held in the system, some DBMS provide a data dictionary query facility. This allows the user to obtain reports extracted from the contents of the data dictionary. Thus the user can obtain some details of the data structuring in the database. However, in addition to it being a separate function, the user is often required to learn a new language, which may be quite different from the query language.

2.4 Validation rules

Data validation is an essential part of any application system. Validation programs often contain large numbers of rules concerning the data. The rules about the existence, format and value ranges of data items are very useful in understanding the data. Rules concerning the relationships between individual entities and attributes provide users with further descriptive information about the data recorded in the system. Apart from validation programs using table driven techniques, which are unusual in current database practice, the user is totally unable to access information of this type. Although the potential value of this type of information is now starting to be recognised, [4], it is virtually unknown in production systems.

2.5 Current user environments

The situation depicted in fig 1, from the point of view of the end user is a mixture of more and less accessible information.

Fig 1. Architecture of Current Database Systems showing the separate interfaces

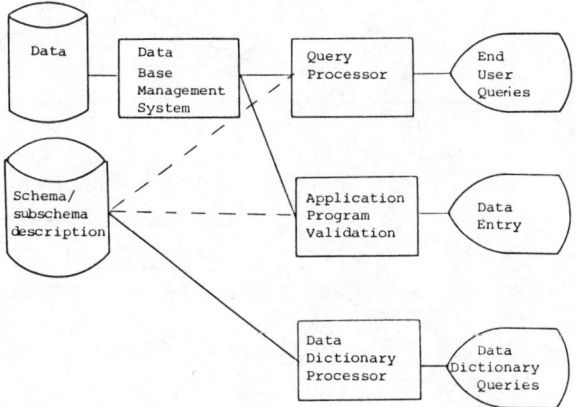

Furthermore the methods of retrieval for the accessible data is very varied. The casual user of the system is, therefore, presented with a range of information that is difficult to obtain and comprehend. It may be compared to pre-database data processing systems, which had no integrated collection of data, and presented the programmer with a range of overlapping and potentially conflicting records and files. As communications develop, so casual use of remote systems is likely to increase. These remote casual users are likely to need much fuller information than currently provided if they are to be able to make full use of the new capabilities. This is discussed further in [7]. In the same way that databases integrated the stored data this paper describes an initial attempt to integrate the users view of data, metadata and consistency rules into one coherent information system.

3. Birkbeck Intelligent Database System (BIDS)

3.1 Overview

The objective of the BIDS project is to provide the casual user with an integrated and intelligent interface to the widest possible range of information about the information held. Firstly, the system provides the user with a view of the system which is essentially a binary relationship model [1]. The example database used throughout this paper is that of a student record system, as shown in fig 2.

Secondly, BIDS allows the user to formulate queries that reference both

Fig 2. A sample BIDS database

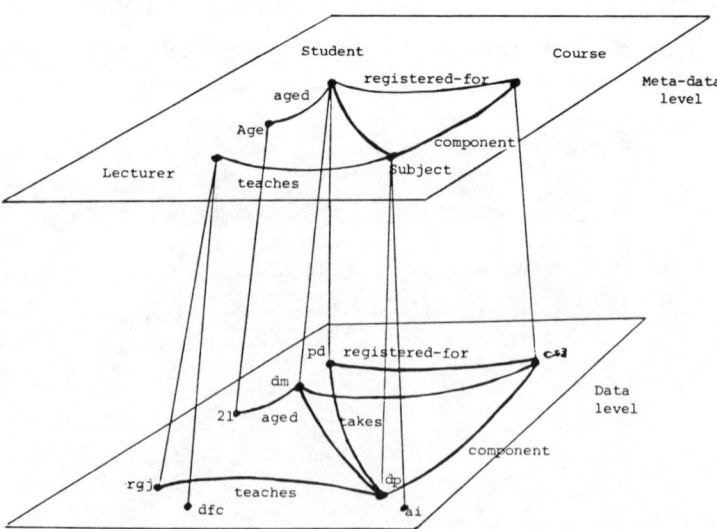

the metadata and data levels. A number of examples of different complexity will demonstrate the facilities. The syntax of the query language is currently being developed. The form shown here is intended to show the facilities provided, but the details are the subject of further work.

3.2 Creating a database

To create the database shown in fig 2 it is necessary to load a series of components into the databasa. The first step is to specify the entities to the system:

```
Entity(STUDENT)
Entity(COURSE)
Entity(LECTURER)
Entity(SUBJECT)
Entity(AGE)
```

The second step is to specify the relationships:

```
Relationship(STUDENT,REGISTERED_FOR,COURSE)
Relationship(SUBJECT,COMPONENT,COURSE)
Relationship(LECTURER,TEACHES,SUBJECT)
Relationship(STUDENT,TAKES,SUBJECT)
Relationship(STUDENT,AGED,AGE)
```

The third stage is to specify the consistency rules. Consider a few examples.

```
A student must be registered for a course
X IS STUDENT IF (X REGISTERED_FOR Y) AND (Y IS COURSE)

A student can take a subject only if that subject is a
component of the course for which he is registered
(X TAKES Y) IF (X REGISTERD_FOR Z)
        AND (Y COMPONENT Z) AND (X IS STUDENT)
```

The final stage is the storing of the occurrences of the entities and relationships.

```
Occurrences of entities

STUDENT(dm)
STUDENT(pd)
LECTURER(dfc)
LECTURER(rgj)
SUBJECT(dp)
SUBJECT(ai)
COURSE(cs3)
COURSE(cs1)

Occurrences of relationships between entities

REGISTERED_FOR(pd,cs3)
REGISTERED_FOR(dm,cs3)
COMPONENT(dp,cs3)
TEACHES(rgj,dp)
AGED(dm,21)
TAKES(pd,dp)
TAKES(dm,dp)
```

Once all the rules and data are loaded, the latter can be validated to ensure that no inconsistent or invalid data has been loaded.

3.3 User facilities

Once the database has been successfully loaded and validated, the user can start querying the information. There now follow some examples of queries, shown in the preliminary version of the language.

```
List all relationships.

Query:    LIST RELATIONSHIP
Results:  STUDENT REGISTERED_FOR COURSE
          SUBJECT COMPONENT COURSE
          LECTURER TEACHES SUBJECT
          STUDENT TAKES SUBJECT
          STUDENT AGED AGE


A request for all relationships involving the entity student.

Query:    LIST RELATIONSHIP ENTITY(STUDENT)
Result:   STUDENT REGISTERED-FOR COURSE
          STUDENT TAKES SUBJECT
          STUDENT AGED AGE


A request for all entities known to the system

Query:    LIST ENTITY
Result:   STUDENT
          COURSE
          LECTURER
          SUBJECT
          AGE


A request for occurrences 'dp' of the entity SUBJECT

Query:    LIST ITEM(dp)
Result:   dp IS SUBJECT            ......(1)
          dm TAKES dp      )
          pd TAKES dp      )       ......(2)
          rgj TEACHES dp   )
```

This example shows a mixture of metadata (1) and data (2) being returned. An unusual aspect of this database is the ability to find out what information is stored about an entity occurrence without obtaining the values.

```
What information is stored about 'pd'?

Query:    LIST RELATIONSHIP ITEM(pd)
Result:   pd IS STUDENT
          pd REGISTERED_FOR COURSE
          pd TAKES SUBJECT
```

This illustrates again the simultaneous use of data and metadata by the user. More traditional queries are readily handled.

```
List all students over 18.

Query:    SELECT ENTITY (STUDENT)
          WHERE (STUDENT AGED AGE) AND AGE>18
Result:   dm


List all lecturers, together with their subjects, who teach 'dm'.

Query:    SELECT ENTITY(LECTURER),ENTITY(SUBJECT)
          WHERE (dm TAKES SUBJECT)
          AND (LECTURER TEACHES SUBJECT)
Result:   rgj    dp
```

3.4 Ad-hoc information

Since the underlying model is a semantic network many of the constraints imposed by other models by the use of record structures are relaxed. In consequence it is very simple to add a new data item to the database. For example, it is possible as shown in fig 3 to add the attribute AGE to one occurrence of the entity STUDENT but not to all occurrences.

Fig 3. Extending the data model

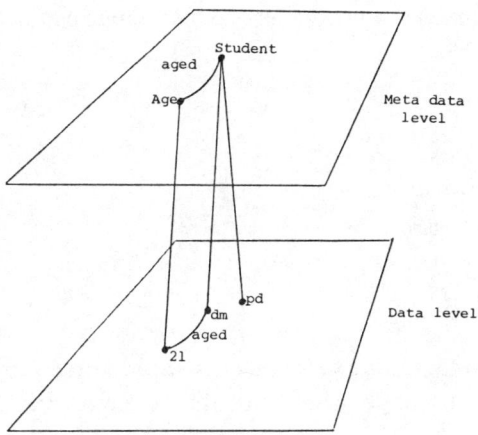

This makes possible the storage of ad-hoc pieces of information. If a piece of information is known about one occurrence of a data item then it can be easily added to the database.

3.5 Aggregation and generalisation

The papers of Smith & Smith [13] on aggregation and generalisation have aroused interest as suggesting an important direction for the next generation of DBMS. The rules facility of BIDS allows the user some facilities of this type. For example, suppose it is decided to generalise the concepts of lecturer and student to that of person. This reflects the existence in the real world of common subsets of attributes which are shared between different entities. In order to incorporate relationships of this type, it is necessary to change the metadata model so that when a user references the entity PERSON the system will recognise that occurrences of PERSON also include the occurrences of LECTURER and STUDENT. This change is shown in fig 4. Further the entity PERSON can be given a relationship LIVES–AT with a new entity ADDRESS.

Fig 4. Meta-data level after inclusion of PERSON

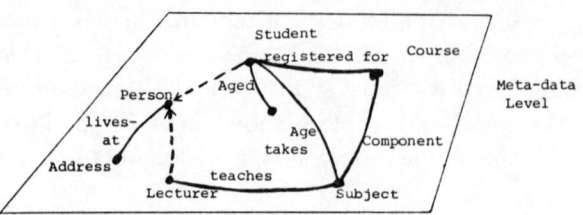

This reflects the real world fact, that both lecturers and students have addresses that can be stored in the system. This change can be made by three simple additions.

```
The new rules are:
X IS PERSON IF X IS STUDENT
X IS PERSON IF X IS LECTURER

The new relationship:
Relationship(PERSON,LIVES_AT,ADDRESS)

Data to populate the new relationship:
LIVES_AT(dm,exeter)
LIVES_AT(rgj,eltham)
```

It is possible, in addition to adding new students and lecturers, to add new PERSON occurrences who are neither students nor lecturers.

```
PERSON(tpj)
LIVES_AT(tpj,woking)
```

If the semantics of the application do not permit this, a new validation rule must be added requiring all persons to be either students or lecturers.

All references in queries to PERSON are understood by BIDS to refer to STUDENT and LECTURER as well.

```
List the name and address of all persons.
Query:   SELECT ENTITY(PERSON),ENTITY(ADDRESS)
         WHERE (PERSON LIVES_AT ADDRESS)
Result:  dm    exeter
         rgj   eltham
         tpj   woking
```

The extension of BIDS to support further facilities in the area of Aggregation and Generalisation is being undertaken.

4. Implementation of BIDS

4.1 Role of Prolog

BIDS is currently written in Prolog [2]. The suitability of Prolog for handling relational databases has been recognised for some time [9].

Prolog consists of a database, and a pattern matcher. The database can store facts and rules. Facts, such as dm is a student are declared to the database. A rule is defined in the database. For example, students and lectureres are people. The pattern matcher can take a 'question', which can be thought of as a part of a fact and search all the stored facts for a successful match or 'answer'. The pattern matcher is sophisticated in that it can divide a question into a series of sub-questions, which if they can be answered will yield an answer to the original question. It can also backtrack through the set of sub-questions and restart using an alternative set of sub-questions. In addition, it has various built-in functions for writing out successful results and listing facts stored in the database.

4.2   Strategy for BIDS

BIDS stores all its data and metadata as PROLOG facts. The validation rules are stored as PROLOG rules. Aggregation is also supported by use of PROLOG rules. Queries are input to PROLOG which interprets themand carries out the appropriate searches of the database, prior to retrieving the answers. At present the query language syntax has been chosen so as to map readily into PROLOG. However, work is being undertaken to improve the syntax of the query language by writing new PROLOG routines.

4.3   Interface to Proteus Distributed Database Project

The Proteus DDB project uses a common network query language. Thus every query entered at each site is translated from that user's local

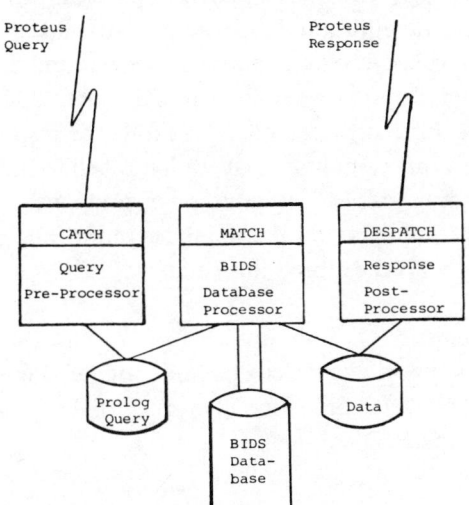

Fig 5. Overview of BIDS DB at Birkbeck Proteus node

querylanguage into the common Proteus Network Query Language (NQL). Requests for data to answer the query are then transmitted to one or more remote sites. When such a request reaches the Birkbeck node, shown in fig 5, it is preprocessed by a Pascal program which generates Prolog assertions.

These are temporarily added to the assertions that form the BIDS database, and the query is then executed. The results are passed to software that adds file headers and other control information, and then returns the results to the querying node.

4.4 *Problems*

The major problems of BIDS is the poor performance of the PROLOG interpreter. This is a well-known difficulty and results from the essentially unstructured storage of facts by PROLOG. Although this leads to poor response times, new versions of PROLOG and potential new hardware architectures should help to overcome these shortcomings. Limitations on memory size also pose limits on the amount of data that can be held in a current PROLOG database. However, although limiting experimental databases, neither of these problems invalidate the conclusions of this paper concerning the contribution of BIDS to the user.

5. Conclusions

This paper has discussed the use of information systems by occasional users. Their difficulties arise mainly from the difficulty in uncovering the structure and semantics of the contents of the database. This paper has described a system which provides more information for the users. In particular, in addition to data, it also makes available metadata and validation rules. The system also supports some features of data abstraction. The BIDS system is implemented in PROLOG so as to support the very general structures needed. This limits the response time, but enhances the system's functionality.   Overall, it is believed that BIDS is a novel system, providing users with features not previously available, and which enable users to understand the database more fully and so to interact more effectively with the stored information.

Acknowledgements

This work was supported by Science and Engineering Research Council grant GR/C/86457. Thanks are also due to Amita Patel for writing software used in the BIDS system.

References

[1] G.Bracchi et al, Binary Logical Associations in Data Modelling, Proc. IFIP Working Conference on Modelling in DBMS, Ed G.M.Nijssen, North Holland, 1976

[2] W.F.Clocksin and C.S.Mellish, Programming in Prolog, Springer-Verlag, 1981

[3] T.Crowe, R.G.Johnson, D.R.Hainline, Query Validation: Reverse translation and the Connection and Selection trap, Proc of 1st British National Conference on Databases, 1981

[4] BCS Data Dictionary Working Party Journal of Development, Summer 1982, British Computer Society, 1982

[5] R.A.Frost, Binary-Relational Storage Structures, Computer Journal, Vol.25, No 3, pp 358–367, August 1982

[6] I.Futo, F.Darnas, P.Szeredi, Applications of Prolog to development of QA and DBM systems, in Logic and Data Bases, ed H.Gallaire and J.Minker, Plenum Press, 1977

[7] R.G.Johnson and M.Agosti, User Views of Distributed Database Systems: The Role of the Data Dictionary, Thames Polytechnic Research Report, CS81-06, 1981

[8] J.J.King, Query Optimisation by Semantic Reasoning, Ph.D. Thesis, Stanford University, Computer Science Dept

[9] R.A.Kowalski, Prolog as a Logic Programming Language, Imperial College, London Research Report No DOC 81/26, July 1981

[10] D.R.MacGregor and J.R.Malone, The FACT Database System, Proc of Symposium on Research and Development in Information Retrieval, Cambridge, Butterworths, 1980

[11] P.Massey, J.Longstaff, C.K.Lam, Inferential Feedback for DBMS User Interfaces, Proc of 2nd British National Conference on Databases, Bristol, 1982

[12] P.Reisner, Human Factors Studies of Database Query Languages: A Survey and Assessment, ACM Computing Surveys, Vol 13, No 1, pp13–31, Mar 1981

[13] J.M.Smith and D.C.P.Smith, Database Abstractions: Aggregation and Generalisation, ACM Trans on Database Systems, Vol 2, No 2, pp105–133, Jun 1977

Do Embedded Dependencies Always Lead to a Wild Goose Chase?

G. Loizou* and P. Thanisch**
* Department of Computer Science, Birkbeck College, University of London, Malet Street, London, WC1E 7HX
**Royal Observatory, Blackford Hill, Edinburgh, EH9 3HJ

The negative results associated with the inference problem for Embedded Multivalued Dependencies (EMVDs) have led researchers to adopt strategies such as pretending that EMVDs do not exist. Herein, we partially rehabilitate EMVDs by establishing the following results: (i) Certain categories of EMVDs can be incorporated into a modified Chase procedure with no loss of efficiency. The resulting modified Chase algorithm, which terminates in polynomial time, can detect the lossless join property whenever the decomposition has certain desirable properties that are similar to the properties of an acyclic database scheme. (ii) We present a lossless Fourth Normal Form (4NF) decomposition algorithm that takes into account projected EMVDs. This algorithm is just as efficient as existing algorithms that only take into account full MVDs (FMVDs).

1. Introduction

Given a decomposition scheme, ρ, for a universal attribute set, $\mathbf{R}$, with a data dependency set, D, the database designer may find it useful to know if ρ has the lossless join property [1] with respect to D. Although a procedure – known as the 'Chase' [11] – tests for this property, if D contains some MVDs (multivalued dependencies), the database designer could be out of luck, as in this case, the Chase has worst-case time and space requirements that are exponential functions of the size of D and ρ [3]. If D contains EMVDs, the database designer's problems are even worse, as the Chase will not necessarily terminate [10]. In Section 2 we present a modified Chase procedure, called ECHASE, that can detect the lossless join property, given a set, F, of FDs (functional dependencies) and a set, D, of FMVDs and EMVDs, for most sensible decomposition schemes. ECHASE has worst-case time and space requirements that are polynomial functions of the size of D and ρ. It should be noted that ECHASE is an extension and generalisation of the algorithms in [9]. The database designer may also have problems finding a lossless join 4NF decomposition when D contains EMVDs. In the following example, no such decomposition exists. **Example 1** Let R = {Course,Student,Prerequisite,Year} and let D = {{Course} $\twoheadrightarrow$) {Student} | {Prerequisite}}. R is not in 4NF, since a non–trivial MVD holds in it, yet there is no lossless decomposition of R. □

A further problem is that there is, as yet, no known algorithm for deciding whether or not a non-trivial EMVD holds in an attribute set, and recent results in this area give no grounds for optimism (see, for example, [12, 13]). Despite this, decomposing as far as possible with respect to any EMVDs that we can detect will still reduce the anomalies described in [10]. In Section 3 we apply ECHASE in a new 4NF decomposition algorithm, LJ4NF. Unlike its predecessors (see, for example, [2, 5]), LJ4NF does not compute large intermediate sets and, in addition, can normalise with respect to certain EMVDs. For example, referring back to Example 1, if we add to D the MVD {Student,Prerequisite} $\twoheadrightarrow$ {Year} | {Course} then the lossless 4NF decomposition algorithms in [2, 5] will be able to decompose R into ρ = {{Student,Prerequisite,Year}, {Course,Student,Prerequisite}}. ρ is not, however, in 4NF since the dependency {Course} $\twoheadrightarrow$ {Student} | {Prerequisite} holds non-trivially in {Course,Student,Prerequisite}. On the other hand, LJ4NF will use the EMVD {Course} $\twoheadrightarrow$ {Student} | {Prerequisite} to decompose ρ into ρ' = {{Student,Prerequisite,Year}, {Course,Student}, {Course,Prerequisite}}. Finally, we observe that even if the set of FMVDs (full MVDs; [9]) in most real-world applications are such that an acyclic database scheme [10] can be found, this does not preclude the existence of EMVDs. Thus a version of LJ4NF could usefully be incorporated into the more restricted 4NF decomposition algorithms that only work for conflict-free sets of MVDs; see [7, 8, 14].

In the sequel, we use the notation and terminology found in [15] wherever possible. We also refer the reader to [10, 15] for tutorial descriptions of dependency theory and the Chase.

2. The ECHASE Procedure

2.1 *A Description of ECHASE*

We use a tableau, T, in the same way as the Chase procedure [11]. In order to make the relationship between attributes and tableau column numbers more straightforward, we represent the attribute set, R, by the integers 1 to k, ie R = {1,2,...,k}.

T is initialised as in [1]. T[i,j] refers to the symbol in row i and column j of T. Similarly, if $X \subseteq R$, T[i,X] denotes the tuple of symbols occurring in the X-columns of row i. Each symbol can only occur in cells in one particular column of T; thus when describing a tuple, say g, generated by an application of the J-rule [11] to rows h and i of T using an FMVD X $\twoheadrightarrow$ Y | Z, we use the notation: h[X]h[Y]i[Z]. When referring to the tuple of symbols T[i,X], we may also use the notation 'a——a' to denote that T[i,X] comprises all 'a' symbols, 'b——b' to denote that T[i,X] comprises all 'b' symbols and 'b–u–b' to denote that T[i,X] comprises only unique 'b' symbols.

Apart from the pseudo-ALGOL code given below, we give the following informal description of three of the functions used by ECHASE:

(a) T[i,S] *subsumes* T[h,S] is true if for rows i and h and attribute set, S, for each j ∈ S such that T[i,j] ≠ T[h,j], T[h,j] contains a unique 'b' symbol.
(b) Match(h,i) is the set of columns in T for which rows h and i have identical entries.
(c) Attr(i) is the set of columns in T in which row i contains an 'a' symbol.

INPUT: The input to ECHASE is an ASC (attribute set collection), ρ, a set, F, of FDs and a set, D = M ∪ E, of MVDs, where M comprises FMVDs and E comprises EMVDs. We let m = $|\rho|$ and as we have seen, k = $|R|$. The FDs are assumed to have single right-hand side attributes.

OUTPUT: The output is a message which says whether or not ECHASE has detected the lossless join property in ρ. (There are lossless ASCs for which ECHASE will be unable to detect this property.)

METHOD: ECHASE is similar to the Chase procedure, except that it does not let the tableau expand. Instead, it checks to see if a generated tuple has made redundant (for the purposes of the Chase) one of the pair of matching rows in the tableau and, if so, replaces the contents of the redundant row with the generated tuple.

T is initialised from ρ and passed to ECHASE, which repeatedly calls INSERT–A and ELIMINATE–B until an iteration occurs in which no changes are made to T. ECHASE returns T to the calling program which checks T for the 'winning' row of 'a' symbols that shows the join to be lossless [11].

Procedure INSERT–A attempts to generate a tuple, say g, from a match involving a pair of rows, numbered h and i, such that Attr(h) is properly contained in Attr(g); in this case, tuple g replaces the contents of row h in T. INSERT–A attempts to replace 'b' symbols with 'a' symbols. It will do this even though it may overwrite non-unique 'b' symbols with new unique 'b' symbols in the columns of T that correspond to attributes outside the context of the EMVD used for the match. (Such new 'b' symbols are generated as a consequence of using EMVDs in the Chase.)

Procedure ELIMINATE–B takes as input D and T (as changed by INSERT–A). It attempts to change T by using an FD with the standard F-rule [11] in order to eliminate a 'b' symbol. ELIMINATE–B will also use an MVD to match a pair, h and i, of rows in T so long as rows h and i contain only unique 'b' symbols in all the columns of T corresponding to attributes that are outside the context of the MVD used. If one of the generated tuples subsumes one of the matching rows, the contents of the row are, in effect, replaced by the generated tuple. ELIMINATE–B may replace a 'b' symbol with either an 'a' symbol or an existing 'b' symbol.

Assuming that $R = \cup R_i, i = 1, 2, ..., m$, then the following fragment of pseudo-ALGOL code initialises T and calls ECHASE:

```
for i := 1, m do
   for j := 1, k do
      if j ∈ R_i then
         T[i,j] := a_j
      else
         T[i,j] := b_{ij}
      fi
   od
od
T := ECHASE(T);
if some row of T contains all 'a' symbols then
   print 'It is lossless'
else
   print 'Losslessness has not been detected'
fi
```

We now give the pseudo-ALGOL code for ECHASE and the procedures INSERT–A and ELIMINATE–B:

```
1   function ECHASE(T);
2   repeat
3      T' := T;
4      INSERT–A;
5      ELIMINATE–B
6   until T' = T;
7   return(T);
8   end ECHASE;
```

```
9   procedure INSERT-A;
10  for each ordered pair, (h,i), of distinct row numbers in T do
11     for each X ↠ Y | Z ∈ D do
12        if (X ⊆ Match(h,i)) and (Attr(h) ⊆ XYZ) then
13           X' := XYZ ∩ Match(h,i);
14           $Y_h$ := (Y ∩ Attr(h)) - X';
15           $Y_i$ := (Y ∩ Attr(i)) - X';
16           $Z_h$ := (Z ∩ Attr(h)) - X';
17           $Z_i$ := (Z ∩ Attr(i)) - X';
18           R' := R - (X'$Y_h Y_i Z_h Z_i$);
19           if $Y_h$ = φ and $Y_i$ ≠ φ then
20              T[h,$Y_i$] := a——a;
21              T[h,R'] := b-u-b
22           fi
23           if $Z_h$ = φ and $Z_i$ ≠ φ then
24              T[h,$Z_i$] := a——a;
25              T[h,R'] := b-u-b
26           fi
27        fi
28     od
29  od
30  end INSERT-A;

31  procedure ELIMINATE-B;
32  for each ordered pair, (h,i), of distinct row numbers in T do
33     for each X → j ∈ F do
34        if X ⊆ Match(h,i) and {j} ⊈ Match(h,i) then
35           if T[h,j] = $a_j$ then
36              newsymbol := T[h,j];
37              oldsymbol := T[i,j]
38           else
39              newsymbol := T[i,j];
40              oldsymbol := T[h,j]
41           fi
42           comment Replace all occurrences of oldsymbol with newsymbol;
43           for g = 1, m do
44              if T[g,j] = oldsymbol then
45                 T[g,j] := newsymbol
46              fi
```

```
47          od
48        fi
49      od
50      comment Check if the contents of rows h and i match for an MVD;
51      for each X ↠ Y | Z ∈ M ∪ E such that X ⊆ Match(h,i) do
52        if (R − XYZ = φ) or (T[h,R − XYZ] = b−u−b) then
53          if T[i,Y] subsumes T[h,Y] then
54            T[h,Y] := T[i,Y]
55          fi
56          if T[i,Z] subsumes T[h,Z] then
57            T[h,Z] := T[i,Z]
58          fi
59        fi
60      od
61    od
62  end ELIMINATE−B;
```

2.2 *A Partial Correctness Proof for ECHASE*

The following lemma justifies the use of the EMVD $X' \twoheadrightarrow Y_h Y_i \mid Z_h Z_i$ in INSERT−A.

Lemma 1 Each EMVD generated by INSERT−A is implied by D.

Proof Let $X \twoheadrightarrow Y \mid Z$ (XYZ) be the EMVD selected on line 11 and suppose that the condition on line 12 evaluates to true. Lines 13 to 17 ensure that $X'Y_h Y_i Z_h Z_i \subseteq XYZ$; lines 14 and 15 ensure that $Y_h Y_i \subseteq Y$. Similarly, lines 16 and 17 ensure that $Z_h Z_i \subseteq Z$. Line 13 ensures that $X \subseteq X' \subseteq XYZ$. Thus, by using the MVD augmentation axiom [12] in the fixed context XYZ, we obtain:

$$\{X \twoheadrightarrow Y \mid Z \, (XYZ)\} \therefore X' \twoheadrightarrow Y \mid Z \, (XYZ).$$

By the EMVD projection inference rule [12], it follows that:

$$\{X' \twoheadrightarrow Y \mid Z \, (XYZ)\}$$
$$\therefore X' \twoheadrightarrow Y_h Y_i \mid Z_h Z_i \, (R - R'),$$

where $R' = R - (X'Y_h Y_i Z_h Z_i)$. □

The following lemma justifies the assignment of 'a' symbols in INSERT−A.

Lemma 2 Let T' denote the state of T as returned by ECHASE. Then for each row, i, of T', the Chase procedure will eventually generate a row with 'a' symbols in a set of columns that contains Attr(i).

Proof Lemma 1 shows that $X' \twoheadrightarrow Y_h Y_i \mid Z_h Z_i \in E^+$. By inspecting lines 13 to 18 it can be seen that the attribute sets X', Y_h, Y_i, Z_h, Z_i and R'

form a partition of R. The E-rule for EMVDs [6] would generate the rows g_1 and g_2 from rows h and i thus:

```
       X'      Yh      Yi      Zh      Zi      R'
       --      --      --      --      --      --
h:   h[X']   a---a   b---b   a---a   b---b   h[R']
i:   h[X']   b---b   a---a   b---b   a---a   i[R']
g1:  h[X']   a---a   b---b   b---b   a---a   b-u-b
g2:  h[X']   b---b   a---a   a---a   b---b   b-u-b
```

Thus, if $Y_h = \phi$ then Attr(h) $\subseteq$ Attr(g_2) and if $Z_h = \phi$ then Attr(h) $\subseteq$ Attr(g_1). INSERT–A puts new unique 'b' symbols in the columns R' so that no illegal combinations of 'a' and 'b' symbols are generated.

Lines 33 to 49 in ELIMINATE–B just implement the F-rule. The condition in line 52 of ELIMINATE–B ensures that if the dependency used is not an FMVD then the row, h, that matches row i has unique 'b' symbols in the columns outside the context of $X \twoheadrightarrow Y \mid Z$. □

A full correctness proof for ECHASE can be constructed using techniques similar to those in [9]. However, the technical details are very tedious so we omit them herein. These results will be published elsewhere.

Lemma 3 The time complexity of ECHASE is polynomial in the size of the input.

Proof Every time the repeat loop on line 2 is executed, T either has a smaller number of different 'b' symbols or a larger number of its cells occupied by 'a' symbols; thus the number of iterations of this loop is bounded by the size of T, ie mk. Since the repeat loop above is executed in polynomial time, it follows that ECHASE has polynomial time complexity □

2.3 Examples

Example 2 In [3] there is a proof that the problem of detecting losslessness in the presence of MVDs is at least as hard as the Travelling Salesman Problem. The example used to illustrate that proof is also an example of where the ordinary Chase procedure can detect losslessness (eventually!), yet ECHASE will fail to detect losslessness. □

Next, we give an example where ECHASE detects the lossless join property in a decomposition, yet the ordinary Chase procedure may not terminate. (Since any particular 'a' or 'b' symbols in T can only occur in one particular column, we simplify the presentation of the contents of T by representing 'a' symbols with zeros and 'b' symbols with non-zero integers.)

```
Example 3   R = {1,2,3,4,5,6},
            ρ = {{1,2,3}, {1,4}, {2,5,6}},
            E = {E1,E2,E3} and
            M = {M1,M2}, where
            E1 = {1} ↠ {5} | {6},
            E2 = {1} ↠ {6} | {2},
            E3 = {2} ↠ {3} | {5,6},
            M1 = {2,3} ↠ {5,6} | {1,4},
            M2 = {1} ↠ {4} | {2,3,5,6}.
```

The tableau for the ordinary Chase procedure may start off as follows:

```
     1 2 3 4 5 6
     -----------
1:   0 0 0 1 1 1
2:   0 2 2 0 2 2
3:   3 0 3 3 0 0
4:   0 4 4 4 1 2  ⎫
5:   0 5 5 5 2 1  ⎭   Rows 1 and 2 match for E₁
6:   0 5 6 6 6 2  ⎫
7:   0 4 7 7 7 1  ⎭   Rows 4 and 5 match for E₂
8:   0 8 8 8 6 1  ⎫
9:   0 9 9 9 7 2  ⎭   Rows 6 and 7 match for E₁
```

and so on, perhaps ad infinitum.

With ECHASE, rows 1 and 3 match for E_3 generating a tuple, 3', that subsumes row 3. Also, rows 1 and 2 match for M_2 generating a tuple, 1', that subsumes rows 1 and 2. At this stage, the contents of T includes the following rows:

```
      1 2 3 4 5 6
      -----------
1':   0 0 0 0 5 5
3':   4 0 0 4 0 0
```

Rows 1' and 3' match for M_1, generating the winning row.

3. The 4NF Decomposition Algorithm

We now use ECHASE in a novel 4NF decomposition algorithm, called LJ4NF. In [5], Grahne and Räihä describe the shortcomings of several published 4NF lossless decomposition algorithms. Two of the algorithms, viz those of Lien [7, 8] and Sciore [14], only work for conflict-free sets of FMVDs. Two other algorithms that work for an arbitrary set of FMVDs, M, and produce lossless 4NF decompositions with respect M^+, are those of Fagin [2] and Grahne and Räihä [5]. Both of these algorithms involve the generation of intermediate sets that could be much larger than the size of the ASC representing the decomposition; moreover, neither of these algorithms takes into account EMVDs. Fagin's algorithm requires that M^+ be computed; the size of this set can be an exponential function in the size of M. Grahne and Räihä's algorithm computes a potentially large collection of attribute sets which are lhs's (left-hand sides) of dependencies in M^+ that may be useful in the decomposition process.

In contrast, LJ4NF does not compute any such large intermediate sets. It checks if any non-trivial FMVDs hold in an attribute set, W, and if so

Embedded dependencies: a wild goose chase?

it finds an FMVD, $X \twoheadrightarrow Y$, that can decompose W into $XY \cap W$ and $X \cup (W - Y)$. An unlucky choice of FMVDs could result in an exponentially large number of decomposition steps, so in order to ameliorate this problem, we have incorporated 4 'clever' features in LJ4NF:

(a) When LJ4NF decomposes W, it selects an FMVD with an lhs, V', such that no FMVD which is non-trivial in W has an lhs that is a proper subset of V'.
(b) When a set, V, is found to be in 4NF, further attributes are added to V until no proper superset of V is in 4NF.
(c) When an attribute set, W, is added to ρ, a row representing W is added to T and ECHASE(T) is computed. LJ4NF halts as soon as ECHASE generates a row of 'a' symbols.
(d) When an attribute set, W, is about to be added to ρ, the tableau, T, is checked. If T contains some row, i, such that $W \subseteq Attr(i)$ then W need not be added to ρ and need not be further decomposed.

In the description of LJ4NF, we refer to a function, BASIS, that returns the dependency basis of an attribute set with respect to M. The dependency basis algorithm used is that in [4]. In order to simplify the presentation of LJ4NF, we assume that the set, F, of FDs is empty.

INPUT: An attribute set, R, and a dependency set $D = M \cup E$, where M comprises FMVDs and E comprises EMVDs.

OUTPUT: A lossless decomposition, ρ, of R that is in 4NF with respect to M (and possibly some of the EMVDs in E, too).

METHOD: LJ4NF picks an FMVD to start the decomposition process, calling procedure DECOMPOSE. DECOMPOSE checks whether V, the attribute set it has been passed, is in 4NF with respect to M. If it is not, it picks an FMVD that is non-trivial in V and uses this FMVD to decompose V. If V is in 4NF with respect to M, procedure EMB–SPLITTER is called to attempt to break down V further using an EMVD whose context contains V. These subsets of V are then added to ρ, and ECHASE is executed in order to see if attribute sets added to ρ so far are sufficient to make ρ a lossless decomposition.

procedure LJ4NF(R,D,ρ);
$\rho := \phi$;
$T := \phi$;
$X :=$ an element of LHS(M) (the set of lhs's in M) with minimum cardinality;

```
for each Y ∈ BASIS(X) do
  if not COVERED(XY) then
    DECOMPOSE(XY)
  fi
od
end LJ4NF;

procedure DECOMPOSE(V);
if FOURNF(V) then
  EXPAND(V);
  EMB-SPLITTER(V,Vsplit);
  for each W ∈ Vsplit do
    if not COVERED(W) then
      ρ := ρ ∪ {W};
      Add ROW(W) to T;
      T := ECHASE(T)
    fi
  od
  if not COVERED(V) then
    Add ROW(V) to T;
    T := ECHASE(T)
  fi
else
  V' := MINIROOT(V);
  for each B ∈ BASIS(V') do
    B' := B ∩ V ;
    if B' ≠ φ and not COVERED(V'B') then
      DECOMPOSE(V'B')
    fi
  od
fi
end DECOMPOSE;

Boolean function COVERED(V);
for each row i ∈ T do
  if V ⊆ Attr(i) then
    return(true)
  fi
od
return(false);
end COVERED;
```

Boolean function FOURNF(V);
for each pair of distinct attributes h,i ∈ V **do**
   V' := V − {h,i};
   if BLOCK(V',h) ≠ BLOCK(V',i) **then**
     return(false)
   fi
od
return(true);
end FOURNF;

function EXPAND(V);
comment Given a 4NF scheme, V, attempt to add attributes to V whilst keeping V in 4NF. No superset of the returned set, V', is in 4NF;
V' := V;
for each i ∈ R − V **do**
   if FOURNF(V' ∪ {i}) **then**
     V' := V' ∪ {i}
   fi
od
return(V');
end EXPAND;

function MINIROOT(V);
comment Return a subset, V', of V such that no proper subset of V' forms the lhs of a non-trivial MVD holding in the context V;
mincard := |V|;
minset := V;
for each pair h,i of distinct attributes in V **do**
   V' := V − {h,i};
   if BLOCK(V',h) ≠ BLOCK(V',i) **then**
     for each j ∈ V' **do**
        V‘ := V' − {j};
        if BLOCK(V‘,h) ≠ BLOCK(V‘,i) **then**
           V' := V‘
        fi
     od
     if |V'| © mincard **then**
        mincard := |V'|;
        minset := V'
     fi

```
      fi
    od
    comment Ensure that no subset of minset splits V;
    for each j ∈ minset do
       W := minset - {j};
       if V - W has a non-empty intersection with two or more blocks in
    BASIS(W)
         then
            minset := minset - {j}
       fi
    od
    return(minset);
    end MINIROOT;


    function BLOCK(V,j);
    comment Return the block in BASIS(V) that contains the attribute j;
    for each B ∈ BASIS(V) do
       if j ∈ B then
          return(B)
       fi
    od
    end BLOCK;


    function ROW(V);
    comment Initialise a new tableau row from attribute set V;
    array Symbsct[1:k];
    comment Set the value of i so as to ensure that 'b' symbols are unique;
    i := (the number of rows in T) + 1;
    for j = 1, k do
       if j ∈ V then
          Symbset[j] := $a_j$
       else
          Symbset[j] := $b_{ij}$
       fi
    od
    return(Symbset);
    end ROW;


    procedure EMB-SPLITTER(V,Vsplit);
    comment Use the EMVDs in E to normalise V into an ASC, Vsplit;
    Vsplit := {V};
```

```
repeat
  Vsplit' := Vsplit;
  for each EMVD X →→ Y | Z ∈ E do
    for each W ∈ Vsplit' do
      if X ⊂ W and W ⊆ XYZ then
        Y' := W ∩ Y;
        Z' := W ∩ Z;
        if Y' ≠ φ and Z' ≠ φ then
          Vsplit := Vsplit − {W};
          Vsplit := Vsplit ∪ {XY',XZ'}
        fi
      fi
    od
  od
until Vsplit' = Vsplit;
end EMB–SPLITTER;
```

3.2 Partial Correctness Proof for LJ4NF

Lemma 4 Procedure LJ4NF halts.

Proof Procedure LJ4NF calls DECOMPOSE once for each element in the dependency basis of the lhs of an FMVD in M; there can be no more than k such elements. Moreover, whenever DECOMPOSE calls itself recursively, the argument it passes, V'B', is always a proper subset of the argument, V, that it has been passed. Thus, as the depth of recursive calls increases, the size of the argument decreases. □

Lemma 5 Let $X' \subset X$. Then each block in BASIS(X) is contained in some block in BASIS(X').

Proof Suppose that there exists a block $B \in$ BASIS(X) such that B is not contained in any block in BASIS(X'). Since $X' \subset X$, it follows that $R - X \subset R - X'$. From the definition of the dependency basis, it follows that $B \subseteq R - X$, so $B \subset R - X'$. The union of the blocks in BASIS(X') is $R - X'$, so if B is not contained in a single block in BASIS(X'), it must be contained in at least two such blocks. Let $Y \in$ BASIS(X') have a non-empty intersection with B. Let $Z = R - X'Y$. Obviously, $B \cap Z \neq \phi$. Now by using the augmentation axiom with the attribute set $X - X'$ on the MVD $X' \twoheadrightarrow Y | Z$, we obtain $X \twoheadrightarrow Y' | Z'$, where $Y' = Y - X$ and $Z' = Z - X$. Since $B \cap Y' \neq \phi$ and $B \nsubseteq Y'$, the result follows by contradiction. □

Lemma 6 V is not in 4NF with respect to M if and only if there exists some attribute pair $h,i \in V$ such that, where $V' = V - \{h,i\}$, h and i are in different blocks of BASIS(V').

Proof Suppose that there exist h,i ∈ V such that h and i are in different blocks of BASIS(V'). Let the block containing h be H and let I = R − HV'. Obviously, V' ↠ H | I ∈ M⁺ and i ∈ I. The projection of this dependency onto V is V' ↠ {h} | {i} (V), which is non-trivial, so V is not in 4NF with respect to M.

Suppose that V is not in 4NF with respect to M. Then there exists some MVD, X ↠ Y | Z ∈ M⁺ that has a non-trivial projection, X ↠ Y' | Z' (V) onto V. Let h and i be arbitrary elements of Y' and Z', respectively; then {h} and {i} are in different blocks of BASIS(X). Let V' = V − {h,i}. Then by applying the root weighting axiom [12] to X ↠ Y' | Z' (V), we obtain V' ↠ {h} | {i} (V). Since X ⊆ V', it follows from Lemma 5 that each block in BASIS(V') is contained in some block of BASIS(X). Thus h and i must be in different blocks of BASIS(X), and consequently in different blocks of BASIS(V'). □

Lemma 7 Let T' the state of T when an attribute set, W, is about to be added to ρ in procedure DECOMPOSE. If COVERED(W) is true, then it is unnecessary to add W to ρ in order that, upon termination of LJ4NF, ρ be a lossless 4NF decomposition of R.

Proof Since COVERED(W) is true, there is a row, i, in T' such that W ⊆ Attr(i). Thus, by Lemma 2, the Chase procedure will eventually generate a row, say g, with 'a' symbols in a set of columns that includes Attr(i), using a tableau initialised from the attribute sets that, upon termination of LJ4NF, are in ρ. Consequently, a row, i, in T with Attr(i) = W would be subsumed by row g. Thus omitting W from ρ will not prevent ECHASE from generating a row of 'a' symbols. □

A full correctness proof of the algorithm will be published elsewhere.

3.3 Examples

In [10], there is given a list of properties that distinguish acyclic database schemes from cyclic ones. One such property is that, if ρ is a reduced, connected acyclic database scheme, then ρ is a unique lossless 4NF decomposition. This characterisation is not so simple when the dependency set includes EMVDs. In the example that follows, the set, M, of FMVDs is NOT conflict-free and there is no unique lossless 4NF

```
Example 4   R = {1,2,3,4,5,6},
            F = φ, D = M ∪ E, where
            M = {M₁,M₂} and
            E = {E₁,E₂,E₃,E₄};
            M₁ = {1,2} ↠ {3,5} | {4,6},
            M₂ = {3,4} ↠ {1,5} | {2,6},

            E₁ = {1} ↠ {4} | {3,5},
            E₂ = {2} ↠ {3} | {4,6},
            E₃ = {3} ↠ {2} | {1,5},
            E₄ = {4} ↠ {1} | {2,6}.
```

decomposition with respect to M. When, however, the set, E, of EMVDs is used for further normalisation, a unique lossless 4NF decompostion is obtained, regardless of the order in which the FMVDs are applied. M_1 and M_2 split each other's left-hand sides, so M is not conflict-free. Depending on which FMVD is applied first in the decomposition process, the decomposition will either be

$$\rho_1 = \{\{1,2,3,5\}, \{1,2,4,6\}\} \text{ or}$$
$$\rho_2 = \{\{1,3,4,5\}, \{2,3,4,6\}\}.$$

When the EMVDs in E are applied to either ρ_1 or ρ_2, the final decomposition is

$$\rho = \{\{1,4\}, \{1,3,5\}, \{2,3\}, \{2,4,6\}\} \text{ in both cases.} \qquad \square$$

The next example illustrates the way in which adding attributes to a 4NF attribute set can reduce the overall size of the decomposition tree.

Example 5 $R = \{1,2,3,4,5,6\}$, $M = \{M_1, M_2, M_3\}$
and $E = \phi$.
$M_1 = \{1,2\} \twoheadrightarrow \{3,4\} \mid \{5,6\}$,
$M_2 = \{2,3\} \twoheadrightarrow \{4,6\} \mid \{1,5\}$,
$M_3 = \{5,6\} \twoheadrightarrow \{1\} \mid \{2,3,4\}$.

Assuming that M_1 is selected in LJ4NF, DECOMPOSE will be passed the set $V = \{1,2,3,4\}$. M_2 holds non-trivially in V, so DECOMPOSE will call itself recursively.

On the first recursive call, the attribute set $V = \{1,2,3\}$ is passed as an argument; $\{1,2,3\}$ is in 4NF, so EXPAND will add the attribute 5 to V. When EXPAND attempts to add either 4 or 6 to V, the resulting set is no longer in 4NF. The set $\{1,2,3,5\}$ is added to ρ and a row with 'a' symbols in columns 1, 2, 3 and 5 is added to T.

On the second recursive call to DECOMPOSE, the attribute set $V = \{2,3,4\}$ is passed as an argument; $\{2,3,4\}$ is in 4NF, so EXPAND is called and adds the attribute 6 to V. The set $\{2,3,4,6\}$ is added to ρ and a row with 'a' symbols in columns 2, 3, 4 and 6 is added to T. ECHASE uses M_2 to match these rows and generates the winning row of all 'a' symbols.

Thus when, in LJ4NF, the block $\{5,6\}$ in BASIS($\{1,2\}$) is assigned to Y, COVERED($\{1,2,5,6\}$) evaluates to true and LJ4NF halts with no further calls to DECOMPOSE. In contrast, the algorithms in [2, 5] would continue the decomposition process until the entire decomposition tree is generated.
$\qquad \square$

References
[1] A V Aho, C Beeri and J D Ullman, The theory of joins in relational databases, ACM Trans. Database Systems, Vol 4, No 3, pp 297–314, 1979
[2] R Fagin, Multivalued dependencies and a new normal form for relational databases, ACM Trans. Database Systems, Vol 2, No 3, pp 262–278, 1977

[3] P C Fischer and D – M Tsou, Whether a set of multivalued dependencies implies a join dependency is NP-hard, SIAM J Comput, Vol 12, No 2, pp 259–266, 1983

[4] Z Galil, An almost linear-time algorithm for computing a dependency basis in a relational database, J ACM, Vol 29, No 1, pp 96–102, 1982

[5] G Grahne and K-J Räihä, Database decomposition into fourth normal form, Proc 9th International Conference on Very Large Data Bases, pp 186–196, 1983

[6] M Ito, K Taniguchi and T Kasami, Membership problem for embedded multivalued dependencies under some restricted conditions, Theoretical Computer Science, Vol 22, pp 175–194, 1983

[7] Y E Lien, Hierarchical schemata for relational databases, ACM Trans. Database Systems, Vol 6, No 1, pp 48–69, 1981

[8] Y E Lien, On the equivalence of database models, J ACM, Vol 29, No 2, pp 333–362, 1982

[9] G Loizou and P Thanisch, A polynomial-time lossless join algorithm for use with a restricted class of multivalued dependencies. Submitted for publication, 1983

[10] D Maier, The Theory of Relational Databases, Computer Science Press, Rockville, Maryland, 1983

[11] D Maier, A O Mendelzon and Y Sagiv, Testing implications of data dependencies, ACM Trans. Database Systems, Vol 4, No 4, pp 455–469, 1979

[12] D S Parker, Jr and K Parsaye-Ghomi, Inferences involving embedded dependencies and transitive dependencies, Proc ACM SIGMOD International Conference on Management of Data, pp. 52–57, 1980

[13] Y Sagiv and S F Walecka, Subset dependencies and a completeness result for a subclass of embedded multivalued dependencies, J ACM, Vol 29, No 1, pp 103–117, 1982

[14] E Sciore, Real-world MVD's, Proc ACM SIGMOD International Conference on Management of Data, pp 121–132, 1981

[15] J D Ullman, Principles of Database Systems (2nd edition), Pitman, London, 1983

A Diagrammer For The Automatic Production Of Entity Type Models

Paul Feldman
School of Mathematics, Statistics & Computing, Thames Polytechnic, London

A strength of Data Analysis is that its resultant Models have diagrammatic representations. However the production and upkeep of these diagrams can be very time-consuming and is error-prone. Due to the prominence and use of these models in Information Systems Development, automation of the diagram production process is highly desirable. This paper describes the implementation and use of a prototype suite of programs to automatically produce these diagrams on a micro-computer. Diagrams which use similar conventions to Entity Model diagrams are capable of being produced.

There are a number of principles and constraints which have shaped the form of the diagrammer. The main constraint is use on a micro-computer, while the main principles are the imitation of human diagram production methods and the minimisation of the number of crossing lines and the length of relationships. The layout of the diagrams can be varied according to a number of criteria and involves a "semi-intelligent' relationship connection algorithm. One of the more contentious issues in the imitation of human methods is the problem of aesthetics. The diagrammer described in this paper deals with aesthetics by producing a number of different diagrams according to a set of user chosen criteria. This method leaves the choice of the most aesthetically pleasing diagram to the human user. The prototype diagrammer has been used by CACI Inc International in various demonstrations.

1.   Introduction

One of the main benefits of Data Analysis is that its resulting models have diagrammatic representations. This is useful because much more information can be meaningfully conveyed by diagrams than by the written word in the same space and is an important consideration because the diagrams are mainly used as communication tools, particularly for validation by users.

The use of diagrams introduces the problems of production and maintenance on which a large amount of Analyst's time can be spent. The production of diagrams may introduce errors due to human fallibility, changing diagrams by hand also increases the chance that errors occur. In addition, redrawing introduces the problem of version control of the diagrams. Thus the manual production of diagrams can lead to a reduction in the quality of information portrayed. A further problem which is encountered when diagrams are hand drawn is a reluctance on the part of a drawer to change their diagram, especially when complex; analysts have been known to argue against change rather than to redraw their diagrams. This paper describes an automated aid for diagram production on a micro-computer; the aid is called a 'Diagrammer'. A joint research project between Thames Polytechnic and CACI Inc International includes the investigation of automated aids for Systems Development; the recognition of the above problems prompted the development of the Diagrammer as part of this project.

The Diagrammer is a suite of programs for the automatic production of diagrams which use the diagrammatic conventions of Entity Models [9]. As such, the work presented in this paper is in the context of producing Entity Models, only. Entity Models are a useful tool for Database Design [7,9] and a 'first cut' design of a Database may be achieved by a simple mapping of Entities to Sets, Relations etc [9] (see, for example, [7]). The value of producing an Entity Model before Database Design is that a knowledge of the conceptual form of the data is gained and a stable, user agreed view of the data in an enterprise is achieved [9]. Diagrams of other types of models such as Bachmann Diagrams [1] and Action Models [6] can be produced with little or no change to the programs.

The use of a diagrammer is analagous to the use of a simple Data Dictionary (ie a Data Dictionary containing just definitions). A Data Dictionary is a central repository of definitions of Data, Functions etc which enables this information to be interrogated [2]. A diagrammer has a central repository of the information to be drawn, eg Entities and their Relationships, Data Sets & their relationships, and produces diagrams for enquiry purposes.

The Diagrammer consists of two PASCAL programs, one to produce the diagrams and the other to view them. It was initially developed on an APPLE II micro-computer and there is an improved development on a SIRIUS micro-computer. An IBM PC version is envisaged in the near future.

This paper first considers the principles and constraints which have affected the design of the Diagrammer. Following this some of the programs' technical details are discussed and some future plans for the Diagrammer are detailed.

2. Diagrammer Principles and Constraints

There are various principles and constraints which have dictated the design of the Diagrammer.

2.1 Diagrammer & Micro-Computers

A requirement of the Diagrammer was that it should be implemented on a micro-computer. The reasons for this are the ability to take a micro-computer into interview situations, the ease of using graphics on this medium, the ubiquitous nature of micro-computers and the portability potential of the program and any diagrams produced.

2.2 Graphics Package Constraints

Any implementation of a diagrammer is heavily constrained by the particular graphics package it interfaces with. However this does not affect the content of a diagram, just how the diagram is viewed. For example, even with the smallest character set available in the graphics package used for the figures in this paper, truncation has been forced in the display of some entity names rather than overwrite symbols; eg TECHNICIAN in Fig 2 appears as TECHNICI. Also, the characters stay the same size when the diagram is scaled up or down.

2.3 Human Imitation

One of the aims of the Diagrammer is to imitate human diagram production methods in producing diagrams and this has been attempted where possible. However the limitations imposed by the use of micro-computers has constrained this aim considerably.

2.4 Diagram Production Methods

There are two reasonable methods of automating the production and maintenance of diagrams: interactive and automatic.

2.4.1 Interactive Diagram Production

There are a number of programs which enable the interactive 'building' of diagrams, for example see [4], and there are also a number under development. The principle behind this method is to interactively 'draw' the diagrams by selecting desired symbols from a menu, eg Fig 1.

The main benefits of this method are ease of input and maintenance and a solution to the version control problem. The main deficiency of this method is that human errors can still be introduced, although the number of such errors will probably be decreased.

2.4.2 Automatic Diagram Production

The second method of diagram production is to automatically produce a diagram from a description of a model; the Diagrammer is based on this method. The description input to the Diagrammer is a list of entities, their relationships, and the optionality and cardinality of the relationships. The output from the Diagrammer is a diagram, eg Fig 2.

Fig 1. A Typical Interactive Building Screen

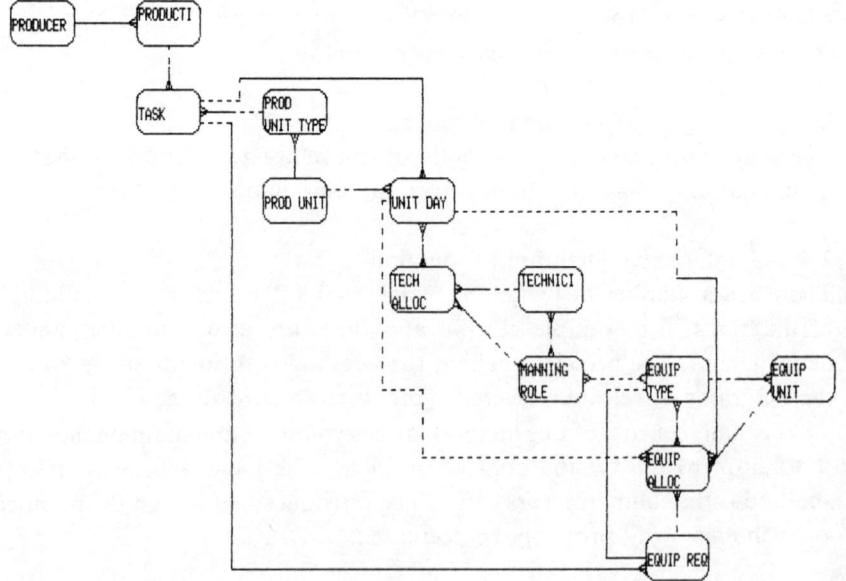

Fig 2. An example of The Output of The Diagrammer

Automatic production of entity type models 61

The main benefit of this method is the lack of human interaction which results in many fewer production and maintenance errors. An automatically produced diagram is a true reflection of the originating input; for example, there is no possibility of forgetting a 'many' symbol, optional line, relationship or entity, all of which can easily be missed in a hand drawn diagram and the only source of errors is in the input itself. Furthermore if mistakes are subsequently detected (eg by further analysis), it is much easier to automatically reproduce a diagram than it is to manually redraw parts of, or even all of a diagram. Diagram version control can also be easily achieved using automatic production.

Ideally, automatic and interactive diagram production methods would be used together; so models would be produced either automatically or interactively, and then interactively manipulated or automatically reformatted as desired. This is intended to be added to future versions of the Diagrammer.

2.5   Criteria For Diagram Production

The main problem with the automatic production of a diagram lies in the nature of the models which are represented. One of the strengths of

Fig 3. Ellis Style Relationship

Fig 4. Example of Isomorphic Diagram
No User Option Chosen

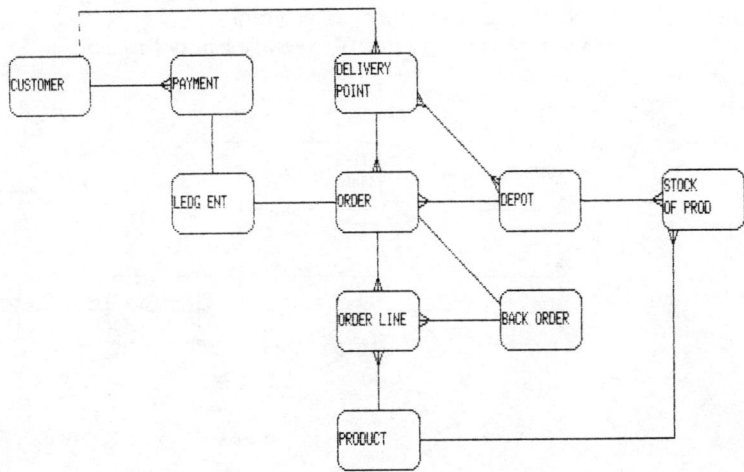

analysis models is that they represent a view of the 'real world' so the diagrams of the models must be able to easily convey any underlying meaning. Analysts achieve this by reflecting the semantics of a model in their diagrams, for example an order line entity would be placed closer to its owner, order, than to the resulting delivery. The Diagrammer does not take this into account because it would require extremely complex semantical representations to be used and processed.

Fig 5. Example of Isomorphic Diagram
User Option – Relationship Priority/Maximum/Entity Priority

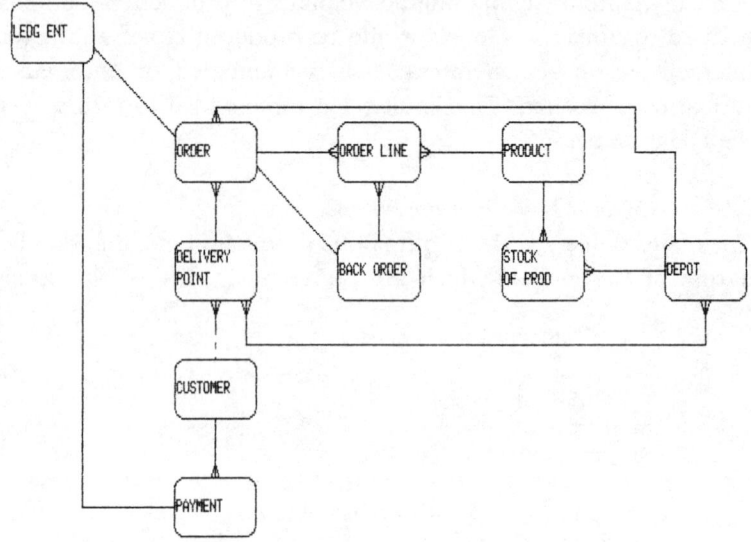

Fig 6. Example of Isomorphic Diagram
User Option – Entity Priority/Average Entity Proximity

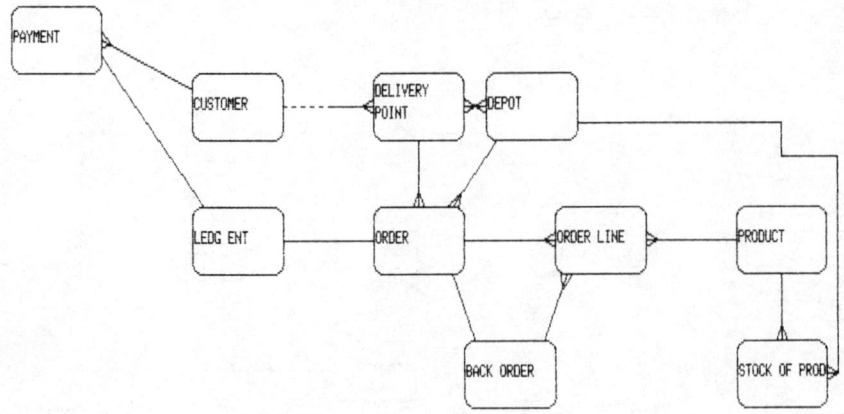

It is just as complex for a computer program to deal with aesthetics; this problem is even difficult for people, eg what makes model A nicer to look at and/or able to communicate more than model B. Every Analyst has their own diagrammatic style: for example, Ellis [5] insists a 1:Many relationship should be drawn with the many on the left wherever possible, eg Fig 3; others will put the entity with the most relationships in the middle of a diagram, as in Fig 4; and so on. The Diagrammer deals with this problem by giving a user a choice of a number of optional guidelines for the layout of a diagram. For example, Figs 4,5 and 6 all depict the same model, ie they are *isomorphic* diagrams. The alternative layouts were produced as a result of different user options being chosen; see 3.2 for an explanation of the options provided by the Diagrammer.

Two criteria which are thought to affect the communication potential of a diagram are the number of crossing lines and the length of relationships. The Diagrammer tries to reduce both of these factors. This is achieved by a 'semi-intelligent' relationship connection algorithm (see 3.3). Various graph theories could have been utilised to achieve a similar result as has recently been done by Tamassia et al [10]. Initial research for the Diagrammer rejected the use of graph theory because it was felt that it would restrict the ability to produce isomorphic diagrams. Furthermore, as very few analysts utilise graph theory in drawing diagrams, it was felt that it should be possible to produce reasonable diagrams without considering graph theory.

2.6 *Diagrammer Input*
The Diagrammer is aimed at the utilisation of information contained in a Data Dictionary-like environment. A separate input interface is provided to enable this. In the prototype the input interface uses a file containing the necessary information. However the interface can be easily adapted to read the required information from any Data Dictionary.

2.7 *Viewing Large Diagrams*
Facilities are required to view any diagram which does not easily fit on a screen. The size of diagram which can fit on a screen depends on the resolution properties of the screen and the graphics package used. The minimum set of viewing facilities are to scroll a diagram left, right, up and down, to zoom in to concentrate on a section of a diagram, or to zoom out to see more of a diagram, and the ability to get hard-copy of the diagram. Optional facilities which may be useful are diagonal scrolling, to be able to scroll pages, or just small amounts, and rotation of the diagram to gain different perspectives.

A problem which has been recognised with viewing diagrams on paper is the difficulty of comprehending large amounts of information in a small space; this problem is intensified when viewing on a screen. For Entity Models this problem can be overcome by the use of a documentary technique called 'Entity Model Clustering' [8]. This technique abstracts parts of a large entity model and has many beneficial side-effects. The technique consists of clustering entities into meaningful groupings and finding the major data of an enterprise. This aids viewing as either the major data, or the major data and its relationships to the clusters, or just a single cluster can be viewed. This is very suitable for automation and solves the problem of viewing large entity models while easing the burden on the production of the diagrams through fewer entities having to appear.

3. Some Technical Details

This section describes the more significant technical issues, since it is beyond the scope of this paper to dwell on the technical design details in any length. Also, as the programs are prototypes, some of the detail may change in the future.

3.1 *Internal Representation of the Diagrams*

As the Diagrammer is aimed at micro-computers, good utilisation of memory is of the utmost importance. To achieve this a diagram is held as a set of linked lists. This is also due to a need for flexibility of different sizes of models. The alternative is to have a fixed size matrix; this matrix would be very sparse, leading to an enormous amount of wasted memory. Various other alternatives were ruled out due to speed considerations.

3.2 *Layout of Entities*

Entities must be placed so as to be close to related entities while avoiding overcrowding. The following describes how this is achieved.

The entities are first ordered according to some criteria; for example the criteria could be ordering by the number of relationships an entity has, or simply the order of input (perhaps enabling some user preferred criteria). The prototype has three options which affect the layout of a diagram. One option affects the ordering; this is Relationship Priority. For this option, the entities are ordered to be in ascending number of relationships (called Minimum), or descending number of relationships (called Maximum, eg Fig 5). These cause the entity with the minimum or maximum number of relationships to be placed on the diagram first. The second option is Entity Priority (eg Figs 5 & 6). This affects the order in which entities are taken from the ordered list. If Entity Priority is not chosen the entities are placed in the order of the list and relationships are only connected to entities already on the diagram. With Entity Priority the entities are also taken in order, but all of an entities' relationships are connected, even if this necessitates the placing of other entities out of a chosen order. If this occurs all of the relationships of the entities which are taken out of order are connected; this may require taking even more entities out of the chosen order, and so on.

The third user option is Average Entity Proximity (eg Fig 6). On layout, each entity is placed as close to an already placed related entity as possible. However, if Average Entity Proximity is chosen, an entity is placed so as to be as close as possible to a position which is the *average* of all the already placed related entities' positions. If no related entity has yet appeared on the diagram, an entity is placed as close to a mythical origin as possible.

The constraints which affect the placing of entities are that an entity must not be placed so as to overlap another entity, or to be on top of a relationship. The search for a free position proceeds in ever increasing circles whose centre is either the related entity, the average position, or the origin. The start point on the initial search circle is varied so as to avoid overcrowding in a particular area.

The introduction of lookahead and/or backtracking techniques has been considered to improve the layout of entities. People tend to employ these techniques when drawing these diagrams. For example, first thought is first given to the effects of putting an entity at a given place on the diagram; if it is felt to be satisfactory the entity will be placed and built round; if the further placing of entities results in the diagram becoming unsatisfactory, much rubbing out and redrawing will occur. Backtracking and lookahead have not been introduced at this stage because it would appear that the vast projected increases in space and time needed to cope with them could be unreasonable.

3.3   *Relationship Connection*

Relationships are drawn so as to meet the aesthetic criteria detailed in 2.5 which are to reduce the length of the relationships and to minimise the number of crossing lines. In addition entity boxes must not be crossed. The connection of relationships is achieved via a spatial search algorithm employing 'tree-pruning'. The algorithm is based on the generalisation that only two of an entities' four sides are useful when aiming towards another entity, one vertical and one horizontal; eg in Fig 7, sides 1 and 2 of A are most suitable for starting relationships towards B.

Four relationship paths are attempted in all – one from the two most appropriate sides of each entity, eg in Fig 7, one from 1 & one from 2 towards B and one from 3 & one from 4 towards A. The path chosen is the one which is most satisfactory. The main aim of the algorithm is to reduce the distance between the current end of a path and the target entity.

First of all a starting place for a path is found on the side to be started from; the path is abandoned if there is no space for any more relationships on that side. Next a path is drawn in an orthogonal direction to the starting side; the point drawn to is the closest point to the target entity which does not lead to the path intersecting any other entities. This process is then repeated with the point just found being substituted for the starting point and the path heading in an orthogonal direction to the previous path. Eventually the path either becomes untenable (ie cannot proceed without crossing an entity box), or the target is reached. A 'score' is calculated while constructing the path to enable the best path to be found, this being the path with the minimum score. The score includes a value for every line in the path to penalise long, complex relationships and a value for every relationship crossed. The search tree is 'pruned' by abandoning the search for a path if its score ever exceeds the minimum score achieved in previous path searches for the relationship. If two paths have the same score, the chosen path is the one which was explored first.

The algorithm considers many special cases. For example, a proposed path might occupy the same space as an already completed relationship. If this occurs, the proposed path is moved to one side and a penalty added to its score to discourage the selection of the path; the selection is discouraged because it can be difficult for a viewer to follow two paths which are close together. Another special case is where a point is reached on a horizontal or vertical line to the target entity, but with an intervening entity, eg Fig 8 (a). If the end of a path is in a direct line to the target any indirect path will increase the distance between them violating the main aim of the algorithm. When this situation is recognised a violation is forced by drawing a line at right-angles to the desired direction, as in Fig 8 (b,c).

Fig 7. Useful Start Sides

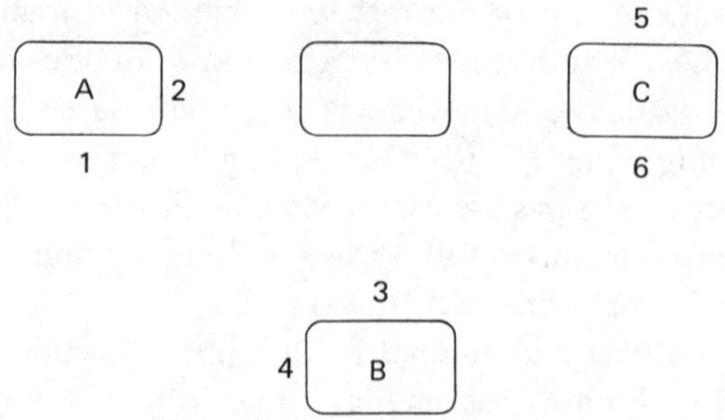

(a) Path can't proceed without increasing distance
(b) Diagrammer draws orthogonal line
(c) Final Result

This also applies to the common case of entities on vertical or horizontal lines with each other but with intervening entities, eg Fig 9. However an extra path is attempted for this case as paths from either parallel entity box side can be equally usable; eg in Fig 7 a path from sides 5 and 6 of C are both of value when heading towards A.

A further special case is where a single diagonal line would suffice between two entities. The use of such a line is very much a matter of personal taste. The Diagrammer searches for such lines before attempting

Fig 8. Intervening Entity Between End Of Path & Target

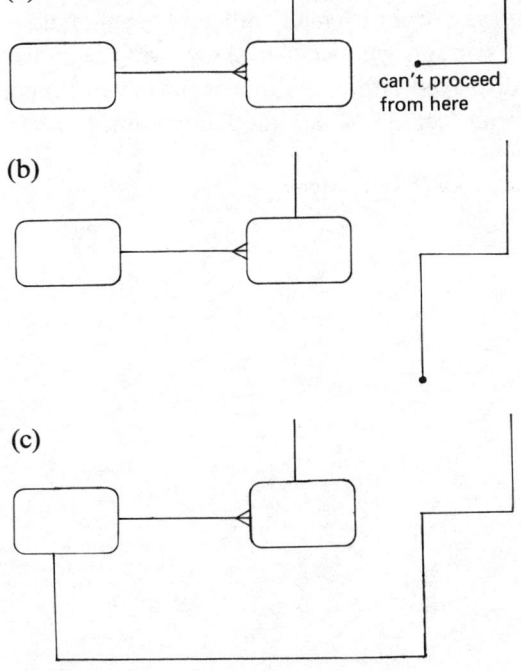

Fig 9. Intervening Entity Between Two Entities

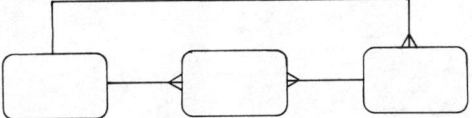

any of the other paths. A diagonal line is drawn if it does not intersect any other symbols, including relationships. Relationships are included in this case due to a widely stated preference that relationships should cross at right angles. Unfortunately this does not stop further relationships crossing an already placed diagonal line. This is discouraged by having a higher penalty for crossing a diagonal line than for a horizontal or vertical line.

3.4 *Viewing Of Diagrams*

The viewing of the diagrams is achieved using a separate program to the construction program. The three main justifications for this are to enable diagrams to be constructed just once, but viewed as often as desired, to enable a common viewing program for different constructing programs, and to enable portability across micro-computers and graphics packages as all the machine dependent and graphics oriented instructions only deal with viewing. The separation has the added advantage that a single construction program can deal with many different types of models as any changes for different symbols will occur in the viewing sections.

The diagrams are displayed with an optional menu of viewing commands, see Fig 10. The viewing facilities which the Diagrammer provides are to

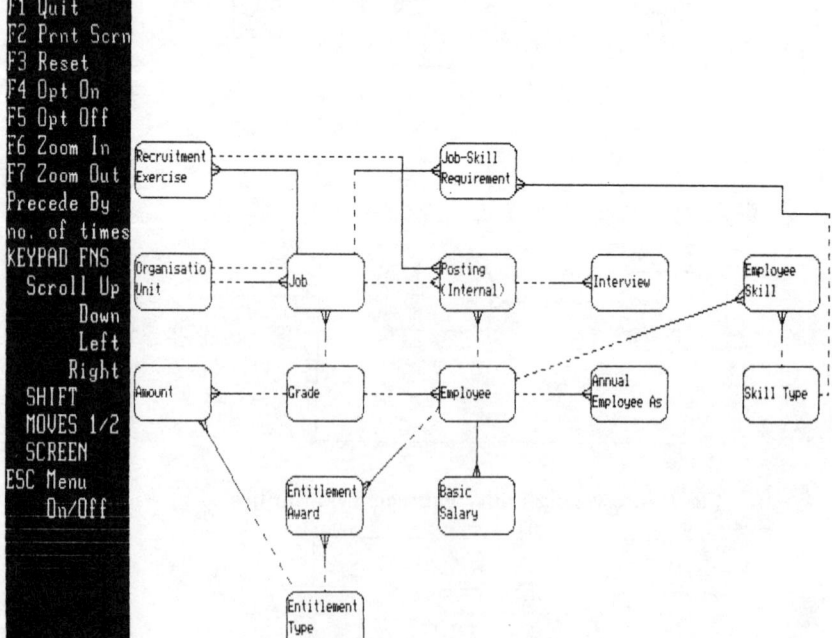

Fig 10. Example Of Facility Menu

zoom in to see less of a model diagram or zoom out; scroll the diagram left, right, up or down, slowly or quickly (dot or half-screen at a time respectively) and diagonally slowly; to enable optionality to be shown on relationship lines or not (eg for a strategy study); and to enable the diagram to be printed out.

4. Future Plans

As has been stated, the Diagrammer is a prototype. Its main purpose is to test the feasibility of producing analysis diagrams on a micro-computer. As such it has been very successful and has been demonstrated by CACI Inc. International. Derivatives of the techniques involved are planned to be used by CACI Inc International to provide a comprehensive micro-computer Graphics interface to their 'Systems Factory' [3].

Future work is planned which will use the Diagrammer in the manipulation of models. This will mainly be to aid the other facets of the research of which the Diagrammer is a part, being Action Modelling [5] and Entity Model Clustering [8]. It is intended to use the Diagrammer in an investigation of the mapping of analysis models into design models, especially for databases.

Other work is intended to:

- add interactive diagram building
- investigate the introduction of graph theory while retaining the ability to generate isomorphic diagrams
- further investigate the use of lookahead and backtracking
- orient the Diagrammer towards Entity Model Clustering
- produce an IBM PC version.

5. Conclusion

A suite of programs has been described for the automatic production and viewing of diagrams of models which use the diagrammatic conventions of Entity Models. The programs have achieved the purpose of proving that it is possible to produce such diagrams on a micro-computer. The need for a tool like the Diagrammer was justified by pointing out that large amounts of analyst's time is spent drawing diagrams and that they often inadvertently introduce errors. Both analyst's time and errors are reduced when using a diagramming aid.

The use of the Diagrammer has ramifications for Database Design. The Diagrammer can be used to produce diagrams of Database models. Also, the use of the Diagrammer can make Analysis models more accurate and usable. Consequently, logical database models and the resulting database will be more accurate and stable.

Context of Research and Acknowledgements

This paper is based on research undertaken at Thames Polytechnic and funded jointly by an SERC CASE award and CACI Inc International. The main thrust of the research is into the CACI Data Analysis Techniques, seeking ways to improve them and to make possible the automation of some aspects. The Clustered Entity Model technique described originally arose out of work done for Whitbread & Co Plc.

The research team also includes G Fitzgerald of the University of Aston in Birmingham, T Crowe of Thames Polytechnic and T Bourne of CACI Inc International. The Clustered Entity Model technique was developed in collaboration with D Miller of Whitbread & Co Plc.

References

[1] C Bachmann, Data Structure Diagrams, Data Base, Vol 1, No 2, 1969
[2] BCS, The BCS Data Dictionary Systems Working Party Report, British Computer Society, 1977
[3] CACI, The Systems Factory, CACI Inc International, 1983
[4] E Chan and F Lochovsky, A Graphical Data Base Design Aid Using The Entity-Relationship Approach, in Entity Relationship Approach to Systems Analysis & Design, Ed P P Chen, North Holland, 1979
[5] H Ellis, A Refined Model For The Definition Of System Requirements, Database Journal, Vol 12, No 3, 1982
[6] P Feldman, Action Modelling, Thames Poly Internal Publication, TP–CS–PBF–8212–1–AO, London, 1982
[7] I Macdonald and I Palmer, System Development in a Shared Data Environment: the D2S2 Methodology, in Information Systems Design Methodologies: A comparative review, Ed T W Olle, H Sol, A A Verrijn-Stuart, North Holland, 1983
[8] D Miller, Whitbread Corporate Data Architecture, Whitbread & Co Plc, Internal Document, 1983
[9] R Rock-Evans, Data Analysis, IPC Business Press, Surrey, 1981
[10] M Tamssia, C Batini and M Talamo, The Automatic Layout Of Entity Models, in Entity-Relationship Approach to Software Engineering, Ed C Davis, S Jojodiu, P Ng, and R Yeh, North Holland, 1983

An analysis of certain data models with respect to their handling of selected integrity constraints

D J Flynn
School of Computing Studies and Accountancy, University of East Anglia, Norwich NR4 7TJ

As the importance of Data Analysis as a modelling technique grows, it is necessary to establish the precise scope of the concepts used. The notion of constraint in this area has been current for some years, and the recent IFIP Conference example is used as a common base to compare the way in which the constraints features of 4 widely-discussed Data Models – ACM/PCM, NIAM, D2S2, and CIAM – are used to model the restrictions in the example. It is found, in general, that the four Data Models are capable of representing the three types of constraint considered. However, the models frequently vary with respect to the manner in which they express the constraints. Four desirable features of Data Models, which are relevant to the expression of constraints, are considered. These are: (1) declarative nature (2) unitary nature (3) orthogonality (4) dependence on change. For every constraint analysed, each Data Model is examined for the way in which it expresses the constraint, from the point of view of each of the four features. Any constraint whose expression in a particular Data Model would conflict with the underlying aim of any of the features is discussed. In the conclusion, the question is posed as to whether some Data Models have fundamentally different aims. Doubt is also cast over the accepted distinction between static and dynamic constraints.

1. Introduction

The aim of this paper is to examine the way in which four currently available data models represent some common real-world constraints, and to draw conclusions about the models from the analysis. Constraints have been selected for emphasis as it is intended to re-evaluate some previous comparisons and their classifications [5, 7].

Traditionally, data models have chiefly been concerned with the representation of the basic objects and associations in the situation being modelled. However, restrictions may occur within this basic structure. For example, a CONFERENCE may have an association with a START-

DATE and with an END–DATE, but a constraint may exist that, for each occurrence of CONFERENCE, the value of END–DATE must be greater than the value of START–DATE.

Hence, the notion of including constraints in data models is broadly that of extending the scope of the models to capture more of the rules and restrictions (the 'semantics') which are inherent in the reality being modelled. This has the advantage that constraints are held in one place only, and are not expressed procedurally – ie, in a program-like manner – but in a more declarative way.

Many data model comparisons have been overly theoretical and too ambitious, attempting to compare the entirety of the model [2, 8] and failing to isolate crucial differences. Many data models exist, but no systematic study of their effectiveness has been made. The intention here is to use a practical example as a common base for the four models. Some important features of the models, which are held here and elsewhere [9] to be desirable features, will be considered. These are:

(a) declarative nature – this has been mentioned above
(b) unitary nature – this feature is concerned with the number of different constructs or sections of a data model which are required to model a given part of the reality. This paper will be particularly concerned with the unitary nature of modelling a given constraint
(c) orthogonality – a data model may be termed orthogonal if different constructs are used for expressing different constraints. There are disadvantages in using a construct for more than one constraint
(d) dependence on change – it is basically desirable that when reality changes, the changes required to be made to the model should be minimal. The data model constructs will be analysed with respect to their performance when common changes are considered

The approach adopted is to use an example presented at the IFIP WG 8.1 CRIS–1 Conference [11], where 13 Information Systems Methodologies submitted their solution to a common problem set by the conference organisers. The problem was to design a system to support IFIP conferences. The example used here is a subset of this IFIP problem, and the constraints that it contains are analysed for the way they are expressed in each of the four data models. This method thus used solutions designed by data model authors. The four models selected are ACM/PCM [3, 4], NIAM [16], CIAM [6], and D2S2 [10], and are intended to cover a fairly wide spectrum of current data models. NIAM is a binary model, while ACM/PCM represents the Semantic Data Model school; CIAM is a product of the

Scandinavian infological approach, while D2S2 is the CACI methodology that has had substantial success over the past 10 years in industry.

Section 2 will briefly discuss the constraint types to be considered, while Section 3 will present the Example and the solutions of the four models. Sections 4, 5, & 6 will discuss the constraints as represented in the models, and Section 7 will draw some conclusions.

2. Types of constraint

The types of constraint compared in the Example may best be discussed, in the absence of a systematic taxonomy of constraints, by considering briefly some rules applying to objects and their relationships that are conventionally represented in data models.

It has been mentioned in the Introduction that data models typically express the fact that certain object types may exist, with certain allowable properties, which are relationships to other object types. These rules are usually considered to be 'structural'. We may now consider restrictions within this structure as constraints. For example:

(a) Some type objects may possess additional properties, forming subtypes. The allowable property combinations are generally specified by a mixture of constraints and structural rules, depending on the model. For example, an object type PERSON may have three subtypes SECRETARY, MANAGER, and ENGINEER, but restrictions exist on the possible combinations – eg, a PERSON who is a SECRETARY and a MANAGER may not also be an ENGINEER. Combinatorial possibilities generally do not make it feasible to list out all the allowable combinations as object types. These types of constraints arise in the example and may be termed Property Constraints.

(b) Between any two related object types, the mapping between the instances may vary. This mapping may be constrained to be any of 1:1, 1:N, or M:N. These are termed Identifying Constraints.

(c) We may introduce an aspect of time into the model, and consider that not all object type combinations may exist simultaneously. Constraints will govern the order in which they are introduced (and deleted). The main reason for this is that when objects are introduced, some or all of their properties are introduced with them. As these properties are associations to other objects, these other objects must either pre-exist or be introduced along with the object in question. These are called Behavioural Constraints.

These are the three types of constraint considered in this paper. It is obvious that they only capture a small proportion of currently identified constraints as, for example, they all are type constraints, applying to all instances of the type. However, they are widely-used and it is thus important to establish how well these 'basic' constraints are represented in the different data models.

3. The example

The example [1, 11] is concerned with three activities: registering Conference papers and authors on receipt, distributing the papers to referees, and assigning accepted papers to sessions. The objects are SESSION, PAPER, ACC–PAPER (paper accepted for a SESSION), PERSON, AUTHOR, REFEREE, SESSION–CHAIRPERSON, CONFERENCE–CHAIRPERSON, and RESULT (result of refereeing a paper).

A SESSION is referred to by a Session-nr, has a Session-Chairperson, and may have more than one ACC–PAPER. The Session-Chairperson is to be introduced together with SESSION.

PAPER is referred to by Paper-title, and when it is introduced, its AUTHOR must also be introduced; an AUTHOR may author many PAPERs. PAPER is refereed by one or more REFEREEs, possibly resulting in its becoming an ACC–PAPER. A SESSION must exist before the relevant ACC–PAPER can be introduced. Many PAPERs may be refereed by a REFEREE as well as being authored by many AUTHORs.

PERSON is referred to by Name. A Conference-Chairperson exists to chair the Conference. An AUTHOR may not be a REFEREE, and AUTHORs may not be the SESSION–CHAIRPERSON of the SESSION to which their PAPER is assigned. Finally, a REFEREE may be a SESSION–CHAIRPERSON but not CONFERENCE–CHAIRPERSON also.

The solutions of the four different data models in this Section are not complete – they consist only of the structural part of the solution. Additional constraints will be added in the sections describing the different constraint types.

3.1   NIAM

The NIAM mapping is shown in Fig. 1. This graphical form of NIAM, termed the Information Structure Diagram (ISD) has been used, as the more formal specification language RIDL is not suitable for an illustration. Briefly, NIAM considers object types and relationships, shown as circles and edges respectively (the rectangles along the edges are for role names and are not considered here). Object types are either NOLOTs (entity types) or LOTs (data items) shown by solid and broken circles

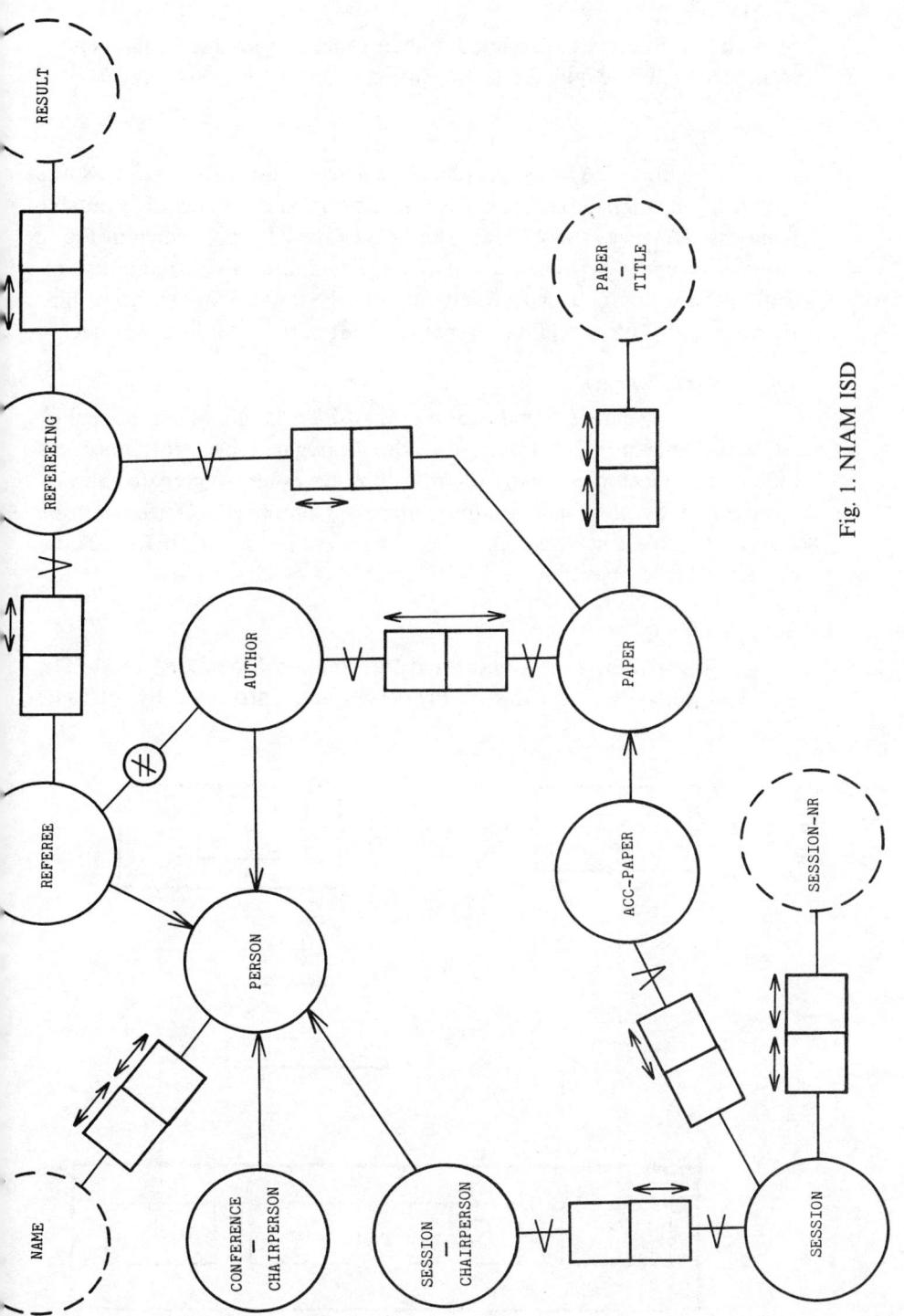

Fig. 1. NIAM ISD

respectively. Subtypes are related to their generic by arrowed edges. Other constructs will be explained as they arise.

3.2 D2S2

As for NIAM, a graphical scheme is used for D2S2 as the specification language is to some extent informal and isn't readily available from the references [10, 13, 14]. The D2S2 Entity Model shown in Fig. 2 consists of entity types shown as rectangles and edges as relationships. Subtypes are rectangles within generic rectangles. Attributes (relationships between entity types and data types) are not part of the Entity Model.

3.3 ACM/PCM

The Structure Specification of the BETA language component of ACM/PCM is in Fig. 3. It considers the Aggregate Object (or Object) as the main Object type, with relationships to other Aggregate Objects represented by their names appearing as Component Objects of the Aggregate Object in question. Subtypes appear in the GENERIC clause of their generic object.

3.4 CIAM

Fig. 4 shows the Conceptual Information Model of CIAM. The major object type is the Entity. Properties are represented by attribute

Fig. 2. D2S2 Entity Model

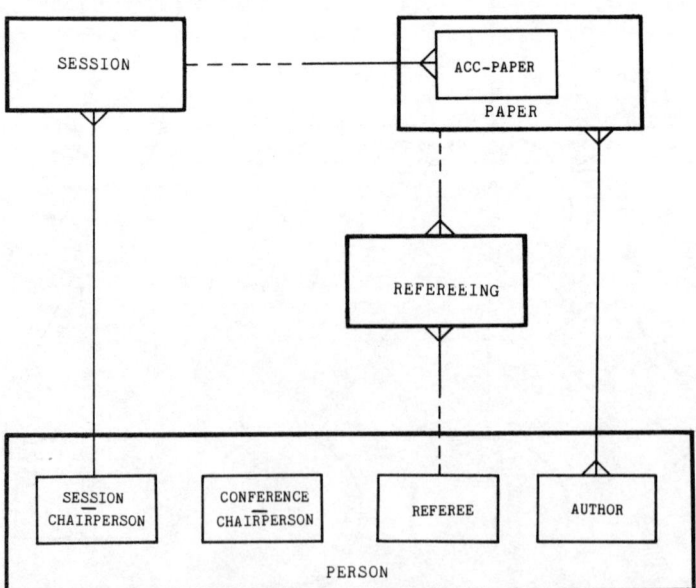

Data models and integrity constraints 77

functions performed on the entities yielding the entity or data type (not shown) in relationship. Each entity has the rules for its existence within the body of the entity object (not all shown). The rules specify the events (procedures) which insert, update, and delete the entity. The event construct will be described later.

4. Property constraints

Three Property Constraints exist in the example:

(1) AUTHOR and REFEREE to be disjoint
(2) REFEREE may be SESSION–CHAIRPERSON but not a CONFERENCE–CHAIRPERSON also
(3) SESSION–CHAIRPERSON and AUTHOR to be disjoint where the PAPER was assigned to the SESSION of which the AUTHOR was SESSION–CHAIRPERSON

Constraints 1 & 2 will be seen to involve simple set operations, while Constraint 3, relying on a common property value (PAPER) is more complex.

Fig. 3. ACM/PCM Structure Specification in BETA language

```
person = OBJECT
  AGGREGATE OF
    name;
      PRIMARY KEY name;
  GENERIC OF
    conference-chairperson : NONEXCLUSIVE;
    session-chairperson : NONEXCLUSIVE
    author : EXCLUSIVE;
    referee : EXCLUSIVE;
END OBJECT;

refereeing = OBJECT
  AGGREGATE OF
    referee;
    paper;
    result;
      PRIMARY KEY referee, paper;
END OBJECT;

paper = OBJECT                          session = OBJECT
  AGGREGATE OF                            AGGREGATE OF
    paper-title;                            session-nr;
    authorship : ESSENTIAL;                 session-papers : ESSENTIAL;
      PRIMARY KEY paper-title;              session-chairperson : ESSENTIAL;
  GENERIC OF                                  PRIMARY-KEY session-nr;
    acc-paper;                          END OBJECT;
END OBJECT;

authorship = OBJECT                     session-papers = OBJECT
  AGGREGATE OF                            AGGREGATE OF
    paper-title;                            session-nr;
      PRIMARY KEY paper-title;              PRIMARY KEY session-nr;
  ASSOCIATION OF author;                  ASSOCIATION OF acc-paper;
    MANUAL membership;                      MANUAL membership
END OBJECT;                             END OBJECT;
```

4.1 NIAM

Property Constraints may be expressed in two forms:

(1) the ISD, as in Fig. 1. Limited to simple constraints only.
(2) the procedurally-oriented language RIDL.

All constraints expressed in the ISD are also expressed in RIDL, as this is the formal language for consistency checking and mapping to a Conceptual Schema. The ISD is manually mapped to RIDL, but automatic mapping from RIDL to the ISD is possible. The ISD is intended chiefly as a vehicle for user-expert communication.

Fig. 4. Conceptual Information Model (CIM) of CIAM

```
entity SESSION;
existence (∀x∀d∃y(SESSION-INTRODUCTION(y)=x ^day(y) <=d --->
          SESSION(x,d)))
attribute functions
    tf   session-nr : SESSION-NR;
    tf   session-cp : SESSION-CHAIRPERSON;
identifier session-nr;
end;

entity SESSION-CHAIRPERSON;
existence (∀x∀d∃y(SESSION-INTRODUCTION(y)^session-chairperson(y)=
          x ^day(y) <=d ---> SESSION-CHAIRPERSON(x,d)));
generics ...
identifier (from PERSON);
end;

entity REFEREEING;
existence ...
attribute functions
    tf   paper : PAPER;
    tf   referee : REFEREE;
    pf   result : RESULT;
identifier (paper, referee);
end;

function AUTHORSHIP;
domains p : PAPER;
        a : AUTHOR;
range   Boolean;
def ...
end;

entity PERSON;                          entity AUTHOR;
existence ...                           existence ...
attribute functions                     generics ...
    tf   name : NAME;                   identifier (from PERSON);
identifier name;                        end;
end;

entity REFEREE;                         entity CONFERENCE-CHAIRPERSON;
existence ...                           existence ...
generics ...                            generics ...
identifier (from PERSON);               identifier (from PERSON);
end;                                    end;

entity PAPER;                           entity ACC-PAPER;
existence ...                           existence ...
attribute functions                     attribute functions
    tf   paper-title : PAPER-TITLE;         tf   session : SESSION;
identifier paper-title;                 generics ...
end;                                    identifier (from PAPER);
                                        end;
```

Constraint 1
A graphic symbol (see Fig. 1) between AUTHOR and REFEREE is used.

Constraint 2
This cannot be expressed either in the ISD or in RIDL, unless a subtype which is the intersection of CONFERENCE–CHAIRPERSON and SESSION–CHAIRPERSON is explicitly modelled. RIDL does not support set expressions, and a procedure must be defined.

Constraint 3
May be expressed in RIDL only.

4.2   D2S2

The Entity Model is the only specification medium for these constraints, and only Constraint 1 can be expressed, as all subtypes must be disjoint in D2S2. Constraints 2 & 3 would have to be expressed in a procedure.

4.3   ACM/PCM

Unlike NIAM, where constraints are expressed in one 'constraints' section of the RIDL language, ACM/PCM uses two sections of BETA, the overall requirements specification language. (These sections are on one level – there is no mapping between them). They are:

(1) Structure Specifications
(2) Assertion Specifications

Constraint 1
Expressed as either an EXCLUSIVE clause in the Structure Specifications (see the PERSON object in Fig. 3), or as a statement in the Assertion Specifications. The Assertion Specifications utilise a predicate calculus-like language which has been modified with the intention of ease of understandability.

Constraint 2
This cannot be expressed in Fig. 2, so the Assertion statement is:
NO p IN person (SOME r IN referee (SOME s IN session-chairperson (SOME cc IN conference-chairperson ((p IS r) AND (r IS s AND r IS cc)))))

Constraint 3
As for Constraint 2, this is:
NO s IN session (SOME ss IN session-papers (SOME ac IN acc-paper (SOME pa IN paper (SOME a IN author (SOME at IN authorship (SOME

sc IN session-chairperson (ss PART OF s AND sc PART OF s AND ac MEMBER OF ss AND pa IS ac AND at PART OF pa AND a MEMBER OF at AND a.name = sc.name)))))))

Simple constraints may be duplicated in the Assertions as a consistency check. The Assertions language is capable of expressing all Property Constraints.

4.4 CIAM

All Property Constraints are expressed in one section of the CIM, Global Constraints. This is similar to the Assertions of ACM/PCM – however, a formal first-order predicate calculus language is used. Constraint 1 is expressed as follows:

$\forall x \forall d\ (AUTHOR(x,d) \rightarrow \bigcap REFEREE(x,d));$

This may be read: 'An entity x of type AUTHOR at day d may not also be an entity of type REFEREE at day d'. Day d is integral to CIAM as it aims to be a time-unrestricted model. This feature will not be considered here.

Constraints 2 and 3 require more complex expressions. For example, Constraint 3 is:

$\forall x \forall y \forall d\ (SESSION(x,d) \bigcap session\text{-}chairperson(x) = y \rightarrow \exists a(PAPER\text{--}TO\text{--}SESSION\text{--}ALLOCATION(a) \bigcap session(a) = x \bigcap authorship(paper(z),y,d)));$

All constraints are expressible – unlike ACM/PCM, they are specified in only one section.

4.5 *Summary*

Considering the Declarative nature of the data models, D2S2 could only express the simplest constraint, while NIAM was seen to lack set expressions. In terms of their Unitary nature, ACM/PCM could duplicate a simple constraint in two sections – this might be useful for consistency checking.

5. **Identifying constraints**
5.1 *NIAM*

NIAM represents these constraints by arrows, varying in number and position, above the edge representing the association between any two objects. See Fig. 1.

Data models and integrity constraints

1:1 An example is SESSION and SESSION–NR, or PAPER and PAPER–TITLE, both with two arrows above the relevant edges. This also designates the identifier.

1:N SESSION and ACC–PAPER is an example. The arrow is placed nearest the object which has the functional association. As the ISD is undirected, an N:1 relationship is simply a 1:N inverse.

M:N Two possible ways exist for modelling this, depending on whether each joint occurrence of the two objects possesses an attribute:
(1) without attribute – modelled as a relationship eg AUTHOR and PAPER
(2) with attribute – modelled as an object eg REFEREEING

These constraints are also expressed in the RIDL language.

5.2   D2S2

Constraints are shown by 'feet' on the ends of the graph edges – see Fig. 2. However, as the graph only shows entities, not data types, all constraints between entities cannot be expressed.

1:1 No example shown – an edge has no feet

1:N An example is SESSION–CHAIRPERSON and SESSION

M:N As for NIAM, two ways exist – as a relationship and as an object. (Unlike other models based on the Entity-Relationship model, relationships are not allowed to have attributes). Examples are AUTHOR and PAPER (relationship) and REFEREEING (object)

The fact that some attributes are not expressed means that constraints will be incomplete. Although, like NIAM's ISD, the Entity Model is meant for user-expert communication only, the fact that the medium to which the Entity Model is mapped is informally specified means that doubt must exist as to how a complete set of Identifying Constraints is expressed. Identifiers are also not in the Entity Model.

5.3   ACM/PCM

1:1 SESSION–NR in the object SESSION is a Component Object of the Aggregate Object SESSION – see Fig. 3. As all Component Objects must be single-valued (and as SESSION–NR is a Data Type) the relationship is 1:1. If SESSION–NR was however an Aggregate Object, then SESSION would have to be a Component Object in it.

1:N There are two ways for this to be modelled. Firstly, the Association construct is used to 'group' occurrences of the identifying object into sets – eg, SESSION, SESSION–PAPERS, and ACC–

PAPER. The set SESSION–PAPERS is modelled as a Component Object of the identified object SESSION. Alternatively, the identified object may be used as a 'foreign key' in the identifying object – eg, REFEREE and REFEREEING. Again, the single-valued nature of Component Objects enforces the constraint.

M:N As for other models, two ways exist. Without an attribute, the Association construct may be used – eg, AUTHORSHIP between AUTHOR and PAPER. With an attribute, an Aggregate Object is used – eg, REFEREEING, between REFEREE and PAPER.

It should be pointed out that if Association is used to model a 1:N relationship, then it is possible for it to become M:N – this is obviously undesirable.

5.4 CIAM

1:1/1:N As for ACM/PCM, attribute functions of Entity types (see Fig. 4) are single-valued and so a 'foreign key' attribute is used for these constraints. Examples are PAPER and PAPER–TITLE, and REFEREEING and REFEREE.

M:N With no attribute, the 'function' object is used – eg AUTHORSHIP. With an attribute, an entity type is used – eg, REFEREEING.

5.5 *Summary*

The notion of dependence on change may be considered in relation to the Association construct of ACM/PCM. This is used for non-functional associations. However, if a 1:N association changed to 1:1, it will be seen later in Section 6 that both structure and behaviour must change.

Two deficiencies were noted:

(1) All models except D2S2 allow all identifying constraints to be modelled on this level.
(2) ACM/PCM is not precise about the Association construct, as it could allow 1:N to become M:N.

6. **Behavioural constraints**

All the Behavioural Constraints considered were related to the order of introduction of two related objects. Two situations apply between any two objects:

(1) Object A constrains Object B that A must pre-exist (or vice versa)
(2) They each constrain each other to exist simultaneously

Data models and integrity constraints

The constraints from the Example are shown below in Fig. 5, separated into those with a constraint on only one of the objects (Single), and those where both objects constrain each other (Double):

Fig. 5. Behavioural Constraints in the Example

CONSTRAINT	OBJECTS
SINGLE	
1	SESSION before ACC-PAPER
2	PAPER before REFEREEING
DOUBLE	
3	AUTHORSHIP and AUTHOR
4	AUTHORSHIP and PAPER
5	SESSION and SESSION-CHAIRPERSON

We will see that all four models use basically the same technique to enforce the Behavioural Constraint statically. The method is to constrain objects to have all the properties of their Object type. This means that other Object types with which they are associated must exist in the database at the time of their introduction. Objects which are not so constrained may however have some of their type properties missing. This situation is commonly described by the terms Total and Partial function. However, it is important to distinguish between two kinds of partial function – Not known, and Not applicable.

If an object has a property that is Not known, the implication is that it will eventually acquire that property. Not applicable, on the other hand, has a completely different meaning – ie, that the object will never possess that type property. In this discussion, only the 'Not known' variation of Partial Function is considered, the author being of the opinion that, for integrity's sake, a subtype should be constructed for objects with 'Not applicable' properties.

6.1 NIAM

NIAM uses only one construct, the Total Role Constraint, to model Behavioural Constraints. If the constraint is that an object A must be introduced before another object B, then the Total Role Constraint does not allow object B to exist without being related to object A. This forces object A to pre-exist object B. Eg, for Constraint 1, the ACC–PAPER relationship has a Total Role Constraint, indicated graphically by a 'V' on the edge. Similarly for Constraint 2. For constraints on both objects, a Total Role Constraint simply applies on both objects' relationships, as shown in Fig. 1 for SESSION and SESSION–CHAIRPERSON.

6.2   D2S2

This approach is identical to NIAM. Each edge in Fig. 2 may be one of two types – contingent, where the line is broken along one half of its length and all occurrences of one type only must participate in the relationship (eg, Constraints 1 & 2), or mandatory, where the line is solid and all occurrences of both entity types must participate (eg, Constraints 3, 4, & 5).

6.3   ACM/PCM
6.3.1   Constraint 1

This is complex, as many different constraints are required.

(a) ESSENTIAL clause is used for SESSION–PAPERS in the SESSION object. This constrains all SESSIONs to be related to a SESSION–PAPERS occurrence.

(b) An ASSERTION specification statement duplicates (a):

ALL s IN session (SOME ss IN session-papers (ss PART OF s))

(c) An ASSERTION statement for SESSION–PAPERS. This constrains all SESSION–PAPERS occurrences to be related to SESSION. Thus the effect of this constraint and that in (a) is to introduce SESSION and SESSION–PAPERS simultaneously.

ALL ss IN session-papers (SOME s IN session (ss PART OF s))

(d) An ASSERTION statement for ACC–PAPER that all occurrences must be related to a SESSION–PAPERS occurrence. From (c), this is obviously equivalent to constraining that they be related to SESSION occurrences.

ALL ac IN acc-paper (SOME ss IN session-papers (ac MEMBER OF ss))

(e) An INSERT SESSION Action is designed to insert a SESSION occurrence. This also has a DEPENDENT ACTION to insert an SESSION–PAPERS occurrence as an empty set. See the example in Constraint 2.

(f) An INSERT ACC–PAPER Action to insert an ACC–PAPER occurrence into the relevant SESSION–PAPERS occurrence. A PRE–CONDITION exists for checking the existence of the relevant SESSION–PAPERS occurrence, using a predicate expressed in the PREDICATE section.

Data models and integrity constraints 85

This constraint has required 6 different statements. To briefly comment:

(1) This example illustrates the undesirability of mixing structure and behaviour. The structural construct Association which is used to model the relationship between SESSION and ACC–PAPER has behavioural consequences. If the reality changed so that SESSION was to be introduced after ACC–PAPER, then Association couldn't be used for the relationship, as the required ASSERTION statements are not possible. Hence, the structure would have to be changed. A similar point was made in Section 5.5.

(2) It isn't clear why some constraints are duplicated and not others. For example, (b) duplicates (a), but (c) is not duplicated. Again, are the ASSERTIONs intended to be in the Conceptual Schema, or to be embedded in Application Programs? If the latter, then (f) duplicates (d).

(3) The complexity of this example is partly due to the Association concept's involvement, but also due to the ambiguity about what parts of ACM/PCM are duplicated for consistency purposes, and what parts are duplicated as they will be implemented in different sections.

6.3.2   Constraint 2

This contrasts with Constraint 1 as Association is not used. The constraint is expressed by an INSERT REFEREEING Action, with a pre-condition that the relevant REFEREE occurrence must already exist. The PREDICATE section is used for the predicates in the PRE– and POST–CONDITIONS. See Figure 6.

Fig. 6. The insert-refereeing ACTION

```
ACTION insert-refereeing (x,y)

IN (x:name, y:paper-title)
OUT (ref:refereeing)
LOCAL (r:referee, pa:paper)
PRE-CONDITION: referee-exist (x)?
               paper-exist (y)?
               no-refereeing (x,y)?
POST-CONDITION: refereeing-exist (x,y)?
DB-OPERATION: INSERT refereeing (x,y);
```

This solution is surprising. The constraint occurs only in the Behavioural part of ACM/PCM, but it should also be in the structural part, perhaps as an ESSENTIAL clause on REFEREE in the REFEREEING object. This adds weight to the view that ACM/PCM is contradictory in its view of its purpose.

6.3.3 Constraints 3 & 4

As these constraints involve the Association construct the solution is again complex, following the lines of Constraint 1. The Double constraint is achieved by a combination of a Dependent Action on the INSERT PAPER Action, to insert AUTHOR, linked with the PREDICATE section which checks that AUTHORSHIP shouldn't contain a null set.

6.3.4 Constraint 5

This is expressed by:

(a) ESSENTIAL clause for SESSION–CHAIRPERSON in the SESSION object
(b) A Dependent Action to insert SESSION–CHAIRPERSON linked to the INSERT SESSION Action.

These two constraints correctly duplicate one another, but the solution is incorrect as a SESSION–CHAIRPERSON occurrence could not be prevented from being introduced before SESSION. It therefore appears that a correct solution to the Double Behavioural Constraint requires the Association Construct.

6.4 CIAM

CIAM uses a Total Function constraint that is similar to the Total Role Constraint, but can only constrain one object, not two. For Constraint 1, Fig. 4 shows how the attribute function session on the entity type ACC–PAPER is total (tf) – this ensures that all ACC–PAPER are related to a SESSION. Constraint 2 is identical. However, it is not clear how CIM would model the constraint if it was reversed – ie, if a SESSION couldn't exist unless its identifier already existed in association with ACC–PAPER.

For Double constraints, CIAM uses a combination of Total Function and Existence Assertions to constrain both objects. Existence assertions (not completed in Fig. 4) specify the events which introduce (and update) entities. An Event is designed which will introduce both objects simul-

Fig. 7. SESSION–INTRODUCTION Event of CIM

```
event SESSION-INTRODUCTION;
    session:SESSION;
    session-nr:SESSION-NR;
    session-chairperson:SESSION-CHAIRPERSON;
    person-name:NAME;
    day:D
identifier session;
occurrence condition:external;
end;
```

Data models and integrity constraints

taneously, and this Event will be the target of the Existence Assertions in both objects. Fig. 7 shows the SESSION–INTRODUCTION Event, which will introduce both SESSION and SESSION– CHAIRPERSON. The Event is referenced in the Existence Assertions of SESSION–CHAIRPERSON and SESSION.

Although CIAM uses a behavioural part of CIM to express the double constraint, it is still in a declarative mode. However, the Total Function for SESSION–CHAIRPERSON is redundant, as the Event duplicates it.

6.5 Summary

Fig. 8 shows the constructs used in the 4 models for these constraints.

7. Conclusions

7.1 Features of Data Models

In terms of deficiencies in the models, D2S2 should add attributes and identifiers to its Entity Model, for completeness, and it is suggested that ACM/PCM review the Association construct, particularly with regard to allowing a 1:N constraint to become M:N.

7.1.1 Declarative Nature

The nature of this feature is that many aspects which were formerly only expressed in programs, in a procedural manner, may now

Fig. 8. Expression of Constraints and Abbreviations in the four Models

CONSTRAINT	NIAM	D2S2	ACM/PCM	CIAM
1	TRC	CON	ESS: ASS: ASSOC: ACT: PRE: PRED	TF
2	TRC	CON	ACT: PRE: PRED	TF
3	TRC	MAN	ESS: ASS: ASSOC: ACT: PRE: PRED	TF:EA:EV
4	TRC	MAN	ESS: ASS: ASSOC: ACT: PRE: PRED	TF:EA:EV
5	TRC	MAN	ESS: PRE: ACT	TF:EA:EV

NIAM	TRC		Total Role Constraint
D2S2	CON		Contingent
D2S2	MAN		Mandatory
ACM/PCM	ESS		ESSENTIAL clause
	ASS		ASSERTION
	ASSOC		Association construct
	ACT		ACTION
	PRE		Precondition
	PRED		PREDICATE
CIAM	TF		Total Function
	EA		Existence Assertion
	EV		Event

be expressed in a static (declarative) manner in a model, parts of which may be mapped to a Conceptual Schema. CIAM and ACM/PCM were found to be highly declarative, with D2S2 not attempting to integrate behaviour in this way – although its Behavioural Constraints were very declarative.

7.1.2 Dependence on Change

ACM/PCM's use of Association was found to cause problems in response to change, as it is used both for Identifying and Behavioural Constraints.

7.1.3 Unitary Nature

ACM/PCM was found to require a large number of constructs to express some constraints, especially the Behavioural Constraints. Some of these may be duplicated unnecessarily – this point implies that the aims of ACM/PCM may be contradictory.

7.1.4 Orthogonality

Another conclusion is that of the undesirability of a data model constraint being used for more than one real-world constraint. This has been termed orthogonality of constraints. At its worst, it occurs when the model constraint has a structural role (eg, an Identifying Constraint) and a behavioural role (eg, order of introduction), as a change to the behaviour in the real-world may necessitate a structural change in the database. This is the case with the Association construct of ACM/PCM. A better strategy would seem to be to design behavioural constraints to sit on top of the data structure, rather than be embedded in it.

7.1.5 Summary

Examination of these features leads to the notion that data models do not all have the same aims. They may, on the one hand, be intended as a specification language basically divided into two parts, one part to be used as a basis for mapping to a Conceptual Schema, the other part to be used as a basis for program design. This may be termed a binary model. On the other hand, their aim may to provide an integrated, highly-declarative specification language aimed to be used as a basis for systems design, without constraining how implementation will proceed. This model may be termed unary. The difference is very important as, for example, it will determine the extent and purpose of constraint duplication. In the binary model, where control will be exerted eventually in two separate regions, constraints should ideally be duplicated in both parts, while in the unary model, constraint duplication should be for consistency checking purposes only. Based on this discussion, CIAM appears to be a unary model, D2S2 and NIAM binary models, while no conclusion can be reached about the intentions of ACM/PCM, as it is frequently contradictory. This point can also make inter-model comparison difficult, if aims are not clearly stated.

7.2 Features of Constraints

No useful distinctioetween static and dynamic constraints as far as representation in data models may be made [5, 7]. A Total function (a static constraint) not only informs us that the total object population is related to another object, it also constrains the introduction and deletion of that object, with respect to the other. In general, a constraint may be expressed statically (in terms of a desired state) or dynamically (in terms of actions which lead to a desired state) – either form is equivalent. A constraint in the real-world may be expressed in either way, but it is more desirable for integrity reasons to express many constraints statically so that they can be enforced within a central Conceptual Schema, where the only copy resides. Application programs run against this Schema thus have less to do (thereby containing less possibility for error) and cannot conflict with each other in their treatment of constraints, as these are held centrally. Work is proceeding on the representation of constraints statically using the value-set construct of the ACS [15].

Further research is necessary as the simplicity of the example here may have led to bias for or against a particular model. More evidence is needed for the conclusions. Also, other constraint types need to be investigated, developing a wider taxonomy.

Acknowledgements

The author would like to acknowledge the contribution [1] to this paper of his colleagues Charles Akinyokun, Marcos Borges, Alberto Laender, Jano de Souza, and Amiya Saha, who are responsible for NIAM, ACM/PCM, and CIAM models which form the basis of the examples used in the text.

References

[1] Akinyokun O C et al. Untitled paper, University of East Anglia, Dec 1982.
[2] H Biller and E J Neuhold. Concepts for the Conceptual Schema. In Architecture and Models in Database Management Systems, pp 1–30, edited by G M Nijssen, North-Holland, Amsterdam, 1977.
[3] M L Brodie. The application of data types to database semantic integrity. Information Systems, Vol 5 No 4, pp 287–296, 1980.

[4] M L Brodie and E Silva. Active and Passive Component Modelling: ACM/PCM. In [11], pp 41–91.
[5] J M de Castilho, M A Casanova, A L Furtado. A Temporal Framework for Database Specifications. Proc International Conference on Very Large Data Bases, pp 280–291, Mexico City, Mexico, 1982.
[6] M R Gustafsson, T Karlsson, J A Bubenko Jr. A Declarative Approach to Conceptual Information Modelling. In [11], pp 93–142.
[7] M Hammer and D J McLeod. Semantic Integrity in a Relational Data Base System. Proc International Conference on Very Large Data Bases, pp 144–172, Framingham, Massachusetts, Sept 1975.
[8] L Kerschberg, A Klug, D Tsichritzis. A Taxonomy of Data Models. In Systems for Large Databases, pp 43–64, edited by P C Lockeman and E J Neuhold, North-Holland, Amsterdam, 1976.
[9] C H Kung. An Analysis of Three Conceptual Models with Time Perspective. In [12], pp 141–167.
[10] I G MacDonald and I R Palmer. System Development in a Shared Data Environment – The D2S2 Methodology. In [11], pp 235–283.
[11] T W Olle, H G Sol, A A Verrijn-Stuart (eds). Information Systems Design Methodologies: A Comparative Review. (Proceedings of the IFIP TC8 Working Conference on Comparative Review of Information Systems Design Methodologies, Noordwijkerhout, The Netherlands, May 10–14, 1982). North-Holland, Amsterdam, 1982.
[12] T W Olle, H G Sol, C J Tully (eds). Information Systems Design Methodologies: A Feature Analysis. North-Holland, Amsterdam, 1983.
[13] R Rock-Evans. Data Analysis. London: IPC Press, 1981.
[14] M J R Shave. Entities, Functions, and Binary Relations: steps to a Conceptual Schema. Computer Journal, Vol 24 No 1, pp 42–46, 1981.
[15] P M Stocker and R Cantie. A Target Logical Schema: The ACS. Proc International Conference on Very Large Data Bases, pp 309–310, Florence, Italy, November 1983.
[16] G M A Verheijen and J van Bekkum. NIAM: An Information Analysis Method. In [11], pp 537–589.
[17] ISO/TC97/SC5/WG3. Concepts and terminology for the Conceptual Schema and the Information Base, edited by J J van Griethuysen, American National Standards Institute, New York, USA, March 1982.

New IDMS Design and Documentation Tools Produced for the FEDOS Database

G Loizou* and El-S N O El-Shebini**
*Department of Computer Science, Birkbeck College,
University of London, Malet Street, London WC1E 7HX
**McDermott Engineering, London, 140 Wembley Park Drive,
Wembley, Middlesex HA9 8JD

FEDOS is an IDMS-based system for managing and controlling large-scale Finite Element structural models. In particular, FEDOS is aimed at the design and analysis of offshore structures in which vast volumes of data are normally involved. In developing FEDOS numerous challenging design problems of a general nature were encountered; the solution of these led to the development of various software tools for use in such areas as the automatic generation of the DDL source code for Schema, DMCL and Sub-schema; the automatic generation of comprehensive 'record' and 'set' documentation; the automatic computation of the exact number of pages and page sizes for each Schema area, ie total disk requirements; and the graphical display of Data Structure Diagrams, based on extended Bachman notation.

The raison d'ietre, design and construction of the said tools as well as the ensuing benefits thereof form the basis of this paper.

1. Introduction and Background

1.1 General

The Finite Element method [23] is a versatile tool used by stress analysts all over the world to determine stresses in structural components for which no mathematically closed form solutions exist. It is only when dealing with large Finite Element models that the real problems of handling vast volumes of data are truly revealed. All well-known Finite Element analysis systems (see, for example, [3, 13, 16, 17, 21]) use some form of a database for storing input data, intermediate calculations and final results. To the average user, however, this database is but a 'black box': data may be stored into and retrieved from this black box by using a set of predefined commands. In addition to being totally dependent on the Finite Element system used, say STRUDL [21], this approach has proved to be very inflexible in practice and has always failed in cases where concurrent access in a multi-user environment is a primary requirement.

In order to eliminate such problems, and indeed to offer a lot more benefits, a radically different approach has been adopted in a *new* system, called SAS (Structural Analysis System), which has been developed at McDermott Engineering, London, and is about to be applied in real life problems. At the heart of SAS is a sophisticated engineering database, hereinafter referred to as FEDOS; it replaces the 'black box' mentioned above and allows us to take advantage of all the benefits of an integrated database environment. (The original idea of FEDOS can be traced back to [18].) FEDOS is basically a serious attempt (cf [10, 11]) to apply database technology to a highly specialised engineering area by utilising one of the well-established database management systems, in our case IDMS [6].

FEDOS is totally independent of associated application programs, including Finite Element solvers; this has been achieved by the introduction of a new, sophisticated, easily expandable, free-format Model Definition Language [19], hereinafter referred to as MDL.

1.2 *MDL and FEDOS interfaces*

All pre-processors, solvers and post-processors available within SAS now use the FEDOS database as a common storage and retrieval source: some of them have direct access to this database, while others use special interfaces. For example, since McDermott Engineering do not have access to the source code for McAuto's STRUDL [21] (which is the main solver used in SAS), an interface CULPRIT [5] program is used to extract the Model data and create a formatted input data file for STRUDL. Similarly, another interface program is used to take STRUDL output results and store them in the FEDOS database. Thus, should it be decided, for example, that SAP6 [17] is to be used as a solver instead of STRUDL, the user need not worry about learning how to code input data for SAP6; he can simply use MDL to define his Model, and it is just a matter of using a different interface program between the FEDOS database and SAP6 to extract the data, and another to store the results. Once results are stored in the FEDOS database they would look the same to the user irrespective of the solver employed.

1.3 *Offshore structures*

Although FEDOS has been designed to handle generalised Finite Element problems, it incorporates very specific features for the design and analysis of offshore structures. For example, FEDOS interfaces with several programs for the generation of fixed offshore steel structures and also Finite Element Models of complex tubular joints. Furthermore, the concept of Super Elements [23] is effectively utilised to split a platform

Model into meaningful Super Elements, such as: Modules; Support Frame; Jacket; Bottle Legs; Piles; etc ... .

FEDOS also incorporates facilities for modelling foundations, which include non-linear soil properties, piles, insert piles, grouted or ungrouted piles, pile groups, etc ... . If it is required, the concept of Super Element images may be effectively used to define all the piles in the Model with minimal effort. Also available are interfaces with several programs for the generation of loads encountered in the design of offshore structures, such as wave, wind and gravity loads.

Moreover, the FEDOS engineering database itself contains additional data items specific to offshore design, such as: cutback values for Bill of Materials or centre of gravity purposes; grouping all Finite Elements which belong to the same physical part, or Finite Elements enclosed within other Finite Elements.

In the next section we describe the software tools which have been constructed in order to aid and speed up the design, development and documentation of the FEDOS database.

2. Computer-based Tools in the Design and Documentation of FEDOS

In the sequel the words *record* and *set* will always stand for *record type* and *set type* [1], respectively. If this is not the case then the full wording will be used, for example, record occurrence.

At the very outset of the database design stage, Schema, DMCL and Sub-schema modules had to be *manually* coded and Data Structure Diagrams had to be plotted by hand. Also, the recommended 'clock rule' method [6] for keeping track of set pointer positions needed in the DDL source code for Schema was very cumbersome indeed. Thus it became clear that the complexity and enormity (19 Schema areas, 85 Schema records, 122 Schema sets, 2000 or so Schema data items, etc) of the FEDOS database, together with its experimental nature, would have made it very difficult to continue its development using the aforesaid methods. Consequently, several database administration software tools have been developed in order to automate the above onerous and tedious tasks. These tools have been continuously enhanced in parallel with the database design and have continued to play a major role throughout the development of FEDOS. The said software tools are:

- DDL program: A DDL generator for Schema, DMCL and Sub-schema source code.
- DOC program: A documentation generator for each Schema record and each Schema set.

- SPACE program: A utility to calculate the physical disk space requirements.
- PLOT program: A plotting program for Data Structure Diagrams, using extended Bachman notation.

These are now described in some detail in the following sub-sections.

2.1 DDL generator (DDL program)

This program is written in PL/1 and although it started life as a one-off development aid, it is now one of the most sophisticated software tools available to Database Administrators within McDermott Engineering.

The program has two input files (see Fig 1):

- Schema definition file: this is a simple fixed-format file in which all the Schema components are defined.
- Run control file: this is a free-format file in which all the run-time parameters and options are defined.

The program produces three output files:

- Schema DDL source code.
- DMCL DDL source code.
- Sub-schema DDL source code.

The DDL source code generated by the program includes all files, areas, records and sets contained in the Schema as well as all possible options allowed by the DDL syntax. Although this, in general, results in the source code being much more than may be actually needed for a given design, it is a fairly simple task to use any online text editor such as TSO/SPF [22, 20] to delete any unwanted code and/or options.

Fig 1. DDL input/output files

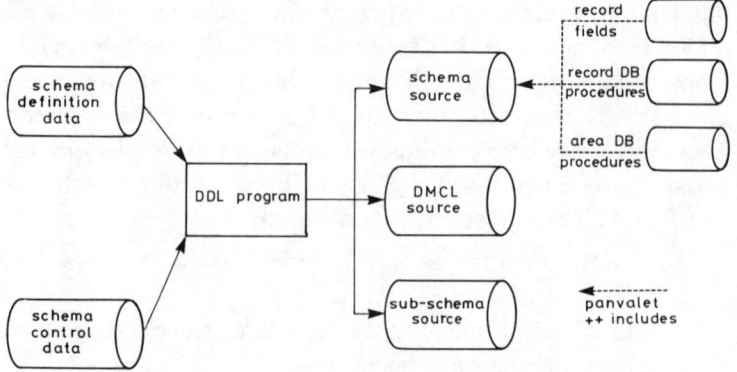

IDMS tools for the FEDOS database

The DDL program offers the following major features and/or benefits:

- The Schema, DMCL and Sub-schema DDL source code is guaranteed to be syntactically correct, according to the latest release of IDMS [7].
- Extensive validation checks are carried out by the program in order to ensure that the Schema DDL source code is error-free before it is passed to the IDMS Schema compiler, thus saving considerable processing time without clobbering the IDMS data dictionary [8] with useless information.
- The automatic calculation and tracking of set pointer positions obviates the need to use the cumbersome 'clock rule' method mentioned earlier. This also makes subsequent Schema design changes in which sets are added, modified or deleted, a simple task, particularly at the early design stages.
- Calls for the database procedures, IDMSCOMP and IDMSDCOM [6], are automatically included in the Schema DDL source code, for all 'Fixed Compressed' (FC) and 'Variable Compressed' (VC) Schema records. For example, IDMSCOMP is invoked to compress a Schema record occurrence before a STORE or MODIFY [1] operation, whereas IDMSDCOM is called after a GET or OBTAIN [14] operation to decompress a record occurrence.
- Absolute page numbers are automatically computed and generated based on relative page numbers or area sizes defined by the Database Administrator. This eliminates some tedious manual calculations and guarantees the correctness of the resulting values.
- Alias area names, based on a one-letter suffix defined by the Database Administrator, may be automatically generated, thus providing a simple, error-free procedure for creating multiple database environments, based on some reference Schema. This particular feature is extremely useful for distinguishing between a production database and one or more test databases, all running under IDMS [7].
- Optional Schema record and/or area database procedures [1, 14] may be automatically included from any externally defined source library.
- A 'minimum space' option allows the Database Administrator to go through the motions of generating the entire DDL source code without having to worry about the exact page numbers or area sizes, which is extremely useful at the early stages of the Schema

design. In this case the program simply defaults all area sizes to the minimum allowed, which for IDMS [6] is two pages.
- The program uses a very convenient identification system, based on 4-digit numbers, prefixed by a *unique* one-letter prefix to refer to Files (F), Areas (A), Records (R), Sets (S) and Members of sets (M). This simple system, which has proved to be very effective for cross-referencing, documentation, plotting, etc ..., is fully described in [19].
- The program includes options for the generation of DDL source code statements required to define different synonyms to be used for different DML languages such as COBOL, PL/1, FORTRAN, ASSEMBLER as well as different headers for OLQ [9] or CULPRIT [5]. These may be later edited using any available online text editor.

2.2   *Record and set documentation generator (DOC program)*

This program, written in PL/1, is essentially part of the previous DDL program which may be invoked by an optional run-time parameter (see Fig 2). If selected, the program produces valuable, properly formatted documentary material for use by the Database Administrator or indeed by anyone interested in the FEDOS database. This documentary material consists of the following components:

- Record documentation: this is one page per Schema record, using extended Bachman notation.
- Set documentation: this is one page per unique Schema set, using extended Bachman notation; multi-member sets appear on multiple pages.

Fig 2. DOC input/output files

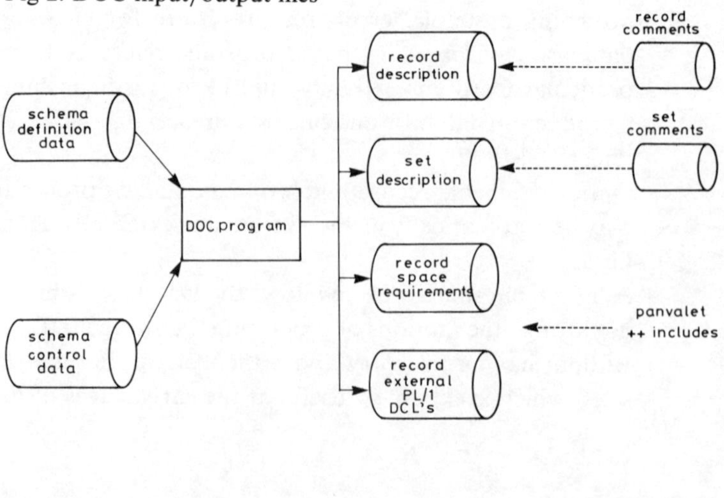

Both files contain necessary INCLUDE [15] statements (or equivalent) in order to include any documentary text created by the Database Administrator and stored externally in a source library. Such text is normally created and maintained using an online text editor such as TSO/SPF [22, 20]. Furthermore, one of the more recent enhancements to the program is a SCRIPT [2] option which outputs the above two files in a form compatible with the IBM mainframe text processing system, SCRIPT/VS [2]. This particular option makes it possible to automatically generate page numbers as well as a useful index based on certain keywords. Finally, the simple 4-digit identification system mentioned earlier is fully utilised here for producing the appropriate page headers and for the automatic generation of index keywords used in SCRIPT [2].

2.3 *Disk space reporter (SPACE program)*

This is a utility program, written in PL/1, and uses the CULPRIT [5] report generator in order to assist the Database Administrator in calculating the exact number of pages and page sizes for each Schema area.

The program has two input files (see Fig 3):

- Record definition file: this is a simple fixed-format file which contains one line per Schema record together with some identification data. Except for the first two fields in each line, the rest of the entries are automatically generated as a by-product of the DDL program. All the Database Administrator has to do is to edit the file online and insert the appropriate values in the two undefined fields which are simply: the expected number of Schema record occurrences and the percentage probability of this number.
- Run control file: this contains only a few optional parameters to control the run.

Fig 3. SPACE input/output files

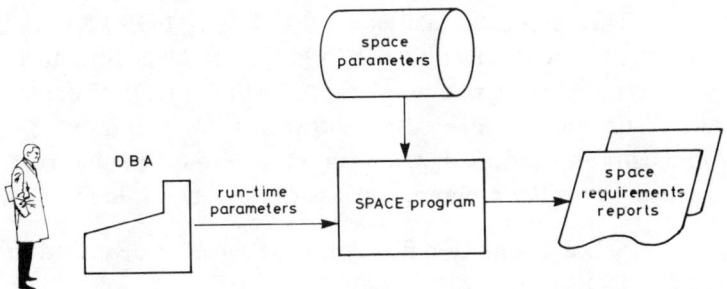

The program produces two output reports:

- Space requirements for each Schema record: this shows the actual Schema record data length and the record overhead (due to set pointers).
- Space requirements for each Schema area: this shows the total number of pages needed by each area to accommodate the various Schema records together with the total space required by the database itself.

The SPACE program offers the following major features and/or benefits:

- The space taken by the set pointers, depending on the pointer options chosen (ie NEXT, PRIOR, OWNER) is automatically included.
- The space taken by the hidden CALC [6] set pointers, maintained internally by IDMS, is automatically accounted for.
- The Space Management Information (SMI) [6] pages which are reserved by IDMS at the beginning of each area are included and properly identified.
- The page overhead reserved by IDMS (eg page header, footer and line index) is also accounted for.
- Any Schema area, which, because of the chosen page size, cannot accommodate a minimum number of Schema record occurrences, is flagged for the attention of the Database Administrator, thus highlighting a potential design inefficiency.
- Similarly, any area page which cannot be fully utilised is flagged for the Database Administrator. This is usually the case when a large page size is used to store very short Schema record occurrences, since IDMS can only store a maximum of 255 lines (ie Schema record occurrences) per page, no matter how large the page is.

2.4   *Data structure diagram plotter (PLOT program)*

This program, written in PL/1 and FORTRAN, is a great productivity tool to facilitate the plotting of Data Structure Diagrams using extended Bachman notation. As with the DDL program, it is now one of the most widely used software tools employed by Database Administrators and Designers within McDermott Engineering.

The input to the program consists of three files (see Fig 4):

- Schema definition file: this is the same file described earlier in the DDL program.

IDMS tools for the FEDOS database

- Plot definition file: this is a fixed-format file defining the general layout of the Schema records and Schema sets to be plotted.
- Run control file: this is a free-format file in which all the run-time parameters and options are defined (eg overall scaling factor, etc ...).

The output from the program usually consists of a plot tape ready for plotting on any Calcomp-compatible multi-pen drum plotter. It is also possible to produce similar plots on a TEKTRONIX graphics display unit by using the appropriate software interface.

The PLOT program offers the following major features and/or benefits:

- The program is driven by the same Schema definition file used in the DDL program to generate the Schema, thus eliminating any possible inconsistencies between the Schema and the corresponding Data Structure Diagram.
- The program includes options to plot the entire Data Structure Diagram or selected portions or views of it (eg Sub-schemas, etc ...).
- The physical plot can be determined by the Database Administrator on choosing the appropriate scaling factors, or may be automatically generated by the program.
- Records, sets, titles, grid lines, etc ... may be optionally plotted in any one of four different colours. For example, this facility may be used to distinguish LINK records from others by plotting them in red and everything else in black.
- Although IDMS/SPF [6] (secondary indexing) is not used in FEDOS, the program automatically recognises 'indexed' sets, and

Fig 4. PLOT input/output files

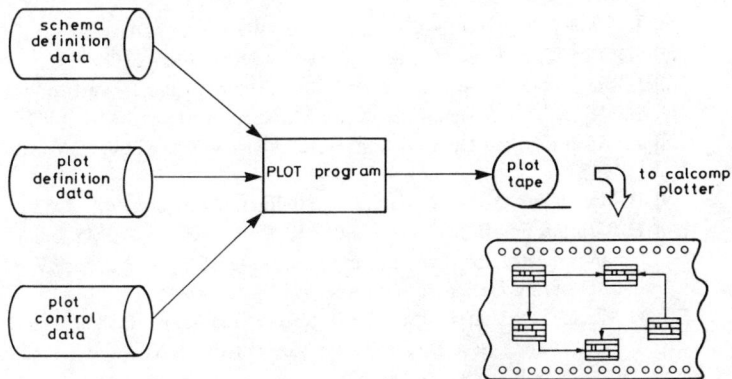

it is thus able to plot the appropriate triangular symbols used to identify such sets [6].
- In addition to plotting the basic information of a Data Structure Diagram, the program also plots the 4-digit identifiers mentioned earlier for convenience and ease of cross-referencing with the Schema DDL source code or other documentation.
- Optional 'summary' plots may be produced on small size paper for quick reference. These are 'skeleton' Bachman plots on which only the Schema record and set names are shown.
- The program includes various run-time options for annotating the Data Structure Diagram with titles, summary of abbreviations, border lines, etc ... . Such annotation is fully controllable in terms of positioning, orientation, size and colour.

A detailed 'extended Bachman' diagram (produced by the PLOT program) of the FEDOS database can be found in [19].

3. Conclusions

We have very briefly introduced the FEDOS engineering database, and have described in some detail the software engineering tools that were constructed in order to aid its design and development and conplete it within a reasonable time scale. FEDOS is now fully operational on IBM mainframe computers running under MVS/TSO [12, 22], and uses most of the IDMS complementary products such as CULPRIT [5], OLQ [9], and ADSO [4] for batch retrieval, online retrieval and online updating, respectively.

References

[1] CODASYL Data Base Task Group Report, ACM, New York, 1971
[2] DCF SCRIPT/VS Reference Manual, IBM, New York, 1978
[3] FEMALE: A Finite Element Modelling and Analysis Language for Engineers, SIA Ltd, London, 1978
[4] IDMS ADSO Features Guide, Cullinet, Westwood MA, 1980
[5] IDMS Culprit User's Guide, Cullinet, Westwood MA, 1982
[6] IDMS Database Design and Definition Guide, Cullinet, Westwood MA, 1982
[7] IDMS DC/CV System Generation, Cullinet, Westwood MA, 1983
[8] IDMS Integrated Data Dictionary Reference Guide, Cullinet, Westwood MA, 1982
[9] IDMS Online Query User's Guide, Cullinet, Westwood MA, 1982.
[10] H R Johnson, J E Schweitzer and E R Warkentine, A DBMS facility for handling structured engineering entities, IEEE Proc Database Week: Engineering Design Applications, pp 3 – 12, 1983
[11] H Matsuka, S Uno and M Sibuya, Specific requirements in engineering data base, in Data Base Design Techniques II (ed S B Yao and T L Kunii), pp 345 – 356, Springer Verlag, 1982

[12] MVS/SP General Information Manual, IBM, New York, 1983
[13] NASTRAN: NASA Structural Analysis, publication No SP−222, NASA, 1972
[14] T W Olle, The Codasyl Approach to Data Base Management, Wiley, Chichester, 1978
[15] PANVALET 10.0 User's Manual, Pansophic, Illinois, 1978
[16] SACS: Structural Analysis Computer System, Engineering Dynamics Inc, New Orleans, 1980
[17] SAP6 User's Manual, SAP6 Users Group, MIT, 1981
[18] N Shebini, Database Techniques for Large-Scale Finite Element Stress Analysis Problems, MSc Project Report, Birkbeck College, London, 1975
[19] N Shebini, FEDOS: A Finite Element Database for Offshore Structures, PhD Thesis, University of London, 1984 (to be submitted)
[20] SPF for MVS General Information Manual, IBM, New York, 1982
[21] STRUDL/DYNAL User's Manual, McAuto, St Louis, USA, 1980
[22] TSO Terminal Session User's Guide, IBM, New York, 1978
[23] O C Zienkiewicz, The Finite Element Method (3rd edition), McGraw-Hill, London, 1977

Logic as a Database Language

Robert Kowalski
Department of Computing, Imperial College, 180 Queen's Gate, London SW7 2BZ

This paper investigates the application of logic to databases in the restricted sense which regards a database as a collection of assumptions expressed in symbolic logic. A database query is regarded as a theorem to be proved from the assumptions. This contrasts with the relational database approach in which a database is regarded as a relational structure and queries are expressed in logic but are answered by evaluating them in the relational structure.

The difference between the two approaches has been characterised by Nicolas and Gallaire as the difference between regarding a database as a theory and regarding it as an interpretation [41]. When a database is regarded as a theory it is natural to describe data both by means of explicit assertions and by means of general rules. The inclusion of recursive definitions can be accommodated without leaving first-order logic.

In contrast, when a database is regarded as an interpretation, it is natural to restrict database description to the explict enumeration of the tuples which belong to the relations in the database. Although general rules defining virtual relations can be incorporated into queries and views, recursive definitions cannot be included without leaving first-order logic.

The use of logic for databases is closely related to its use as a programming language. Thus we shall review the main features of logic programming. Because logic programs and databases do not allow destructive assignment, we need an assignment-free method for dealing with database updates. For this purpose we make time explicit and we combine object language with metalanguage. The explicit treatment of time, needed to avoid the use of destructive assignment, has several incidental advantages. It imposes a semantic structure on updates and it distinguishes between the time at which an event takes place and the time at which it is recorded.

1. Historical background

Although the relational view of databases as interpretations has been the dominant theoretical model of databases since its introduction by Codd [13] in 1970, the view of databases as theories goes back at least to the question-answering systems of the 1960's. After a brief flurry of activity initiated by the application of resolution theorem-proving [46] to question-answering by Green [24], The application of logic to question-answering declined during the 'declarative versus procedural' debate which seemed to dominate the field of artificial intelligence during the first half of the 1970's.

Partly in response to the proceduralist criticism of logic, several researchers [26, 31] advanced the view that the better resolution theorem-provers behave as program executors.

Declarative statements of the form (called **Horn clauses** or **definite clauses**)

>*A* **if** B **and** C **and**...

in particular, behave as procedures which reduce problems of the form

>*A*

to subproblems of the form

>*B* **and** C **and**...

Such theorem-provers had in fact already been in existence since the mid 1960's [38].

However, it was not until 1972 that Colmerauer and Roussel [17] designed and implemented a practical language, PROLOG (PROgramming in LOGic), based upon the procedural interpretation of definite clauses as a development of an SL-resolution theorem-prover [37]. Further improvements to the implementation of PROLOG were made by Pereira, Pereira and Warren [51] who implemented a PROLOG compiler in PROLOG and showed that it compared in efficiency with compiled pure LISP. During the second half of the 1970's logic programming attracted adherents slowly and mostly in Europe. By 1980, however, interest had become more wide-spread [39], and in October 1981 the Japanese announced their decision to use logic programming as the foundation for their Fifth Generation Project.

The procedural interpretation of logic has been applied to many areas of computing. It has been particularly successful for program verification and program synthesis [7, 28, 29, 36]. When logic is used as both specification language and programming language, verification and synthesis both reduce to derivation of the program as a logical consequence of the specfication. The usual need to define the semantics of the programming language in terms which are compatible with the specification language is entirely circumvented.

PROLOG has contributed to significant practical advances in natural language processing. Again the lead has come from Marseille. Colmerauer's logic grammars [16] and analysis of natural language semantics [15] have provided the starting point for many of these systems [14, 18, 52].

PROLOG has also been used for many other applications. In this paper, however, I shall concentrate on the application of logic programming to database problems. The use of logic for database description is implicit in many PROLOG applications. The symbolic integration programs written in Marseille [2] and the drug analysis programs written in Budapest [20] are good examples. They combine programs which compute information with tables which store information explicitly.

In this paper I shall investigate some of the extensions of definite clauses which are needed for database applications as well as some of the current problems of database theory – such as incomplete information – from a logical point-of-view. An earlier version of this paper was presented in 1981 at a workshop on the Theoretical Foundations of Databases in Cetraro, Italy. The main difference between this version and the previous version is in the treatment of time in historical databases. For additional material the reader may wish to consult the book 'Logic for Problem Solving' [33]. The papers by Gallaire [22] and Reiter [45] are also a useful supplement to the material presented here. A more general, recent survey of logic and databases can be found in [23].

2. Definite clauses

The simplest definite clauses express that a relationship holds among individuals. For example, the assertion

$$Parents(John\ Mary\ Baby)$$

might express that

John is the father and Mary the mother of Baby.

In general an **assertion** consists of the name of a relationship, say P, applied to the appropriate number of names, say $t_1, ..., t_n$, of individuals. Such an assertion can be written in the form

$$P(t_1 \ ... \ t_n)$$

A more general form of definite clause is the implication, a clause of the form

$$A_1 \text{ if } B_1 \text{ and } B_2 \text{ and } ... \text{ and } B_n$$

where the **conclusion** A and the **conditions** $B_1, ..., B_n$ are all **atomic**, i.e. have the form

$$P(t_1 \ ... \ t_n)$$

where the expressions t_i are terms (defined below). For example, the implication

Mother(y z) **if** Parents(x y z)

expresses that

> for every x, y, and z
> y is mother of z if x and y are the parents of z.

Here x, y and z are **variables** which refer to arbitrary individuals, whereas 'John', 'Mary' and 'Baby' are **constants** which refer to particular individuals. In this paper we shall employ the convention that **variables** are strings of lower case letters (e.g. x, y, a, b, fred) and **constants** are non-negative integers (e.g. 0, 21, etc.) or strings of letters, the first of which is upper case (e.g. X, Fred, John).

In general the **terms** t_i which appear in an atomic conclusion or condition can be either

> constants, variables or expressions of the form $f(t_1 \ldots t_n)$ where f is a function symbol and $t_1, \ldots, t_n$ are terms.

For example, we could use function symbols 'dad' and 'mum' to name fathers and mothers. The implication

(1) Parents(dad(x) mum(x) x) **if** Human(x).

expresses that every human has a father and a mother. In the standard form of logic we could express such information using the **existential quantifier** $\exists$ (there exists)

(2) $\forall x \exists y \exists z$[Parents(y z x) **if** Human(x)]

$\forall$ is the universal quantifier (for all).

Sentences (1) and (2) are related to one another by a relationship called **Skolemization**. (1) logically implies (2) as a logical consequence, but not vice versa. (1) refers to individuals by means of names (e.g. dad(John), mum(Baby)), whereas (2) refers to individuals anonymously. The so-called 'clausal form' of logic without existential quantifiers (exemplified by (1)) is logically as powerful as the standard form of first-order logic (exemplified by (2)).

Although clausal form does not allow explicit use of existential quantifiers, in some contexts it is implicit. Given any clause C containing variables x1, ..., xn we read it as expressing

$$\forall x_1 \ldots \forall x_n \, C.$$

However if a variable x occurs in the conditions, but not in the conclusion, of C, then it can be read equivalently as existentially quantified after the 'if'. For example

$\forall x \forall y \forall z$ [Mother(y z) **if** Parents(x y z)]

is equivalent to

$\forall y \forall z$ [Mother(y z) **if** $\exists x$ Parents(x y z)].

3. Clausal Form

Only a slight extension of definite clauses is needed to obtain the full expressive power of first-order logic. It suffices to admit sentences of the form

A_1 **or** ... **or** A_m **if** B_1 **and** ... **and** B_n

which contain more than one alternative conclusion. Here, as before, the conclusions A_i and conditions B_j are atoms. If $n=0$ we may omit the vacuous 'if'. The use of alternative conditions allows databases to deal with incomplete information. For example

Martin teaches hardware or Morris teaches hardware.

In this example as elsewhere below we have taken the liberty of employing the more readable infix notation for binary relations.

More generally, it is often convenient to employ distributed infix notation for multi-place relations: for example

$x + y = z$ *instead of* Plus(x y z),
x supplies y to z instead of Supplies(x y z)
etc.

We shall not investigate full clausal form further in this paper, limiting attention instead to definite clauses and various extensions other than full clausal form. This is not entirely satisfactory as it limits our ability to deal with incomplete information. However, definite clauses have many compensating advantages. They provide great expressive power with remarkable simplicity; systems using them can be implemented efficiently.

4. Goal statements and denials

The degenerate cases (where $m=0$ or $n=0$) of the general form

A_1 **or** ... **or** A_m **if** B_1 **and** ... **and** B_n

have special significance. We have already seen the case n=0. In the case m=0 we can read such a clause as expressing that

>for all $x_1, ..., x_k$ it is not the case that B_1 **and** ... **and** B_n

where $x_1, ..., x_k$ are all the variables occurring in the clause. Such a clause is said to be a **denial**.

Given a collection of definite clauses as assumptions, a denial behaves as a challenge to show that it is inconsistent with the assumptions. In other words it functions as a **goal statement** of conditions to be achieved. For example, given the definite clause assumptions

>Adam supplies Sweets to Eve
>Eve supplies Apples to x **if** x supplies Sweets to Eve

the clause

>**if** Eve supplies x to Adam

denies that

>Eve supplies anything to Adam

which is obviously inconsistent with the assumptions. It is possible to extract from the proof the reason for the inconsistency:

>x = Apples

The denial functions as a query:

>Eve supplies what to Adam?

In the sequel, where all assumptions are definite clauses, we shall write denials

>**if** B_1 **and** ... **and** B_1

in the form

>B_1 **and** ... **and** B_n?

5. Terms as data structures

Terms in definite clauses can be used like data structures in programming languages. A term such as

>$cons(s\ t)$

for example, could be used to name a list

whose first element is named s, followed by the list named t. If the constant NIL is used to name the empty list, then the term

> *cons(D cons(A cons(T cons(A NIL))))*

names the list of characters

> *D A T A.*

It is convenient to use infix notation for two-place function symbols, writing

> *s.t instead of cons(s t).*

It is also useful to reduce the number of parentheses by employing conventions such as

> *r.s.t stands for r.(s.t).*

Thus we can simply write

> *D.A.T.A.NIL instead of*
> *D.(A.(T.(A.NIL))) instead of*
> *cons(D cons(A cons(T cons(A NIL)))).*

6. Recursion

It is commonly believed that recursion cannot be expressed in first-order logic. This view is expressed, for example, by David Harel [25] in his critical review of the book 'Logic and Data Bases' [21].

Consider, however, the following two definite clauses

> *x belongs to x.y*
> *x belongs to u.y* **if** x belongs to y.

For practical purposes these two clauses constitute a usable recursive definition in the definite clause subset of first-order logic of the membership relation for lists. Not only can they be used for such elementary purposes as showing that

> *A belongs to D.A.T.A.NIL*

but they can also be used to find an x which satisfies several constraints

> *x belongs to D.A.T.A.NIL and*
> *x belongs to A.N.S.W.E.R.NIL?*

In this respect the recursive definition behaves like a relational database which can be queried in different ways.

7. The procedural interpretation of definite clauses

Definite clauses of the form

A if B_1 and ... and B_n

can be interpreted efficiently as procedures which respond to procedure calls of the form A by replacing them with the collection of procedure calls

B_1 and ... and B_n.

PROLOG is based upon the procedural interpretation of definite clauses. For the sake of both simplicity and efficiency, it executes procedure calls left-to-right and tries alternative procedures one at a time. The order of execution of both procedure calls and alternative procedures is determined by the order in which they are written.

Given the problem of finding an x in both D.A.T.A.NIL and A.N.S.W.E.R.NIL, the procedural interpretation as realised in PROLOG behaves like a double loop. The outer loop generates consecutive elements of the first list and the inner loop searches sequentially for such elements in the second list.

8. Algorithm = Logic + Control

A collection of definite clauses alone does not fully specify an algorithm in the conventional sense. The clauses determine only the logic of an **algorithm**. The remaining component is supplied by the proof procedure which **controls** the way the clauses are used to solve problems [34].

The advantages of decomposing algorithms into logic and control components are two-fold.

(a) Algorithms can be developed from specifications and can be modified by ignoring the control component to begin with, reasoning with the logic component alone.
(b) Different algorithms can be obtained by altering the control component, leaving the logic component alone.

The use of deduction to derive the logic component of algorithms from specifications expressed in logic has been investigated by several authors [7, 28, 29, 36]. Their techniques resemble the program transformation methods, developed for recursion equations by Burstall and Darlington [5]. They are similar also to methods used for query transformation.

Improving the control component of an algorithm provides an additional tool for improving efficiency. Perhaps the most obvious improvement is the one which is obtained by executing procedure calls in a more flexible manner than that determined by left-to-right text order. IC–PROLOG [9], for example, allows users to annotate procedure calls for the purpose of executing them as coroutines and pseudo-parallel processes. The control features of IC–PROLOG have been incorporated into the truely parallel language of Clark and Gregory [10], which is the basis of both concurrent PROLOG [48] and Parlog [11]. Selective backtracking [4, 42] is another control improvement which is especially useful for database applications. Loop detection, macroprocessing and limited use of bottom-up execution have also been investigated.

In addition to improved control facilities implemented in software, many research groups are now investigating the design of parallel logic programming machines. Such machines are the main goal of the Japanese Fifth Generation Project.

9. Negation as failure

It is useful to extend definite clauses by allowing the negation of atomic conditions. In the procedural interpretation, a procedure call

not B

succeeds if and only if all the ways of trying to execute B terminate in **finite failure**. For example, given the assumptions

> *Bob supplies Pens to Mary*
> *Mary needs Money*
> *John supplies x to Mary* **if** *Mary needs* x **and not** [*Bob supplies* x *to Mary*]

the query

> *u supplies v to Mary?*

has two answers

> u = *Bob*, v = *Pens* **and** u = John, v = Money.

The second answer is obtained by using the third assumption to reduce the query to the two subgoals

> *Mary needs x* **and not** [Bob supplies x to Mary]?

Solving the first subgoal leaves the second subgoal which succeeds because the subgoal

> [*Bob supplies Money to Mary*]?

fails.

Negation as finite failure was first introduced by Hewitt in the AI programming language PLANNER [27]. Keith Clark [8] has shown that it is consistent with the standard meaning of negation. Roughly speaking, given a proof of **not** B by finite failure using clauses

$$B \text{ if } B_1, B \text{ if } B_2, ..., B \text{ if } B_n$$

there exists a structurally similar classical proof of **not** B using the if-and-only-if form of the definition of B:

$$B \text{ iff } B_1 \text{ or } B_2 \text{ or } ... \text{ or } B_n$$

together with appropriate axioms of equality.

There is one complication, however. To be correct, all variables $x_1, ..., x_k$ in a negative procedure call

not B

when it is selected for execution must be understood as existentially quantified

not $\exists x_1 ... \exists x_k$ B.

This is not always the intended reading. Consider, for example, the clause

A customer is category A if he has no debts, i.e.
x is category A **if not** *[x owes y].*

Suppose

John owes 10p
Bob owes 5p

The answer to the query

Mary is category u?

is correctly given as

$u = A.$

However, the query

who is category A?, i.e.
x is category A?

reduces to

not *[x owes y]?*

which succeeds if and only if

x owes y?

fails, which it does not. The query is incorrectly determined to have no answer.

Logic as a database language

The problem can be solved in several ways. Perhaps the simplest solution, though not necessarily the most efficient or most elegant, is to follow the lead of the relational calculus. A procedure call such as

>   **not** [x owes y]?

which contains a variable x which occurs elsewhere in the same clause should not be executed until it is instantiated. In our example, this necessitates introducing another condition which restricts the type of the relevant variable.

>   *x is category A* **if** x is a Customer **and not** [x owes y]

Membership in the type needs to be defined either by explicit enumeration

>   *Bob is a Customer*
>   *John is a Customer*
>   *Mary is a Customer*

or by general laws

>   *x is a Customer* **if** x purchases y
>   x is a Customer **if** x has account y

or by a combination of the two.

Using enumeration in this example, the answer to the query

>   *x is category A?*

is now correctly given as

> $x = Mary.$

It is worth noting that the complications which arise with negation as finite failure do not arise with the standard notion of negation. On the other hand, at the present time, negation by failure has the virtue that it can be implemented much more efficiently than standard negation.

10. Definite clauses as conditions

Negation as finite failure can be used to implement efficiently the execution of procedure calls which themselves have the form of definite clauses. A simple example is (the if-half of) the definition of subset:

>   *x is a subset of y if every member of x is also a member of y i.e.*
>   *x subset of y if* $\forall$ u [u belongs to y if u belongs to x]

Equivalently

>   *x is a subset of y if there is no u which belongs to x*
>   *but does not belong to y, i.e.*
>   *x subset of y* **if not** [u belongs to x **and not** [u belongs to y]]

Using the procedural interpretation of definite clauses and of negation as finite failure, the definition of subset behaves as a procedure which

> *given x and y*
> *shows x is a subset of y by*
> *finding all u which belong to x and*
> *showing each such u belongs to y.*

Executed sequentially in PROLOG-fashion this becomes a double nested loop. The outer loop generates successive elements of x and the inner loop tests whether they belong to y. The behavior of the procedure can be improved by improving the efficiency of its control component. In particular, given the availability of multi-processor architectures and associative memories,

> *members u of x could be generated in parallel by several processors and the test that such members belong to y could be made without search by look-up in an associative memory.*

Notice, however, that the remarks made earlier concerning the limitations of negation as finite failure apply also to definite clauses as procedure calls. As it stands the definition does not behave correctly when required to generate subsets or supersets of a given set. If the type restrictions

> *Set*(x) **and** Set(y)

are added as extra conditions then the definition behaves correctly but inefficiently.

Sentences which contain conditions having the form of definite clauses occur commonly both in database queries and in program specifications:

For example,

(Q) Find all suppliers which can supply all parts needed for project X. i.e. Supplier(x) and $\forall$ u[x can supply u if u is needed for X]?

(S) An element of a list is its maximum if it is greater than or equal to all elements in the list. i.e. u is maximum of x **if** u belongs to x **and** $\forall$ v [u $\geqslant$ v **if** v belongs to x]

Interpreting queries, such as (Q) above, as programs is accepted practice in relational database systems. Interpreting specifications, like (S), as programs is more unusual [36, 49].

11. Sets and aggregation

In database applications it is often necessary to generate and manipulate sets of answers to a query. Several programming languages, such as SETL [19], and HOPE [6], as well as most PROLOG implementations, provide a set constructor for this purpose.

The introduction of set construction can be justified within a first-order axiomatisation of a fragment of set theory:

> *For every formula F(x) containing at most one free variable x, there is an axiom which states the existence of a set Y such that x belongs-to Y **if-and-only-if** F(x).*

The collection of all such axioms is called the **axiom schema of comprehension**. Special care needs to be taken in its formulation to avoid the paradoxes of naive set theory.

In practice it is convenient to use a predicate

Setof (T Form Set)

which holds when

> *Set names the set of all instances of the term named T which satisfy the formula named Form in the current database.*

For example, given the set of assumptions

Adam supplies Sweets to Eve
Eve supplies Apples to x **if** x supplies Sweets to Eve

The query

Setof(u.v.w[u supplies v to w]s)?

has answer

$s = (Adam.Sweets.Eve).(Eve.Apples.Adam).Nil$

where the set s is represented by a list.

Given a formula F named Form and term t named T (all of whose variables occur in F) the obvious way to answer the query

Setof (T Form set)?

is to find all variable-free distinct solutions

$x = S_1, ..., x = S_n$

to the query

F and x = t?

and collect them into a list

$set = S_1.S_2 ... S_n.NIL$

This deals satisfactorily with the case where F has only finitely many answers. By using lazy evaluation as in PARLOG [11] it is also posible to deal with the case where F has infinitely many answers.

Other aggregation relations can be defined in terms of 'Setof'. For example:

>Cardinality(x f c) **if** Setof (x f s) **and** Length (s c)
>
>>Length (NIL 0)
>>Length(one.rest v) **if** Length(rest u) **and** u+1=v
>
>Total(x f t) **if** Setof(x f s) **and** Sum(s t)
>Sum(NIL 0)
>Sum(one.rest v) **if** Sum(rest u) and one + u = v

In the inventory example, later in the paper, we need a more complicated aggregation relation to add all the quantities of items sold between two dates. Given the assertions

>Sale(Apples 10 1.Jan.81)
>Sale(Oranges 5 1.Jan.81)
>Sale(Apples 2 2.Jan.81)
>Sale(Apples 10 1.April.84)

for example, the query

>Total(quantity Sale(Apples quantity time) x)?

gives the incorrect answer

>x = 12

because the Setof predicate gives the set {10 2} of all quantities of Apples sold. This can be corrected by generating instead the set {10.(1.Jan.81) 2.(2.Jan.81) 10.(1.April.84)} of all quantity-time pairs and then summing up the first elements of the pairs. The predicates Total* and Sum* meet this purpose:

>Total*(x y f t) *if* Setof(x.y f s) and Sum*(s t)
>Sum*(Nil 0)
>Sum*((one.index).rest v) *if* Sum(rest u) and one + u = v

The query

>Total*(quantity time Sale(Apples quantity time) x)

gives the correct answer

>x = 22.

Logic as a database language

12. Amalgamation of object language and metalanguage

Set construction can be formalized either in first-order set theory or in an amalgamation of object language and metalanguage. However, many practical applications of logic are most naturally catered for by amalgamating the two levels of language. In the case of databases, in particular, it is necessary both to describe and query databases in the object language as well as to construct and manipulate databases in the metalanguage. The amalgamation of object language and metalanguage which we propose is similar to the language FOL of Wehyrauch [53]. It uses the 'reflection rules' of FOL, in particular, to link the two levels of language. The amalgamation of object language and metalanguage is similar also to the use of 'eval' in LISP. Further discussion of the amalgamation logic can be found in [3, 33, 35].

The metalanguage can be interfaced with the object language by means of a four place 'Demo' predicate. The Demo predicate is defined in the metalanguage by means of axioms Pr such that

Pr implies Demo(A' Control' Concl' Result') in the metalanguage

if and only if

the attempted proof of the conclusion Concl, from the assumptions A, using control Control, results in output Result in the object language, where the **terms** *A', Control', Concl', Result' name the* **expressions** *A, Control, Concl, Result respectively.*

Thus the definition Pr of Demo in the metalanguage faithfully describes the input-output behavior of the object level proof procedure. Both the object language and metalanguage can be of sublanguages full first-order logic.

In theory the metalanguage, using Pr, can simulate the object language, making the object language unnecessary. In practice, however, it is useful to allocate work to both languages using **reflection rules** to communicate problems and their solutions between the two:

(1) Given A', Control' and Concl', the problem

Demo(A' Control' Concl' x)?

using the metalanguage can be replaced by the problem

Concl?

using A + Control in the object language. The name Result' of the output is returned to the metalanguage as result

x = Result'.

(2) An object level problem

> Concl?

to be solved using assumptions A and control Control can be replaced by the problem

> Demo(A' Control' Concl' x)?

in the metalanguage. The result

> x = Result'

in the metalanguage identifies the result Result to be returned to the object language.

The two reflection rules are so formulated that they do not alter the theorems which can be proved without them.

Set construction can be defined in terms of the Demo predicate:

> *Setof(t form set)* **if** CurrentTheory (assumptions)
>   **and** Demo(assumptions All(t) form set).

Here the predicate 'CurrentTheory' holds for, and accesses, a name of the current global database of assumptions and the control annotation All(t) specifies that a representation of the set of all distinct solutions of the query named form for the term named t is required as output.

The method of answering queries of the form

> *Setof(T Form set)?*

outlined in the preceeding section can be regarded as a special application of reflection rule (1).

13.   Database updating

The amalgamation of object language and metalanguage is useful for managing the way a database changes in time. Before defining this formally, we shall discuss the problem informally.

In relational databases, alterations of a database are generally associated with change of state. The time period for which a relationship holds is dealt with implicitly by adding the relationship to the database at the time it begins to hold and by deleting it when it ceases. This makes it impossible to distinguish between a deletion which marks the cessation of a relationship and one which simply removes erroneous information. It makes it difficult to distinguish between an addition which marks the beginning of a relationship and one which simply amplifies information about the current database.

Logic as a database language

An alternative is to include an explicit time parametas an argument of every time-varying relation. This is done in effect in Legol [30], a relational algebra based language intended for formalising laws and regulations. Marek Sergot [47] has shown how the treatment of time in Legol can be formulated in logic programming terms.

Explicit treatment of time has the advantage that addition and deletion of data can be freed from its associations with implicit recording of time periods and can be used for augmenting, correcting and logically reorganising the data. Information about start and end times can be dealt with uniformly by adding event descriptions to the database and can be structured by defining change of state as a logical consequence of events taking place. The following simplified personnel database illustrates the differences between the two approaches.

Suppose a personnel database contains a relation

EmployeeRecord(employee rank)

which holds between an employee and his rank (e.g. lecturer, professor, etc.). The relation needs to be updated every time an employee is hired, promoted, or leaves. Depending on which of these takes place, the update consists of an addition, replacement or deletion. Other tuples of other relations, dealing with employee salary, home address or immediate supervisor, for example, might also need to be updated. Because time is not explicit it is impossible to distinguish between the time at which a promotion is decided, the time at which it takes effect and the time its record is incorporated into the database.

Consider the alternative formulation in which time is made explicit. The additional parameter in the relation

EmployeeRecord(employee rank period)

records the total period for which the employee has a given rank. For example, the database might contain the historical information

(1) EmployeeRecord(Mary Lecturer P1)
(1a) $start(P1) = 1.Jan.80$
(1b) $end(P1) = 1.Jan.81$
(2) EmployeeRecord(Mary Professor P2)
(2a) $start(P2) = 1.Jan.81$

where P1 and P2 are constants and the equalities

$start(period) = time$
$end(period) = time$

can be regarded as functional syntax for binary relationships

> *Start(period time)*
> *End(period time)*

respectively. That Mary is still a professor is reflected by the absence of any information about the end of period P2.

If Mary leaves the firm, then a record of the event can be explicitly added to the database

> (L) Leave(Mary 1.April.84)

and the end of period P2 can be derived by the general rule

> (3) end(u) = v **if** Leave(x v)
>   **and** EmployeeRecord(x y u) **and** start(u) = z **and** z < v
>   **and** not [end(u) = w **and** w < v]

which express that an employee record ends on a date v when the employee leaves, if the employee record is not known to have ended earlier. (2), (3) and (L) logically imply

> (4) end(P2) = 1.April.84

However the attempted derivation in PROLOG of (4) from (3) goes into an infinite loop, because the subgoal end(u) = w of (3) reinvokes (3) without end. This can be cured in a variety of ways. But the modifications necessary are too complicated to enter into here.

Notice that the formulation using an explicit representation of time is more expressive than a representation in which time periods are implicit. It allows us to keep historical records and is a more accurate model of reality. Notice too that sentences such as (3) can be entirely hidden from the user who queries and updates the database. Moreover, all updates can be expressed as event descriptions such as (L). The derivation of relationships such as (1), (2) and (4) can be performed without the user knowing.

For example, suppose Mary was hired as a Lecturer and was promoted to Professor. The information (1)–(2) can be implicitly added to the database by explicitly adding instead the event descriptions

> (H) Hire(Mary Lecturer 1.Jan.80)
> (P) Promote(Mary Lecturer Professor 1.Jan.81).

(1) and (2) can then be derived by using general rules:

> (5) EmployeeRecord(x y period(H x y z)) **if** Hire(x y z)
> (6) start(period(H x y z)) = z

Logic as a database language 121

> (7) EmployeeRecord(x z period(P x y z u)) **if** Promote(x y z u)
> (8) start(period(P x y z u)) = u
> (9) end(u) = v **if** Promote(x y z v)
>   **and** EmployeeRecord(x y u)
>   **and not** [end(u) = w **and** w < v].

Here the terms period(H x y z) and period(P x y z u) name time periods which exist as a result of hiring and promoting events respectively. They can be thought of as being obtained by the use of Skolemization to eliminate existential quantifiers.

This formalization of state change is similar to the formulation of the plan-formation problem in [33, Chapter 6]. Clauses (7),(8) and (9), for example, describe the information **deleted** and **added** when an **action** of promotion is performed. What is remarkable in this formulation is that we have no analogue of the frame axiom, which states that any fact which holds in a state and is not affected by an action also holds in the new state which results when the action is performed. The frame axiom gives rise to the computationally expensive **frame problem** [43] of explicitly reasoning about facts which are not affected by actions. This is avoided in the formulation above by associating local time periods with time-varying relationships rather than global states. It is possible that local time periods can be used as local states to combat the frame problem in plan formation.

14. Another example

In this next example of an inventory database a simpler treatment of time is possible. Like the personnel database before, however, change can be dealt with simply by adding event descriptions to the database.

We can describe sales and purchases by means of relations

> *Sale(item quantity time)*
> *Purchase(item quantity time)*

A more realistic formulation would include extra parameters for sale number or order number. However, the simpler formulation presented here is sufficient for our purpose.

The Inventory relation can be defined in terms of the Sale and Purchase relations. Here it is intended that the relation

> *Inventory(item totalquantity time)*

describes the total quantity of any item in stock at any particular time. For the sake of simplicity arithmetic relationships are expressed in an abbreviated form.

Inventory(item totalquantity time)
  if Inventory(item oldquantity oldtime)
  and Total*(sold time1 [Sale(item sold time1) **and** oldtime ⩽ time1 < time] sold*)
  and Total*(bought time2 [Purchase(item bought time2) **and** oldtime ⩽ time2 < time] bought*)
  and totalquantity = oldquantity + bought* − sold*

In addition it is necessary to assert the initial inventory explicitly, e.g.

Inventory(Apples 10 1.*Jan*.81).

In a Prolog system the general Inventory rule would be used exclusively top-down to compute inventories when they are needed. Logically, however, the same rule could also be used bottom-up to generate new inventories which are then stored explicitly. Clearly in this example bottom-up execution would save much recomputation.

15. Formalization of database maintenance

The preceeding two examples motivate treating database maintenance as the problem of assimilating information into a database. They also suggest separating the database which describes the data from the integrity constraints which constrain it.

Since assimilation is a relationship between linguistic objects we shall formalize it in the metalanguage. The following formulation is a slight elaboration of that given in [3]. Here it is intended that

Assimilate(currdb constraints input bound newdb)

describes when assimilation of an input sentence into a given current database with given integrity constraints results in a new database within specified bounds on the deductive processing of the input. We use the control parameter of the Demo relation to communicate the bound to the object level proof procedure. Thus

Demo(db goal bound result)

holds when the attempt to derive a **goal** from a **database** within a specified **bound** outputs a corresponding **result**. In particular, if a goal is implied by the database but its proof cannot be obtained within the given bound, then the result will be 'No'. Here the following infix function symbols are used:

set-element names the set which results from deleting an element from a set,
set+element names the set which results from adding an element to the set,
*set*1 ∪ *set*2 names the union of set1 and set2, and
Yes(proof) names the proof which results from a successful call of the Demo relation.

(A1) Assimilate(currdb constraints input bound currdb)
    if Demo(currdb input bound Yes(proof))

(A2) Assimilate(currdb constraints input bound newdb)
    if info belongs to currdb
    and interdb = currdb-info
    and Demo(interdb+input info bound Yes(proof))
    and Assimilate(interdb constraints input bound newdb)

(A3) Assimilate(currdb constraints input bound newdb)
    if Demo(currdb   constraints not(input) bound Yes(proof))
    and AnalyseFailureRestoreConsistency(currdb constraints proof newdb)

(A4) Assimilate(currdb constraints input bound currdb+input)
    if Independent(currdb constraints input bound)

(A1) deals with the case in which the input is derivable from the current database within the given bound. The new database is then identical to the current database.

(A2) deals with the case in which the input implies information already in the current database. The proof of implication needs to be derived within the given bound and other parts of the database can contribute to the derivation. The definition is recursive because more than one item of information might be derived from the given input. In this simplified formulation the same bound is used for every attempted demonstration of information in the database. In a more realistic formulation the given bound would be shared among the subderivations.

(A3) is the most interesting case. The input is inconsistent with the current database and the integrity constraints. In the simplest case it is sufficient to reject the input. More generally, however, any part of the database might be abandoned or modified to restore consistency. We have assumed that the integrity constraints themselves are not subject to modification, although this need not be the case.

(A4) is the simplest case. The input is logically independent from the current database within the given bound. The new database is then the current database plus the input. The calls to the Demo predicate can be executed by using the metalanguage definition of Demo. It would be more efficient, however, to use the reflection rule. In fact it is even possible to use a single proof procedure at both the object and metalanguage levels. It is necessary only to ensure that the object level and metalevel databases are kept distinct.

16. Model Theoretic Semantics

As our final topic we shall discuss the theoretical differences between relational databases and logic databases. We shall argue that a relational database is best regarded as a relational structure and answering a query is evaluating a sentence (or formula) in a relational structure. A logic database, on the other hand, is a collection of sentences, also called a theory. Answering a query is proving that a sentence corresponding to the query is a logical consequence of the theory.

The distinction between these two views of databases is due to Gallaire and Nicolas [23]. It was a failure to distinguish between these two views which seems to have lead Harel [25] to argue that logic databases cannot be formulated in first-order logic. We shall also show, however, that it is possible to interpret a relational database as a particularly simple logic database consisting of finitely many variable-free atomic sentences with negation interpreted as finite failure.

A **relational structure** is simply a collection of individuals together with functions and relations over them. An interpretation of a collection of sentences S is a relational structure together with a correspondence between individuals in the structure and constants in S, functions in the structure and function symbols in S, and relations in the structure and predicate symbols in S.

We are interested in what it means for a sentence to be true in an interpretation. This allows us to define the answer to a yes-no query for a relational database to be the truth value of the query in the database regarded as an interpretation. It also allows us to define the notion of logical consequence. A sentence C is a **logical consequence** of a set of assumptions S iff (if and only if) C is true in all interpretations which are models of S. A **model** of S is an interpretation in which all the sentences which belong to S are true.

In a logic database S, a yes-no query C can have three kinds of answers: 'Yes' if C is a consequence of S, 'No' if **not** C is a consequence of S, or 'Don't know' if neither C nor **not** C is a consequence of S. In contrast, in a relational database a yes-no query can have only two kinds of answers: 'Yes' or 'No', corresponding to the two truth values of two-valued logic.

Logic as a database language

In the case where S is a set of clauses rather than a set of sentences in standard form, we can simplify both the notion of interpretation and the definition of truth. In particular, we can restrict the individuals in a relational structure I to be the variable-free terms constructible from S. This restricts the interpretations of S to so-called **Herbrand interpretations**. A Herbrand interpretation I is simply an assignment for every variable-free atom constructible from the vocabulary of S of exactly one of **true** or **false**. It can be shown that for every interpretation I of a set of clauses S there exists a Herbrand interpretation I* of S such that

S is true in I iff S is true in I*.

This has the immediate consequence that

S has no model iff it has no Herbrand model.

It is this fact which allows us to restrict attention to Herbrand interpretations. It has the consequence, however, that in order to use Herbrand models to show S logically implies C, it is necessary to show that S together with **not** C has no models and therefore has no Herbrand models.

It remains now to define the notion of truth for arbitrary clauses by reducing it to the notion of truth for variable-free atoms.

> *A set of clauses S is* **true** in an Herbrand interpretation I iff every clause in S is **true** in I and is false otherwise. A clause C is **true** in I iff every variable free instance of C is **true** in I and is **false** otherwise. A variable-free clause
>
> A_1 or ... or A_m **if** B_1 and ... and B_n
>
> is **true** in I iff at least one of the conclusions A_i is **true** in I or all of the conditions B_j are **false** in I and is **false** otherwise.

The following example illustrates the application of these semantic notions to the distinction between the relational database and logic database approaches.

The set of clauses

L1 John likes Mary
L2 Mary likes x **if** x likes Mary
L3 John likes John **or** Mary likes Mary

has exactly three Herbrand models. The variable-free atoms

John likes Mary
Mary likes John

are assigned the value **true** in all three models. One assigns **true** to

John likes John.

Another assigns **true** to

Mary likes Mary.

The third assigns **true** to both.

In the logic database approach, a set of sentences such as L1–3 is a **database**. A query such as

Mary likes John?

is answered by determining whether it is true in **all models** of the database. Because of the **completeness** of first-order logic, such questions can be answered by using proof procedures rather than the semantic definition of truth.

Notice that in this example the question

John likes John?

gets neither a 'Yes' nor a 'No' answer because it is true in some models but not in others.

In the relational database approach, a database is a relational structure. A formalization of the preceeding example by means of a relational database must choose one of the three models of L1–3 even though the current state of knowledge may not warrant such a choice. Once a relational structure has been chosen every yes-no query has a definite 'Yes' or 'No' answer. This makes it difficult for the relational database model to deal with incomplete information. Attempts to solve the problem by employing a three-valued logic while retaining the database as a relational structure do not have the power of the logic database approach. Query evaluation still reduces to unwinding the truth definition, whereas in a logic database it potentially involves the full problem-solving resources of a deductive proof procedure.

17. Definite clauses and minimal models

The distinction between the two views of databases becomes less clear cut if we limit attention to definite clause databases. This is because among all the Herbrand models of a set of definite clauses S is a single distinguished **minimal model M** [1, 50], which has the property that

a variable-free atom is true in **M** *iff it is true in all Herbrand models of S.*

Logic as a database language

More generally, a definite clause logic database S is **equivalent** to the relational database **M** which is its minimal model as far as

positive answers to first-order queries which can be constructed without negation and universal quantification

are concerned.

Consider, for example, the following simple definite clause database, a variation of L1–3 before,

L4 John likes Mary
L5 Mary likes x **if** x likes Mary
L6 Mary likes X **if** John likes X

This has exactly two Herbrand models. In one the variable-free atoms

John likes Mary
Mary likes John
Mary likes Mary

are assigned **true** and all others are assigned **false. This is the minimal model M**. In the other

John likes Mary
Mary likes John
Mary likes Mary
John likes John

are assigned **true** and all other variable-free atoms are assigned **false**.

Both the logic database and the relational database consisting of the minimal model give the same positive answers to queries without negation and universal quantification. For example:

Mary likes John?
  'Yes'
x likes John?
  'Yes', x = Mary
x likes x
? 'Yes', x = Mary
x likes y **and** y likes x?
  'Yes', x = John and y = Mary
    or x = Mary and y = John.

With the classical notions of negation and universal quantification the two databases can give different answers. A question such as

not[John likes Mary]?

has the same answer in both databases, but for different reasons:

> '*No*' *in the logic database because the unnegated query has answer* '*Yes*'. '*No*' *in the relational database because it is false in the database.*

Similarly

$$\forall x \text{ [Mary likes x \textbf{if} x likes Mary]}?$$

has answer

> '*Yes*' *in the logic database because it is a* (*trivial*) *logical consequence of it.* '*Yes*' *in the relational database because it is* **true** *in it (because both variable-free instances are true).*

The question

not [John likes John]?

however, is answered 'Yes' in the relational database (because it is **true**) and 'Don't know' in the logic database (because although it is true in one model, the minimal model, it is false in the other). For similar reasons

$$\forall x \text{ [Mary likes x]}?$$

is answered 'Yes' in the relational database but 'Don't know' in the logic database. Although this sentence is true in both Herbrand models, there exist non-Herbrand models in which it is false. Or to look at it differently, the Skolem form of the negotiation of the sentence, i.e.

not [Mary likes A]

is consistent with L4 – 6.

The situation is further complicated if in the logic database approach we interpret negation as finite failure. As already noted this is equivalent to the classical interpretation of negation where if-halves of definitions are reexpressed in if-and-only-if form and the appropriate equality assumptions are made explicit. If we do this for the definite clause database L4 – 6 we obtain the new logic database

> y likes x **iff** [y = John and x = Mary]
> **or** [y = Mary and x likes Mary]
> **or** [y = Mary and John likes x]
> **not** [John = Mary]
> **not** [Mary = John]
> x = x

Logic as a database language

If we now ask the question

not [John likes John]?

of the new database, we get the same answer as we did of the relational database. We need Reiter's [44, 45] domain closure axiom,

$x = John \; x = Mary$

and the axioms of equality, however, if in addition we want to obtain the same positive answer to the question

∀x [Mary likes x]?

as we did of the relational database.

The relational database and logic database approaches converge to an even greater extent when we focus attention on logic databases described by means of finitely many variable-free atoms. Or, to look at it from a different point-of-view, instead of regarding a relational database as a relational structure, we can regard it as the logic database consisting of all the variable-free atoms which are true in the relational structure. If in addition we interpret negation as finite failure and employ the domain closure axiom and the axioms of equality then

> all queries expressed in first-order logic evaluate to the same value whether we interpret the relational database as a relational structure or a logic database.

Thus we have two distinct ways of regarding a relational database from a logical point-of-view. In practice both ways give rise to the same results as far as the evaluation of queries is concerned. They differ greatly, however, in the extensions to the relational database model which they suggest for dealing with incomplete information. Treating relational databases as relational structures suggests handling incomplete information bymeans of many-valued logic and 'anonymous individuals'. Treating them aslogic databases suggests using disjunctions in conclusions, relaxing the'closed world assumption' associated with negation by finite failure andreferring to unknown individuals by existential quantifiers and Skolem functions. The first approach has been extensively investigated by relational database theorists and has not led to satisfactory results. If the second approach were adopted then the relational database model would be subsumed by that of logic databases.

18. Conclusion

We have sketched a logic programming approach to databases. From a practical point-of-view, logic databases have the advantage that

(1) they combine data definition, data query, data manipulation and programming language in one uniform formalism,
(2) they combine explicitly defined data with data defined by general rules which behave like programs, and
(3) they can deal with incomplete information by using disjunction and existential quantifiers and by relaxing the closed world assumption without altering the underlying formalism of logic.

Acknowledgement

This research was supported by the Science and Engineering Research Council. Marek Sergot has contributed to many useful discussions about the treatment of time and Sandra Evans has patiently and efficiently seen this paper through many intermediate drafts and revisions.

References

[1] Apt, K. R. and Van Emden, M. H., Contributions to the theory of logic programming. JACM Vol. 29, No. 3, pp 841–862, July, 1982

[2] Bergman, M., Kanoui, H., Application of mechanical theorem proving to symbolic calculus. Third international symposium on advanced computing methods in theoretical physics, C.N.R.S., Marseilles, June 1973

[3] Bowen, K. A. and Kowalski, R. A., Amalgamating language and metalanguage in logic programming. Logic Programming (K. Clark and S.-A. Tarnlund Eds.). Academic Press, 1982

[4] Bruynooghe, M., Analysis of dependencies to improve the behaviour of logic programs. 5th conference on Automated Deduction (W. Bibel and R. Kowalski, Eds.). Springer-Verlag, 1980

[5] Burstall, R. M., Darlington, J., Transformation for developing recursive programs. J. ACM Vol. 24 No. 1. pp 44–67, 1977

[6] Burstall, R. M., NacQueen, D. B. and Sannella, D. T., HOPE: an experimental applicative language. Proc. Lisp conference, Stanford, pp. 136–143, 1980

[7] Clark, K. L. and Sickel, S., Predicate logic: A calculus for deriving programs. Proc. 5th Int. Joint Conf. on Art. Intell. Cambridge, Mass., 1977

[8] Clark, K. L., Negation as failure. Logic and data bases. (H. Gallaire and J. Minker, Eds.)., Plenum Press, New York, pp. 293–322, 1978

[9] Clark, K. L. and McCabe, F., Control facilities of IC-Prolog. Expert Systems in the micro-electronic age. (D. Michie, Ed.). Edinburgh University Press, 1979

[10] Clark, K. L. and Gregory, S., A relational language for parallel programming. ACM Conference on Functional Programming Languages & Computer Architecture, October 1981

[11] Clark, K. L. and Gregory, S., PARLOG: parallel programming in logic. Research report DoC 84/4, 1983

[12] Clocksin, W. F. and Mellish, C. S., Programming in Prolog. Springer-Verlag, 1981
[13] Codd, E. F., A relational model for large shared data bases. CACM Vol. 13, No. 6 (June 1970), pp. 377–387, 1970
[14] Coelho, H., A program conversing in Portugese providing a library service. Ph.D thesis. University of Edinburgh, 1980
[15] Colmerauer, A., An interesting natural language subset. Logic Programming (K. Clark and S.-A. Tarnlund, Eds.). Academic Press, 1982
[16] Colmerauer, A., Metamorphosis Grammars. Natural language communication with computers, (L. Bolc, Ed.), Lecture notes in computer science No. 63, Springer-Verlag, Berlin, Heidelberg, New York. pp. 133–189, 1978
[17] Colmerauer, A., Kanoui, H., Pasero, R., Roussel, P., Un systeme de comunication homme-machine en Francais. Rapport, groupe intelligence artificielle, Universite d'Aix Marseille, Luminy, 1973
[18] Dahl, V., Quantification in a three-valued logic for natural language question-answering systems. Proc. 6th IJCAI, Tokyo, 1979
[19] Dewar, R. B. K., Grand, A., Liu, S-C., Schwartz, J. and Schonberg, E. Programming by refinement, as exemplified by the SETL representation sublanguage. ACM Transactions on programming languages and systems, Vol. 1, No. 1, pp. 27–49, 1979
[20] Futo, I., Darvas, F., Szeredi, P., The application of PROLOG to the development of QA and DBM systems. Logic and data bases. (H. Gallaire and J. Minker, Eds.), Plenum Press, New York, pp. 347–375, 1978
[21] Gallaire, H., Minker, J., (Editors), Logic and data bases. Plenum Press, New York, 1978
[22] Gallaire, H., The impact of logic on database. Seventh international conference on Very Large Data Bases. Cannes, 1981
[23] Gallaire, H., Minker, J. and Nicolas, J. M., Logic and Databases. University of Maryland, Technical Report, 1983
[24] Green, C. C., Theorem proving by resolution as a basis for question-answering systems. Machine intelligence 4, Edinburgh University Press, New York, (B. Meltzer and D. Michie, Eds.). pp. 183–205, 1969
[25] Harel, D. Review of the book Logic and Databases. Computing reviews, Vol. 21, No. 8, pp 367–369, 1980
[26] Hayes, P. J., Computation and deduction. Proc. 2nd MFCS symps. Czechoslovak Academy of Sciences, pp. 105–118, 1973
[27] Hewitt, C., PLANNER: A language for proving theorems in robots. Proc. IJCAI, Washington, D. C., pp. 295–301, 1969
[28] Hogger, C. J., Program synthesis in predicate logic. Proc. AISB/GI conf. on AI, Hamburg, July, pp. 18–20, 1978
[29] Hogger, C. J., Derivation of logic programs, JACM, Vol. 28, No. 2, pp. 372–392, 1981
[30] Jones, S., Mason, P. J. and Stamper, R. K., Legol-2.0: A relational specification language for complex rules. Information Systems, Vol. 4, No. 4, 1979
[31] Kowalski, R. A., Predicate logic as programming language. Proc. IFIP 74, North Holland Publishing Co., Amsterdam. pp. 569–574, 1974
[32] Kowalski, R. A., Logic for data description. Logic and data bases. (H. Gallaire and J. Minker, Eds.), Plenum Press, New York, pp. 77–102, 1978

[33] Kowalski, R. A., Logic for problem solving. North Holland Elsevier. New York, 1979
[34] Kowalski, R. A., Algorithm = Logic + Control. CACM, Vol. 22, No. 7, July 1979
[35] Kowalski, R. A., Logic Programming. Proceedings of IFIP Congress. Paris, France, September 1983
[36] Kowalski, R. A., The relationship between logic programming and logic specification. The Royal Society Discussion Meeting, February 1984
[37] Kowalski, R. A. and Kuehner, D., Linear resolution with selection function. Artificial Intelligence, Vol. 2, pp. 227–260, 1971
[38] Loveland, D. W., Mechanical theorem proving by model elimination. JACM 15, April 1968, pp. 236–251, 1968
[39] McDermott, D., The Prolog phenomenon. SIGART Newsletter, No. 72, pp. 16–20, 1980
[40] Mendelson, E., Introduction to Mathematical Logic. Van Nostrand, Princeton, N.J, 1964
[41] Nicholas, J. M., Gallaire, H., Data base: Theory vs. Interpretation. Logic and data bases, (H. Gallaire and J. Minker Eds.), Plenum Press, New York, pp. 33–54, 1978
[42] Pereira, L. M. and Porto, A., Selective backtracking for logic programs. 5th conference on Automated Deduction (W. Bibel and R. Kowalski, Eds.). Springer-Verlag, 1980
[43] Raphael, B., The frame problem in problem solving systems. Artificial intelligence and heuristic programming. (Findler, N. V., Meltzer, B., Eds.), Edinburgh University Press, Edinburgh, pp. 159–169, 1971
[44] Reiter, R., On closed world data bases. Logic and data bases, (H. Gallaire and J. Minker, Eds.), Plenum Press, New York, pp. 55–76, 1978
[45] Reiter, R., Towards a logical reconstruction of relational database theory. In 'On Conceptual Modelling' (M. Brodie, J. Mylopoulos, J. W. Schmidt, Eds.) Springer Verlag. To appear
[46] Robinson, J. A., A machine oriented logic based on the resolution principle. J. ACM Vol. 12, pp. 23–41, 1965
[47] Sergot, M., Programming Law: Legol as a logic programming language. Dept. of Computing, Imperial College, 1980
[48] Shapiro, E., A subset of Concurrent PROLOG and its Interpreter. ICOT technical report TR–003, 1983
[49] Turner, D., Functional programs as executable specifications. Royal Society Discussion Meeting, February 1984
[50] Van Emden, M. H., Kowalski, R. A., The semantics of predicate logic as a programming language. J. ACM, Vol. 23, No. 4, pp. 733–742, 1976
[51] Warren, D. H., Pereira, L. M., Pereira, F., PROLOG– The language and its implementation compared with LISP. Proc. Symp. on AI and programming languages, SIGPLAN Notices, Vol. 12, No. 8, and SIGART Newsletters No. 64, pp. 109–115, August 1977
[52] Warren, D. H., Efficient processing of interactive relational database queries expressed in logic. IEEE Proc. 7th Conf. Very Large Databases, pp. 272–281, 1981
[53] Weyhrauch, R., Prolegomena to a theory of mechanical formal reasoning, Artificial intelligence, Vol.13, pp. 133–170, 1980

HERCULES: Database query using natural language fragments

R.N. Cuff
IBM United Kingdom Laboratories Ltd., Product Assurance Laboratory, Hursley Park, Winchester, Hampshire SO21 2JN UK

Most, if not all, of today's database retrieval systems are hard for a casual, non-programming user to work with. They often presuppose that the user can deal with a logical or programming-like formalism, and nearly always force a knowledge of the structure and naming of database components. At the other extreme, such a user may have different problems with a free-form natural language (NL) interface, which prevent it from being as convenient as is sometimes supposed.

This paper proposes a query interface, HERCULES, intended especially for such users. It combines menus with fragments (phrases or clauses) of NL that the user enters against particular menu items. These items are short descriptions of the information held in the database, relating to particular entities. The user is unaware of database structure and the names of components such as relations or attributes. Before data are retrieved, HERCULES feeds back an NL restatement of the query for confirmation.

Heuristics are included to propose information to be retrieved beyond what the user asks for explicitly; and to rank alternative interpretations of potentially ambiguous input.

We describe in outline a prototype implementation, and discuss in some detail the data collections needed to support the interface. The prototype is intended to show that the HERCULES approach can succeed using simpler implementation techniques than are needed by other NL understanding systems.

1. Introduction

Casual or infrequent users, especially those with no programming skill, are likely to have difficulty with many present-day database systems. They may be required to know the database structure and be able to navigate around it; and use formal manipulative techniques to extract data. In such cases there is a mismatch between the user's needs and the system's procedures. After reviewing this imbalance, this paper proposes a new interface, HERCULES, for making database queries. (The name is an acronym for HEuristic Retrieval: a Casual User LanguagE System.)

HERCULES combines ideas from menu-driven systems and natural language (NL) understanding systems. A prototype has been partially implemented.

2. Casual users and today's systems

[4] depicts casual users as having certain important features in common. (For simplicity, we shall concentrate discussion on relational databases, but this is not an important restriction.)

(a) Casual users do not work regularly and frequently with the system. They tend to forget details about it and to retain only a few simple concepts.
(b) They tend to make errors easily. The more opportunities for error that a system provides, the more errors are made.
(c) They may not know or remember how the database is organised. A casual user should not need to know how to navigate through relations, or to talk about relation or attribute names.
(d) Often a casual user will have little or no programming skill.
(e) Casual users tend to forget to fill in all the details of what they want from a database query. For instance, a literal treatment of a formal query equivalent to "Which employees earn more than Lewis and work in a department that sells fish?" would list only employee names, whereas there is a good chance that the salary and department of each identified employee would also be useful things to list. Nearly every query system today requires its users to ask for these attributes explicitly.
(f) What evidence there is on the matter suggests that casual users do not form complex queries. Although the evidence is hardly conclusive, it lends credence to the view that many casual users will wish to pose only queries that could be stated simply in English. More complicated problems will be tackled, if at all, through consecutive simpler queries.

Many existing query systems, including those described as research vehicles, do not suit this profile well. In particular, languages such as SEQUEL [2] or Query-by-Example [17] require the user to know the relational composition of the database; to know the system's names for the relations and their attributes; and, to a greater or lesser extent, to be able to link them together in a methodical way rather as in programming. The burden of creating the query is very much the user's. Because the query has to be expressed in terms of the relational organisation, one must break the original question into parts that may not flow naturally from its English form.

For instance, consider the following database (used throughout the rest of the paper), which gives information on the people employed by a department store and the items sold there.

```
EMP     (NAME, SAL, MGR, DEPT)
SALES   (DEPT, ITEM)
SUPPLY  (ITEM, SUPPLIER)
TYPE    (ITEM, COLOUR, SIZE)
```

In Query-by-Example (QBE), for instance, the question "List departments with their suppliers" involves using three example elements and creating a temporary table, as in Fig 1.

Further, "Which departments have more than eight employees?" involves nested built-in functions, a condition-box, and double underlining (the QBE way of grouping relational tuples that have a common value for some attribute) — see Fig 2.

Each of these queries has potential pitfalls for the casual user, for whom these methods do not provide a natural way of thinking about the problem.

It is not surprising, then, that research on natural language (NL) query interfaces has flourished during the past decade. Examples include LIFER, part of the LADDER system [9]; PLANES [15]; RENDEZVOUS [3]; ROBOT [8]; EUFID [13]; and TEAM [7].

Experimental studies of how well potential users can work with such systems are not as plentiful, but there have been reports on LADDER [1, 10] and PLANES [14]. Commercial versions of ROBOT have been available for some years. A special issue of the SIGART Newsletter [12]

Fig 1. QBE: "List departments with their suppliers"

SALES	DEPT	ITEM
	toy	ink

SUPPLY	ITEM	SUPPLIER
	ink	mmm

	p.toy	p.mmm

Fig 2. QBE: "Which depts have more than 8 employees?"

EMP	NAME	SAL	MGR	DEPT	CONDITION
	all.x			p.t	cnt.all.x>8
				—	

in 1982 included outlines of many projects in progress, and a recent overview of modern NL processing systems is [6].

There are some daunting practical problems with an NL interface:

(a) It encourages an unrealistic expectation of the system's power.
(b) The linguistic limitations of such a system are not as well defined as they are with a formal language. They can appear, sporadically and unexpectedly, when the system rejects an unknown word or a grammatical construction, or when it lacks background knowledge.
(c) NL's richness often makes sentences ambiguous. One has to rely on the implementation being prepared to consider all possibilities, a situation that does not arise with a formally-defined language.
(d) Because much of the vocabulary and knowledge that people want to use when querying a particular database may be specific to it, an NL system has to be partly recast for each domain of discourse.
(e) There are several technical problems, such as anaphora and ambiguity, requiring effort in areas that do not concern more formal systems. If it is to have an acceptable interface, an NL system is inherently more complicated to implement. If too much of this burden is put back subtly on to users (as, for instance, in lengthy attempts to remove ambiguity via dialogue), they may react against it.

3. HERCULES

HERCULES is a database interface that offers a partial NL capability in a novel way. It operates within a menu-based framework that shields the user from the relational structure of the database.

3.1 Example 1

Here is a query against HERCULES, equivalent to the question, "Who earns more than Lewis and works in a department that sells fish?". It shows one way in which this question could be answered using a partly implemented prototype, discussed later. (In this example, the user's input is shown in single quotation marks for clarity. We shall drop this convention subsequently.)

```
Which of these topics are relevant to your problem?
Select one or more by number.

1. Employees
2. Items sold or supplied

'1'
```

HERCULES: query using natural language

```
%The screen is cleared before the following appears
EMPLOYEE              *
  Name                :
  Salary (pounds)     : '> lewis'
  Department          : 'selling fish'
  Manager             :

* * * * * * * * *
Using this specification:

EMPLOYEE's salary is more than LEWIS' salary; his/her
department is department selling the FISH.

List for each such EMPLOYEE:
  (1) his/her name
  (2) his/her salary
  (3) his/her department
List for each such LEWIS:
  (4) his/her salary

Is this interpretation OK?
1. Acceptable as it stands
2. Acceptable, but some output fields should be omitted
   or listed in a different order.
3. No - I want to alter my specification
4. No - HERCULES should offer a different meaning

--- etc ---
```

Had the user declared an interest at the beginning of this interaction in both employees and items sold or supplied, a different menu would have been displayed at that point, and the user could have used rather different NL fragments (see Example 2).

Note that in a strict calculus sense, " lewis" is not well-formed, since "lewis" is a string, not a number. QBE or SEQUEL would force a more indirect way of expressing this constraint.

A QBE user seeking to answer the question would need to know that two table-skeletons, for EMP and SALES, should be requested; and would then enter something like Fig 3.

Fig 3. QBE: "Who earns more than Lewis & works in a dept that sells fish?"

EMP	NAME	SAL	MGR	DEPT
	p.	p.>$\underline{sl}$		p.$\underline{d}$
	lewis	p.$\underline{sl}$		

SALES	DEPT	ITEM
	$\underline{d}$	$\underline{fish}$

Note that the QBE user would have to decide in advance which attributes should be displayed, and ask for them all explicitly.

3.2 Example 2

Here is another way of asking the same question as above:

```
EMPLOYEE                   *
   Name                    :
   Salary (pounds)         : more than lewis
   Department              : =
   Manager                 :
ITEM                       *
   Name                    : fish
   Colour                  :
   Size                    :
   Department              : =
   Supplier                :
```

The user has told the system which attributes of each entity should be equated. If he/she had not done this, the prototype would have offered guidance:

```
         Please select one or more of the following. Do you intend
that:

         1. Department selling the FISH is EMPLOYEE's department
         2. No such link applies
```

3.3 Example 3

"Who earn more than Lewis' manager, and where do they work?"

```
EMPLOYEE                   *
   Name                    :
   Salary (pounds)         : > lewis' manager
   Department              : ?
   Manager                 :
```

The question-mark is the convention by which the user can ask explicitly for a particular attribute to be included in the list to be retrieved.

Fig 4 shows what this would be like in Query-by-Example.

Fig 4. QBE: "Who earn more than Lewis' manager, & where do they work?"

EMP	NAME	SAL	MGR	DEPT
	p. lewis x	p.n>y y	x	p.

It may be interesting to see how V2 would feed back its interpretation:

```
EMPLOYEE's salary is more than EMPLOYEE_B's salary.
EMPLOYEE_B is LEWIS' manager.

List for each such EMPLOYEE:
   (1) his/her name
   (2) his/her salary
List for each such EMPLOYEE_B:
   (3) his/her name
   (4) his/her salary
```

3.4 Example 4

The most straightforward form of certain queries may involve NL fragments that seem more appropriate to an entity itself (considered as a unit) rather than to any of the ordinary menu leaves. It is legitimate to treat the entity-name as a leaf (it is known as an entity-leaf, and owns the ordinary leaves immediately following it):

"Who, other than Smith's manager, works in the toy department?"

```
EMPLOYEE          * not smith's manager
  Name            :
  Salary (pounds) :
  Department      : toy
  Manager         :
```

3.5 Example 5

"Which departments have more than 8 employees?"

```
EMPLOYEE          *
  Name            :
  Salary (pounds) :
  Department      : with > 8 employees
  Manager         :
```

The actual total of employees would also be offered to the user. See section 2 of this paper for the QBE version of this request.

3.6 Example 6

"Who is managed by Cox or Smith?"

```
EMPLOYEE          *
  Name            :
  Salary (pounds) :
  Department      :
  Manager         : cox or smith
```

Table 1 shows examples of NL fragments acceptable to the prototype if entered against the 'Manager' menu leaf under the EMPLOYEE entity.

Table 1: Some inputs accepted by the prototype

```
carter
= carter
smith's
of· smith
manager of smith
smith's manager
managing smith
who manages smith
not bailey's
who does not manage bailey
who is managing the hardware department
in the hardware dept
who works for the hardware department
who works for robinson
of smith's manager's department
earning £12000
earning more than 10,000
earning between 12000 and 15000 pounds
with at most 8 employees
of a department selling rice
of an employee who earns more than chapman
of a department selling an item supplied by Acme
```

The main characteristics of a HERCULES session are as follows.

(a) The user is never concerned with the way in which the database is split into relations or attributes, or even that it is a relational database at all. Relation- and attribute-names are not exposed.

(b) The user is encouraged to think of the database as describing entities. (The Database Administrator (DBA) judges what the entities are, when creating a description schema – see section 5.)

(c) The menu of entities focuses attention on those aspects of the database (those entities) pertinent to the user's current interest.

(d) The bottom-level (leaf level) menu describes, in a series of short noun phrases, information held in the database that relates directly to the chosen entity or entities. A leaf corresponds to one or more attributes in the database (for example, "Name" of ITEM corresponds to SALES.ITEM, SUPPLY.ITEM and TYPE. ITEM). Note that this is fundamentally different from systems that expose the database's relational structure.

(e) The user enters a short NL phrase or clause against each of zero or more leaves. Certain other conventional characters may be entered: see '=' and '?' above.

(f) HERCULES may then ask for guidance on the manner in which entities are to be linked, if the user has not already specified the links (see Example 2). When setting up the description schema, the DBA defines which attributes in which relations have domains overlapping with some other attribute. This information provides the basis for HERCULES to decide which linkages to offer in the current menu.

(g) HERCULES feeds back its best interpretation of the user's intention, couched in stylised English. It offers to list appropriate values corresponding to one or more leaves, having included those leaves that it judges may be of interest, besides any that the user may have asked for explicitly (using the '?' control convention).

(h) The user may accept this interpretation, in which case it is mapped internally to a query in the formal language used for the underlying database management system interface, and despatched for execution. Alternatively, the user may want to exclude or reorder some of the offered attributes before agreeing to the interpretation.

(i) A third option allows the user to ask for another interpretation from HERCULES. If HERCULES can suggest one (perhaps derived from an alternative parsing of the input, if multi-word

HERCULES: query using natural language

phrases or clauses appear in it), it will produce what it judges to be the next most likely interpretation, and so on.

At each point during linguistic processing at which some ambiguity is noted, HERCULES assigns a heuristically based likelihood to each possibility. When processing is complete, the most likely alternative is selected for feedback first. Examples of potential ambiguity include:

(a) (against EMPLOYEE Name) "employee managing xxxx" – is xxxx an employee name or a department name? The DBA will have supplied an estimate for the relative likelihood of these possibilities (based on an assessment of typical user queries) as part of the entry for 'manage' in the lexicon.

(b) "manager of (Smith's department)" or "(manager of Smith)'s department"? The semantic filtering component in the prototype was designed to reflect some features of idiomatic English, and would give a slight preference to the first of these.

4. Appropriateness for casual users

In section 2, we commented on some of the attributes that casual users tend to share. The HERCULES interface appears to fit many of the requirements implied by these attributes, although of course this needs to be tested in practice. Commenting on the list at the beginning of section 2:

(a) There are only a few simple concepts to remember with HERCULES: knowing how to enter NL fragments against menu leaves; and the meaning of the conventional control characters '?' and '='. Everything else is introduced in menu form, and in words appropriate to end users. Even the case of '=' can be avoided, and an extra level of system-initiated menu dialogue used instead.

(b) A menu approach offers smaller scope for user error.

(c) The various levels of menu guide the user to the aspects of data relevant to the problem. At no time is the relational structure observable. Menu leaf descriptions are noun phrases rather than database attribute names.

(d) No programming-related skills are needed.

(e) The HERCULES prototype includes heuristics to decide which attributes should be offered for display in response to any particular query. Included will be any attribute mentioned in an NL fragment or implied by use of a menu leaf; and the 'key' attribute(s) of each entity in the menu (eg, 'Name' for the EMPLOYEE entity).

(f) A query stated simply in English stands a good chance of being represented by short and simple NL fragments against HERCULES.

Section 2 also pointed out some of the problems associated with orthodox NL interfaces to a database. Some of these are reduced in HERCULES. For instance, getting away from a linear, sentence-based query statement provides a constant reminder that this is an artificial system, without the full inferential power of a human being.

5. A prototype implementation

A prototype implementation has been designed and partially implemented. Some important areas of NL coverage were excluded, notably quantifiers and a full treatment of logical operators. The prototype was not formally tested in a real user environment, as it was able to carry only simple queries through the complete interpretation process. However, there are tentative plans for a reimplementation, when users' reactions could be studied properly.

The prototype described here was written at the Man-Machine Systems Laboratory in the Dept. of Electrical Engineering Science at the University of Essex. The implementation language was ULISP [11] running on a PDP 11/45 under UNIX. The target language into which it translated a query was QUEL. A full account of the implementation can be found in [5].

HERCULES input is intended to be short, and simply descriptive; further, because it occurs in the context of a particular leaf, the description on the menu leaf ("Department", etc) can usually be omitted from the input, making it shorter still.

If in fact the nature of HERCULES means that a restricted NL range is all that is required, then the techniques needed to process it should be less complex than with a full NL query system. The prototype was a deliberate attempt to use straightforward processes as a test-bed. Five main stages are involved:

5.1 *Lexical*

Using the lexicon, each input word is reduced to one or more standard forms, each being tagged with a syntactic category and perhaps a value. Any word which cannot be so reduced is assumed to be a data string-value.

5.2 Syntactic

The standardised input is parsed using a database-independent augmented transition network (ATN) [16]. Parsing is syntax-based: no reference is made to the lexicon, and no semantic criteria appear in the ATN's arc-tests. Several parse structures may be produced.

5.3 Semantic

Using the lexicon again, each parse is analysed for semantic plausibility. At the same time, it may be partially restructured, expanded into two semantically different structures, or discarded as invalid. Each surviving interpretation (by now unambiguous) emerges tagged with a numerical relative likelihood.

5.4 Feedback

The interpretation-structure bearing the highest likelihood is selected from each leaf, and converted to an internal form that can readily be mapped into stylised English feedback. If the user accepts the ensuing interpretation, events proceed as in the next stage. If not, a combination of structures with the next highest likelihood is chosen, if one exists, and this stage repeated until the user accepts or changes the query.

5.5 Program synthesis

The same internal form used in the feedback stage is used as input to an algorithm for synthesising a QUEL program to carry out the actual data retrieval and presentation.

6. Description schema

The prototype uses two data collections to represent the outside world. The first is a description schema, which describes the database structure, and how it is to be represented to the user as a set of entities with their attributes.

We shall list briefly the main components of a description schema, with examples in a suitable LISP-based syntax referring to the sample database.

(a) The name by which each relation or attribute is known to the DBMS: eg,

```
<relations emp sales supply type>
<attribs   emp name sal mgr dept>
```

(This latter describes the relation EMP as consisting of attributes NAME, SAL, etc.)

(b) Logical relationships between the domains of each attribute. For instance, a manager is also an employee: so that the set of values from EMP.MGR is a subset of that from EMP.NAME:

```
<subset     emp mgr emp name>
<intersect sales item supply item>
```

(c) The entities that the DBA decides should be represented in this view of the database; some simple facts about each entity, to help in producing idiomatic English feedback; and a short descriptive phrase to appear in the entity-level menu:

```
<entities employee item>
<emark employee person singular>
<emark item thing singular>
<nlent employee "employees">
<nlent item "items sold or supplied">
```

(d) The contents of each entity's leaf menu. This is the way in which the user's entity-oriented view of the data is mapped into relational attributes by HERCULES – eg, how the entity ITEM is reflected in parts of the relations TYPE, SALES and SUPPLY.

Each leaf has a list of database attributes directly semantically connected with the usage identified by the leaf description in the context of the entity. For instance, the "Department" leaf of EMPLOYEE is directly connected with EMP.DEPT, but not SALES.DEPT, because the latter's role in this view of the database is directly related to ITEM and not to EMPLOYEE.

```
<menu employee 1 (emp name)
               2 (emp sal)
               3 (emp dept)
               4 (emp mgr)>
<menu item     1 (type item
                  sales item
                  supply item)
               2 (type colour)
               3 (type size)
               4 (sales dept)
               5 (supply supplier)>
```

(e) A NL descriptor for each leaf. The descriptor is used for several purposes, including message entries and English feedback, and may be required to produce a slightly different external result for each. Consequently, it has a structure rather than being a simple string. However, we shall not go into details here. As an example, the NL descriptor for "Department" (the fourth leaf) of ITEM is:

```
<nlattr item 4 "department" "selling the *">
```

This may be shown externally, depending on the context, as, for instance:

```
department
department selling the item
department selling the FISH
```

7. Lexicon

The second data collection is the lexicon. This is a less fixed creation than a description schema is. It is up to the DBA to decide such issues as which words the user can employ in leaf input, or which links between leaves and/or entities may be described. The DBA will use a mixture of common sense understanding of how people refer to things (for example, money received by an employee is usually called 'salary' or 'pay' or 'wage', but not 'manager' or 'halibut'), and knowledge or surmise about how the local users employ words in a HERCULES framework. Obviously, this can be refined, and the lexicon suitably modified, through experience. This is directly comparable to the situation obtaining with any NL-based system. In the HERCULES case, the simplicity of leaf input makes the DBA's task relatively easy once the basic rules have been grasped.

The prototype's lexicon identifies six major syntactic categories – comparative, built-in function (such as "average"), Boolean operator, leaf (with entity as a special case), link, and data value – and some minor ones such as preposition and noise word. A noise word is one ignored in a HERCULES context – for instance, the definite or indefinite article.

The main components of the lexicon are as follows, again with examples.

(a) A syntactic category is supplied for each valid syntactic role that each input word may have. If an input word has meanings in several categories, each is given a different (internal) token, which is then treated separately elsewhere in the lexicon.

```
<ambig from between in>
<range between>
<link employee in department>
```

This represents the facts that "from" can be a range-indicator carrying the meaning "between" (as in "from 10 to 20"), or can be a synonym for the "in" link (see later) connecting "employee" with "department" (as in "Smith from/in the hardware department").

(b) If two words share a meaning (at least, if the meanings can be treated as the same in a HERCULES context), that meaning is represented by a single token.

```
<alias employ manage>
```

(c) Most tokens are associated with a value of some kind, taken from a specialised domain appropriate to the token's syntactic category. For example, comparatives draw from the set (lt, nlt, gt, ngt, eq, neq), and built-in functions draw from the set of aggregate functions valid in QUEL. In cases such as these, assigning a value to a token allows a parametric approach when producing QUEL or NL feedback.

(d) The remainder of the lexicon contains the relationships between the tokens for entities and leaves. We showed above that the description schema associates each entity with an ordered list of database attributes, which form the basis of the leaf menu. Using the same numbering, the lexicon associates each leaf with a token. This token, if appearing in the output from the lexical stage of NL processing (ie, if some input word has been lexically transformed to this token) and in the context of the present entity, will be taken as referring to the identified leaf of the menu. For example,

```
<leaves of employee are 1 name
                       2 salary
                       3 department
                       4 manager>
```

As elsewhere, different external words may refer to the same leaf or entity, but be represented internally by the same token.

We mark those leaves that draw values from an ordered domain. Only against these will operations such as "greater than" or "minimum" be sensible.

Further, we specify the unit, if any, in which the values of each leaf are measured. The semantic stage may be able to use the appearance of a unit-token in its input as an aid for disambiguating that input.

(e) A relationship between two topics (the generic name for an entity-or a leaf-token) may be found in either of two forms.

The first is where topic1, besides any other role it may play, is also a special case of topic2. So a "manager" is also an "employee".

```
<assume manager is employee>
```

The second form is where the topics are related by a link. This is a token corresponding to a word such as "earns"; in the sample database, this can only validly occur as part of a user input involving (or implying) the topics "employee" and "salary":

```
<link employee earn salary>
```

A given link may relate more than one pair of topics. For instance, a manager may employ an employee; a department may employ an employee; and a manager may employ (manage) a department. The syntax used is:

```
<link 100 manager employ employee>
<link  90 department employ employee>
<link  80 manager employ department using employee
          where (1 employ (3 in 2))>
```

The third of these recursively defines "manager managing a department" as being true if the manager (1) employs an employee (3) who is "in" (which is another link) the department (2).

The integers 80, 90, 100 are likelihood factors, used as follows. If several meanings for a particular link survive to the end of the semantic stage, this must be because the input has insufficient internal evidence for HERCULES to decide what the user means. For instance, if the input against the "Manager" leaf is "managing xxx", the data value xxx might validly represent an employee or a department. Here we appeal to an external knowledge source – the DBA's previous judgement on the relative likelihood of each possibility. This judgement will be based on predictions about the relative frequency of different types of query, knowledge of colloquial English usage, and good guessing. It can be refined when HERCULES is monitored in a working environment.

The DBA adds a likelihood factor into each meaning clause to reflect this. Only the ratios of competing likelihoods are important, not their absolute values. Likelihood factors are used in calculating a numerical assessment $L(i,j)$ of how likely it is that the generated meaning-structure $M(i,j)$ reflects the user's intention for leaf input $IN(i)$. The $M(i,j)$ with the highest $L(i,j)$ will be the first to be tried out in NL feedback. If that is rejected, others may then be used.

8. Summary

The HERCULES interface combines menus, fragmentary NL input, and stylised NL feedback, all couched in user-oriented terms. The dialogue focuses the user's attention methodically but swiftly on the particular areas within the database that are of interest for the present query. The user is in charge throughout, but strongly guided. Substantial feedback is provided, notably in HERCULES's restatement of the query in English terms.

The user needs no knowledge of databases or how they are organised. Ordinary menus, leaf menus and feedback contain no names of system objects; the user is told what information is available, but not how it is reflected in the database. Since the leaf menu describes all the data available about an entity type, the user may be less inclined to try to ask queries impossible to answer within the semantics of the database.

Experience with the prototype suggests that simple NL-handling implementation techniques are enough to provide a practically useful interface. The ATN that is the main information structure of the syntactic stage remained compact and easy to extend, because no semantic information had to be carried around.

Large data structures and complex processing were not required (although this must be qualified, since not all the semantic stage was implemented). The savings here over other NL systems stem from the fact that only limited fragments of NL need to be dealt with. So a small number of primitive word categories proved to be all that was necessary, and this made possible an ATN that is database independent and has relatively few nodes. Because of the restricted nature of CU queries against databases when guided by the HERCULES interface, the impedimenta of verb tenses, cases, and pronoun reference could be dropped.

HERCULES certainly has some limitations. It is poorly equipped in its present form to handle problems that need to connect separate leaves by a Boolean OR — for instance, "Who earns more than 10,000 dollars or works in the Toy department?". Unless two separate queries are issued, this can be posed only clumsily:

```
EMPLOYEE            * paid > 10,000 or in toy dept
   Name             :
   Salary (dollars) :
   Department       :
   Manager          :
```

Problems that require an OR-connection between values against a single leaf are easily dealt with (such as "Who is managed by Smith or Cox?").

Other limitations and possible ways of alleviating them are discussed in [5].

Acknowledgements

I am grateful to Prof. Ian Witten, now at the University of Calgary, for discussions while the work reported here was in progress, and for his comments on a draft of this paper.

References

[1] C L Blais, A natural language query system to aid in Navy command and control; concepts for modifying LADDER for the retrieval of information in an operational environment, Tech Rpt 374, Naval Ocean Systems Center, San Diego, California, 1979

[2] D D Chamberlin, M M Astrahan, K P Eswaran, P P Griffiths, R A Lorie, J W Mehl, P Reisner and B W Wade, SEQUEL2: a unified approach to data definition, manipulation, and control, IBM J of Research and Dev, Vol 20, No 6, pp 560–575, 1976

[3] E F Codd, R S Arnold, J-M Cadiou, C L Chang and N Roussopoulos, RENDEZVOUS Version 1: an experimental English language query formulation system for casual users of relational data bases, Res Rpt RJ2144, IBM Research Lab, San Jose, California, 1978

[4] R N Cuff, On casual users, Int J of Man-Machine Studies, Vol 12, No 2, pp 163–187, 1980

[5] R N Cuff, Database queries using menus and natural language fragments, PhD thesis, Dept of Elec Eng Science, University of Essex, 1982
[6] W B Gevarter, An overview of computer-based natural language processing, NASA Tech Memo 85635, Washington DC, 1983
[7] B J Grosz, TEAM, a transportable natural language interface system, Proc Conf on Applied Natural Language Processing, Santa Monica, California (Assoc for Computational Linguistics), pp 39–45, 1983
[8] L R Harris, The ROBOT system: natural language processing applied to data base query, Proc ACM Annual Conf, pp 165–172, 1978
[9] G G Hendrix, Human engineering for applied natural language processing, Proc 5th Int Joint Conf on Artificial Intelligence, pp 183–191, 1977
[10] R L Hershman, R T Kelly and H G Miller, User performance with a natural language query system for command control, Interim Rpt TR 79–7, Navy Personnel R&D Center, San Diego, California, 1979
[11] R L Kirby, ULISP for PDP–11's with memory management, Rpt TR6, Comp Sci Center, University of Maryland, 1977
[12] Newsletter of the ACM Special Interest Group on Artificial Intelligence, No 79, pp 27–109, 1982
[13] M Templeton and J Burger, Problems in natural language interface to DBMS with examples from EUFID, Proc Conf on Applied Natural Language Processing, Santa Monica, California (Assoc for Computational Linguistics), pp 3–16, 1983
[14] H Tennant, Experience with the evaluation of natural language question answerers, Proc 6th Int Joint Conf on Artificial Intelligence, Tokyo, Japan, 1979
[15] D L Waltz, An English language question answering system for a large relational database, Comm ACM, Vol 21, No 7, pp 526–539, 1978
[16] W A Woods, Transition network grammars for natural language analysis, Comm ACM, Vol 13, No 10, pp 591–606, 1970
[17] M M Zloof, Query-by-Example: a data base language, IBM Sys J, Vol 16, No 4, pp 324–343, 1977

The Construction of Interfaces to Triple Based Databases

N J Martin
Birkbeck College, University of London, Malet Street, London
WC1E 7HX

In recent years there has been a resurgence of interest in the implementation of database systems using an underlying 'triple' storage structure. In contrast, there has been less work on the design and implementation of end user and application programmer interfaces to such systems.

This paper examines the implications of adopting a triple storage structure on the design of such interface software. The problems arising both from stores designed to embed data semantics and semantic free triple stores are demonstrated. The consequences of particular semantic embedding models are discussed.

The paper describes a triple model which has been designed specifically to enable the construction of flexible interfaces. The design principles and implications for interface construction are identified. Triple store database interface software using this model, which is at present in the course of implementation, is discussed.

1. Introduction

There has been interest for many years in the use of binary relationships in the implementation of database systems. They have been considered both as a conceptual or data modelling construct and as the basis for a database storage structure. The fundamental construct of the binary relationship approach to conceptual modelling is the binary relation between types or categories of entities. The work of Abrial [1] and others has been influential in this context. The ISO report [10] provides a thorough review of this approach.

Binary relationships have also been considered as a modelling construct at the entity instance rather than type level. Such binary relationships can clearly be represented as a triple of elements. Storage structures adopting such a triple format have been called binary-relational storage structures. Frost [5] reviews work on such structures. 'Triple' storage structures can of course be considered without any interpretation of the elements by reference to a binary relationship model. For this reason the term 'triple store' is used hereafter for such structures. The purpose of this paper is to consider specifically the construction of interfaces to triple store databases.

2. Triple Stores

2.1 Basic concepts

A triple store can be thought of simply as a data structure for the storage of triples together with basic operations for manipulating those triples. The nature of triple elements is not specified. Basic operations for triple manipulation are 'insert', 'delete' and 'retrieve'. The first two operate on a specified triple in the obvious way. The 'retrieve' operation retrieves those triples from the store matching a given triple. Each element of the given triple may specify a particular element value or a 'match any' value. Clearly there are eight possible permutations of 'match any' elements in the given triple ranging from none to all three elements being so specified. Whether the resultant eight forms of the retrieval operation are all actually available as basic operations in a given triple store implementation depends on the particular method of implementation.

The notation for representing triples adopted in this paper is angled brackets with commas separating triple elements, for example:

```
<x, y, z>
```

2.2 Recent work

Since Frost's survey in 1980 [5] of triple store implementations and applications, work has continued on a number of projects. These are briefly reviewed below with particular reference to work on interfaces.

2.2.1 The Fact machine

The Fact machine [15][16] has been developed at the University of Strathclyde. Although included here as a triple store, the basic units of information manipulated by the machine are numbered triples giving rise to a quadruple structure called 'facts'. The triple part consists of two entity symbols and the symbol for a directed relation between them. The latter is itself an entity symbol. A valid fact is (extending the triple notation to quadruples):

```
<1, the moon, is made of, cheese>
```

Here character strings rather than the corresponding entity symbols are illustrated. As the example shows there is no necessity for a fact to represent true information. A fact number may be used as a triple element of another fact. In this way it is sought to represent information of arbitrary complexity. Hence, given the example fact above, the information that 'John believes that the moon is made of cheese' can be represented by the fact:

```
<2, John, believes, 1>
```

Frost [5] has noted in particular the emphasis in this project on the use of set membership information to enable the expansion of reference to an entity 'upwards' to references to all sets containing that entity and 'downwards' to all entities representing subsets of that entity. Work on the implementation of this 'generic' information via a generic associative matrix chip in VLSI is reported as progressing well [16]. The first chip set was delivered in October 1982.

In addition to basic triple store operations 'generic' operations are provided to take advantage of generic information. For example a 'generic retrieve' operation expands the reference to each element in the given triple as indicated above. Facts which have elements in each of these expanded search sets are retrieved. From an interface point of view therefore, a powerful retrieval operation is directly available. As noted by McGregor and Malone [16], relevant information, which is stored in a more particular or general form than that specified in a query, can be returned to a user.

Generic information is also used in internal data reorganisation and hypothesis formation. McGregor and Malone [15] discuss these and other novel features such as the use of a particular class of facts as integrity rules and the tagging of facts with procedures of Fact machine instructions.

2.2.2 IFS

IFS (Intelligent File Store) is a triple store system being developed at the University of Manchester [3][14]. It has a particular underlying data model called the Semantic Binary Relationship Model (SBRM), some features of which are here outlined.

SBRM is an extension of the binary relationship model to include a number of entities and relationships with predefined semantics, such as the familiar 'IS A' relationship. Unusually, a distinction is made between meta-information and meta-meta-information.

Classes (sets) and relationships are viewed as entities at the meta-level. Classes are ordered in a subclass or generalisation hierarchy by the predefined 'IS SUB' relationship. The most general class is 'THING'. Other classes with predefined semantics such as 'LEXICAL' are below in the hierarchy with user defined classes lower still. Property inheritance from class to subclass is supported.

Classes of meta-level entities are viewed as entities at the meta-meta-level. Therefore meta-meta-level entities are either classes of classes or classes of relationships. Users do not have access to the meta-meta-level at which six entities with predefined semantics exist. These are used to express integrity constraints on meta-level entities. For example in the case of the meta-meta-level entity 'CLOSED CLASS', a class 'IS A' 'CLOSED CLASS' if members may not be added to or deleted from the class.

Integrity constraints can also be specified by the use of predefined relationships and user defined rules. In addition inference rules can be user defined. Both inference and constraint rules are expressed in Horn clause form.

The interface partly described by Azmoodeh and Lavington [3] provides restriction, intersection and union operations on classes. These are used to specify entities required by a query. The possibility of naming classes defined by subqueries is noted. These names can themselves be used in a query thus avoiding complex nested queries. Lavington and Azmoodeh [14] have noted the need for other external models of data to be supported, the coexistence approach [18]. SBRM is proposed as a suitable coexistence conceptual data model [3].

A conceptually conventional triple store is used as storage structure for the SBRM. Triple elements are integers, lexical entities being given internal integer identifiers. A hardware approach to the implementation of the store is adopted for performance reasons [3].

2.2.3 NDB

Work continues on NDB [23] at IBM UK Laboratories, Hursley Park. This represents a software approach to triple store implementation via list structures as described by Frost [5].

Both application program and end user interfaces to NDB have been described [21][23]. These have adopted a binary relationship view of data in terms of relationships between entity types. The application program interface consists of PL/1 function references and procedure calls providing access to entities and relationships at both type and instance levels.

More recently, the support of basic triple operations 'insert', 'delete' and 'retrieve' has been considered [9]. Also query languages, intelligent user interfaces, interactive graphics, graphic query languages and business chart production have been studied via experimental applications [9]. An application program interface approach has been described [20] which presents data in a triple store as a conventional file which can be accessed by operators equivalent to record input/output on a file. Although the file does not physically exist in the triple store, a query is used to define a 'virtual file' which may be accessed by conventional operations on 'virtual records'.

2.2.4 Other work

Frost et al. [6][7] have described Schemal, a conceptual schema definition and constraint language for triple stores adopting a binary relationship model of data. Schemal is first order predicate calculus based and consequently an algorithm adopting theorem proving methods has been designed to enforce the constraints. Statements in Schemal are not restricted to Horn clause form. Nevertheless Frost has noted the expressive limitations of the language. The work on Schemal has been predominantly concerned with the implementation of integrity constraints. The possibility for statements also to be interpreted as inference rules has been noted [7] and that area is being pursued.

Giles et al. [9] have considered the suitability of triple stores for knowledge representation. An equivalence between triples and first order predicate calculus is drawn by demonstrating that formulae in the clausal form of first order logic can be represented by triples. Giles [8] has also considered how triple stores may be used to represent a number of data models.

3. Triple Store Interfaces

3.1 *General considerations*

In considering triple store interfaces, a neutral position is taken on the actual method of implementation of the underlying store. The choice between hardware and software approaches is not discussed here.

A triple store supporting the basic operations referred to in section 2.1 is assumed. No assumption is made as to the nature of triple elements. Clearly there is a possibility for these to be character strings, internal surrogates or objects themselves having some structure. Triples are not assumed to be numbered in the manner of the Fact machine.

In the event that triple elements are 'meaningful' character strings, the basic operations could be made directly available to an end user. Such a user could then add, delete and retrieve triples such as:

```
<John, is a, employee>
```

The ability of triple stores to represent and process information is sometimes illustrated with examples of basic operations on such triples. Basic operations could also be made directly available for use with surrogate based triples, if a simple symbol table mechanism is used to convert between internal surrogates and corresponding external character strings.

The desirability of a database user having freedom to select his own mental model of data has been argued by Nijssen [18]. As noted in section 2.2.2, IFS is intended to support this coexistence approach. The possibility of triple stores supporting flexible interfaces following the coexistence approach is now examined.

3.2 Interface requirements

An interface must provide operations for the manipulation of data within the triple store. Manipulation is used here to cover both the retrieval of stored data and modification of that data. Operations, however, manipulate a particular perception of the structure of the data; relational query languages manipulate relations and so on. 'Data model' is often used to refer to the definition of the structure of data together with the associated operations. The structure of a data model typically implicitly constrains the information that can be represented within the model. Other constraints are explicitly specified.

The ability of a triple store to support data models in the above sense is therefore at issue. This is true whether or not the operations are available at an application program or an end user interface, although the suitability of the model depends on which is being considered. The specific problems of embedding operations in an application programming language are not considered here.

3.3 Triple stores and data models

Two main approaches to the support of data models by triple stores can be identified:- semantic free and semantic embedding.

In the first approach, the triple store is considered as representing no particular data model. This, following Giles et al. [9], is referred to as the semantic free approach since triples cannot be interpreted by reference to the structure or constraints of such a model. A semantic free triple store will support interface data models through the definition of mappings direct from each model's concepts to triples.

The alternative approach is to consider the triple store as representing a particular data model, called here the embedded model. Triples are interpreted by reference to the semantics of the embedded model since triples embed the structure and constraints of that model. Hence the structure and constraints of any interface data model which it is required the triple store to support must be mapped to those of the embedded model. In terms of the ANSI/SPARC framework [2] the embedded model

Interfaces to triple based database

can be equated with the conceptual schema and interface data models to external schemas. There is no reason why the embedded model should not be directly available at an interface however. IFS is a clear example of this approach to triple stores, SBRM forming the embedded model. Hereafter, interface data models are referred to simply as data models.

Candidate embedded models considered below are a simple sentence model and a binary relationship model. These are by no means the only possible approaches. Others could be semantic network models or explicitly first order logic based.

Candidate data models for support might be the 'traditional' models (hierarchy, network and relational) as well as newer models such as the functional model [22]. The relational model is considered in particular. Figure 1 shows simple relations used as examples below.

3.3.1 The semantic free approach

Without the structure and constraints imposed by an underlying model, it is clear that there will be no unique way of mapping any particular data model to triples. Giles [8] has considered one way of mapping in the case of the relational model. His method applied to the relation 'order' produces triples shown in figure 2. As can be seen, each tuple ti of relation R generates a triple:

    <ti, belongs-to, R>

For each attribute A and corresponding value V of ti, a triple is generated:

    <ti, A, V>

Constraints are also specified to represent, for example, the existence of relational keys and the uniqueness of tuples. This aspect is not pursued here.

Fig 1.

order

supplier	part	quantity
Jim	bolt	43
Fred	nail	65

manager

name	age
Joe	43
Tim	49

employee

name	manager
Bill	Tim
Don	Joe

The triples generated contain 'relational' elements 't1', 't2' and 'belongs-to' which can only be interpreted by reference to the original relation. There is no doubt that software can be written which generates triples from relations according to this algorithm, reconstitutes relations from triples and implements relational operations. However following the coexistence approach, software implementing any other model of this data must reflect the purely relational semantics of the 'relational' elements. Hence the relational model becomes the de facto embedded model. The same argument holds for whichever model is originally considered. In practice therefore, a coexistence approach to semantic free triple stores is not possible.

Whether the relational model is a suitable embedded model is another matter. The arguments of many authors, for example Kent [11], suggest that it is not.

3.3.2 The semantic embedding approach

To support the coexistence approach, the aim must be to restrict as far as possible the extent to which the user is forced to have knowledge of embedded model concepts which are unnatural to his chosen model. Inevitably the embedded model will restrict the chosen data model structure and operations which can be supported. The embedded model choice is crucial to minimise unnatural restrictions.

The simplest form of embedded model might well be one based on the notion of simple sentences of subject-verb-object form, mapped directly to triples, for example:-

```
<John, is a, employee>
<John, lives in, London>
```

With only the informal concept of a simple sentence however, no structure or constraints exist as targets for the structure and constraints of data models to be supported. At the very least, a notion of type is required. This could be introduced by formalising the 'is a' verb. Interface software will itself have to embed a notion of type by recognising 'is a' if it does not exist already in the model. Otherwise it is difficult to see how data models utilising types or sets can be supported. Hence the model would

Fig 2.
```
<t1, belongs-to, order>
  <t1, supplier, Jim>
    <t1, part, bolt>
      <t1, quantity, 43>
<t2, belongs-to, order>
  <t2, supplier, Fred>
    <t2, part, nail>
      <t2, quantity, 65>
```

de facto embed the concept. Interface construction is clearly simpler if the embedded model itself has such a concept formally at the outset.

Whilst such an informal model as simple sentences cannot be defended as an embedded model, it does have two attractions. First, simple sentences can be understood by a user. Hence it might be hoped that it could be possible to generate such sentences to give meaning to information represented by data models above such a model. This follows the aims of work on reverse query translation [4] and inferential feedback [17]. Second, the absence of a strict type structure suggests such a model could support non-conventionally structured data. The cost of the lack of concepts to handle structured data seems too high however.

A conventional binary relationship model based on the definition of relationships between entity types certainly provides structure and constraints for interface models to map to. The ability of such a model to support a relational interface model is examined in particular.

Given an explicit binary model the work of Pelagatti et al. [19] shows that structural mappings can be defined for particular relations. The mappings are in terms of explicit operations on the binary model. These must be severely restricted to enable operations on relations to be mapped uniquely to operations at the binary level. This is of course the problem of the update of relational views. Relations that can be defined are therefore restricted. It is not clear whether it is envisaged in this work that a user himself could define relational mappings. An explicit knowledge of the binary model and operations, which are relatively complex, would be needed. Otherwise relations are restricted to those predefined by the mappings or obtainable via the predefined operations on those relations. This limits severely the flexibility of any interface constructed in this way. For example, it would be impossible to create entirely new relations or add new attributes to existing relations.

Considering the problem the other way round, that is generating the embedded model from relations, some progress is possible. Structure only is considered here.

In generating a binary relationship model from the relation 'order' of figure 1, it seems most natural to identify relationships 'supplier', 'part' and 'quantity' from entity type 'order' to entity types of the same names as the relationships. The immediate problem is to identify members of the type 'order'. One approach is to system generate surrogates which may or may not be user visible as 'order numbers'. Assuming 'is a' as the type membership relationship the following triples would then be amongst those generated to represent relationships at the instance level.

```
<1, is a, order>
<Jim, is a, supplier>
<1, supplier, Jim>
```

As in the semantic free approach, triples with surrogate elements seem directly to arise from the purely relational concept of a relation name. The same comments therefore apply.

The need for the generation of surrogates can be viewed in embedded model terms however, namely in the distinction between lexical and non-lexical entities typically supported by binary relationship models. Relation names could be considered as defining non-lexical entity types without introducing relational model semantics.

Again, however, this structure in the embedded model will constrain the interface model. Triples generated from Relations 'manager' and 'employee' in figure 1 in this way include:-

```
<100, is a, manager>
<Joe, is a, name>
<100, name, Joe>
        .
        .
<Joe, is a, manager>
```

The lexical/non-lexical distinction between a manager and his name is not maintained and assuming binary relationship constraints on membership of the type manager, the two relations cannot be supported. The inconsistency at embedded model level however produces no inconsistency in terms of relational constraints. Even assuming a domain constraint on the attribute 'manager' no concept of relational name domain constraints exist.

Another approach suggested by this example is to abandon relation names and use a relational model where attributes define relationships on the type named by the first attribute. Relations in figure 3 illustrate this. Whilst the manager problem has gone, it has now been necessary to

Fig 3.

order	supplier	part	quantity
32	Jim	bolt	43
33	Fred	nail	65

manager	age
Joe	43
Tim	49

employee	manager
Bill	Tim
Don	Joe

introduce a new attribute 'order' since quantity cannot be considered a relationship from supplier alone. This is the familiar problem of modelling inherently n-ary relationships with binary relationships. Here 'order' values are shown as visible, but they could be represented by hidden surrogates.

It can be seen that general properties of the embedded model are fundamentally affecting how data can be seen at the interface model. A relation user must understand the distinction between lexical and non-lexical entities or be forced to deal with explicit entity names throughout. He must also understand the inherent n-ary relation problem. Interface software must be constructed in such a way that structures and operations at the interface model level which produce inconsistencies at the embedded level are recognised and action taken to reconcile the inconsistency. This implies interaction with the user and should be in terms of concepts understandable at the user model level.

It can be concluded from the foregoing that the ability of a user to see data according to his own model may be severely restricted even with an underlying triple store. One approach, as adopted by Pelagatti et al. is to explicitly define the structures and operations available to a user. Alternatively the user can be made to interact directly with embedded model concepts, namely entity types and relationships in the case of the binary relationship model.

A triple model is now presented which is being developed specifically to simplify the construction of interfaces enabling triple store users to view data with as few restrictions imposed by the underlying model as possible. Two points are stressed at the outset. First, the model is intended as a target embedded model, not as a data model itself to be directly available at a user interface. Second, the description in terms of tables defining mappings is not meant to suggest that an implementation should adopt a fixed length record approach corresponding to the logical model.

4. The Model

4.1 Main features

The model assumes an underlying conventional triple store except that triples are uniquely identified with triple identifiers as in the Fact machine. A two stage mapping is defined from external character strings to stored triple elements. This enables uniform treatment of both lexical and non-lexical entities.

Triples are interpretable as subject-verb-object sentences to gain the benefits of simple sentence embedded models outlined in section 3.3.2. However as in binary relationship embedded models, entities are typed.

Entities may belong to more than one type. Types may be defined explicitly by 'rules' in terms of other types and their relationships. Relationships may be defined at the entity instance level.

4.2 The character string to triple element mapping

All character strings are transformed by a simple symbol table mechanism to internal string identifiers. This mapping is represented below by the string table. At this level therefore, homonyms and synonyms are not supported. Triple elements do not consist of these string identifiers however. Instead they are entity and relationship identifiers.

4.2.1 Entity identifiers

An entity is identified by its relationship to other entities. Examples are 'the teacher who teaches the subject french' or 'the teacher named Bill'. Naming is a special relationship in that the distinction between an entity and its name is typically not explicitly made, and we say 'Bill is a teacher'. Considering 'the subject french' one could either take the view that 'french is a subject' or 'french is the name of a subject'. Hence this naming ambiguity is not restricted to distinct physical entities. The model does not force a distinction to be made between entities and their names. In considering the relational model on top of an embedded binary relationship model, it was seen that a strict distinction in the embedded model can cause difficulties.

Entity identifiers are mapped to string identifiers by a mapping represented below by the entity table. This reflects the way of identifying entities noted above. An entity identifier consists of a type identifier and either, or both, a name identifier and triple identifiers. A type identifier is the string identifier corresponding to the type of the entity, for example 'teacher'. A name identifier is the string identifier corresponding to the name of the entity, for example 'Bill' or 'french'. Triple identifiers are the numbers of triples representing relationships identifying an entity. Hence an entity such as 'subject french' is mapped to the type identifier for 'subject' and the name identifier for 'french'. Triple identifiers are null. Conversely an entity such as 'the teacher who teaches the subject french' is mapped to the type identifier for 'teacher', a null name identifier, and a triple identifier for a triple representing the identifying relationship. The identifying relationship itself must contain named entities, not entities themselves identified by a relationship. The entity table illustrated below provides for three triple identifiers. Therefore each entity must be identified uniquely by not more than three relationships to other entities. The choice of a maximum of three relationships here is of course arbitrary,

Interfaces to triple based database 163

and an implementation need not necessarily impose such a limit. However it seems unlikely that more than three relationships would be needed to identify any entity.

4.2.2 Relationship identifiers

Relationship identifiers are of two kinds. Consider the sentences 'the teacher Bill lives in the city London' and 'the teacher Bill has father Jim'. The first can clearly be represented by a relationship 'lives in' between the particular teacher and city. By a similar process, a relationship 'has' can be identified between the particular teacher and father. For reasons identified later, relationship 'has' is not permitted in the model. The type of the following entity is adopted to form a compound relationship, in this case 'has father'. The relationship entity representing 'lives in' is mapped to the type identifier for 'lives in' For 'has' relationships the corresponding relationship entity is mapped to the type identifier for 'has' and the name identifier for the adopted type, 'father'.

4.3 *Examples*

In figure 4 entity and relationship identifiers are denoted by a preceding '–' and triple identifiers by a preceding '*'. Figure 4 shows the triple model representation of the sentences 'the teacher who teaches the subject french lives in city London' and 'the teacher Bill has father Joe'.

Considering the first example, the subject entity is 'the teacher who teaches the subject french'; the relationship is 'lives in' and the object entity 'city London'. This sentence is represented by triple *2. 'lives in' and 'city London' are transformed to entities –4 and –5 in a straightforward way by the entity table. The entry for the subject entity –1 shows type 2, that is 'teacher', and identifying triple *1. Triple *1 has the same entity –1 as subject. Relationship and object are simply transformed from 'teaches' and 'subject french'. Entity –1 is therefore interpretable as 'the teacher identified by [teaches the subject french]'. Triple *1 in isolation is interpretable as 'the teacher identified by [teaches the subject french] teaches the subject french'. The sentence whilst not particularly informative is clearly true. All triples can be interpreted in the same way even if they come into being as an entity identifying triple. The information that this teacher teaches french will still be recorded even if the relationship which identifies him subsequently changes. The second example can be interpreted similarly.

Information in the entity table could itself be represented in triple form. For example the SBRM model has a system defined class 'DIST.REL' used to identify the relationships uniquely determining the members of a particular entity set. Here the distinction can be made at the entity instance level and this information is, together with type and name information, separated from the triples. As a result, all elements in the triple store are uniformly interpretable and external string representations of triples can be generated in a uniform and simple way. Pursuing an approach of storing all information in the triple store would result in triple elements consisting of entity, string and triple identifiers, each requiring a different method of interpretation. It can be noted that any of the triple store implementation methods could be used in respect of the entity table. Entity table information is available through the basic model interface uniformly with information stored in triple form.

The model simplifies the treatment of homonyms and synonyms. Problems such as identifying whether one or two Bills are referred to in the following triples can be reconciled easily.

```
<Bill, lives in, Watford>
<Bill, works in, London>
```

Types and relationships distuish the Bills at the entity level and each has a distinct entity identifier.

Fig 4.

String Table

String	String Identifier
has	1
teacher	2
lives in	3
city	4
London	5
teaches	6
subject	7
french	8
Bill	9
father	10
Joe	11

Entity Table

entity	type	name	trip1	trip2	trip3
-1	2	-	*1	-	-
-2	6	-	-	-	-
-3	7	8	-	-	-
-4	3	-	-	-	-
-5	4	5	-	-	-
-6	2	9	-	-	-
-7	1	10	-	-	-
-8	10	11	-	-	-

Triple Store

*1	-1	-2	-3
*2	-1	-4	-5
*3	-6	-7	-8

Interfaces to triple based database

4.4 Operations

The model has the basic operations of add, retrieve and delete. However these operations apply to simple sentences, not triples directly. The syntax at present adopted for the sentence 'the teacher that teaches the subject french lives in the city London' is:

```
teacher : [<teaches> subject : french]
          <lives in> city : London
```

The 'add' operation applied to such a sentence results in each entity first being checked individually to establish that such entities are already stored in the model. For relationships and entities identified simply by name this can be done via the string and entity tables alone. For entities identified by relationships, the identifying reference is treated as a query. In each case if no such entity exists in the model, such an entity is created by entries in the entity table and string table if necessary. If one entity exists satisfying the reference, the corresponding entity symbol can be used in the triple to be created. If more than one entity exists, the user must be presented with the description of each such entity, generated from the entity table information, to enable him to indicate the required one.

The 'retrieve' command uses the same sentence syntax with a '?' symbol indicating the required information. For example, to produce the names and descriptions of teachers teaching the sentence french, the following syntax is used.

```
teacher : ? <teaches> subject : french
```

The 'deletion' command checks that a unique triple is referenced by the simple sentence. It must also be checked that the triple to be deleted is not a triple used as an entity identifying reference. This is simply done since any such triple will have an element entity referencing the triple itself. Another problem is that simple sentences can represent triples which are implied by type definition 'rules' discussed below, rather than explicitly stored triples. An attempt to delete a referencing or implied triple indicates an inconsistency with other data stored. Interaction with the user is needed to amend the identifying relationship in the first case and the offending rule or an actual stored triple causing invocation of the rule in the second case.

Operations are also required to enable the insertion, retrieval and deletion of data in the entity table. Names can be manipulated by normal operations applied to sentences with the relationship has name which has predefined semantics, for example:

```
teacher : [<teaches> subject : french]
          <has name> name : Bill
```

Special operators are required to amend the identifying triples of entities and the membership of entities to types. An operation is also required to establish the equivalence of two entities previously considered as distinct.

4.5   Rules and constraints

The model at present does not include general rules and constraints. This area is the subject of further work. Some of the considerations involved are outlined here with details of rules that the model at present supports.

The inherent structure of the model itself provides constraints on the data that can be stored. As noted, entities are uniquely identified by a combination of name and relationships to other entities. An attempt to enter information relating to an ambiguously referenced entity, or the deletion of information thereby creating an ambiguously referenced entity will be prevented.

Explicit general constraints are not yet provided however. A particular need is a capability to define functional constraints. These could be considered as part of wider cardinality constraints on types and relations.

It is not yet clear that a language based on first order logic is necessarily a sufficient basis for constraint and rule definition. Frost's comments on the expressive limitations of Schemal were noted in section 2.2.4. However against the expressive limitations must be set the availability of well understood theorem proving algorithms in first order logic.

Some constraints could naturally be expressed by small extensions to the sentence language outlined. For example, to specify that every maths student must be a person registered for the exam in maths, a syntax such as the following could well be adopted:

```
maths_student =>
         person <registered_for> exam : maths
```

As a constraint this would be used to prevent the recording of information about a maths student without the prior recording of the exam information. Alternatively the sentence can be interpreted as an inference rule enabling the exam information to be deduced about any maths student. Both interpretations are not possible simultaneously. The ambiguity results from the ambiguity in the logical 'only if' as discussed by, for example, Kowalski [13]. The sentence can also be interpreted purely as data to enable positive response to the query 'is every maths student a person registered for the exam in maths?'.

Whilst the area of appropriate concepts at the model level for expressing rules and constraints is therefore the subject of further work, the model does incorporate rules of the form:

```
A <=> B
```

Interfaces to triple based database 167

Here A represents a single triple statement and B a conjunction of triple statements as illustrated below. Such rules could be interpreted as constraints. The effect would be to ensure that triples derivable from the left hand side of the rule were represented within the model before those represented by the right hand side could be and vice-versa. Hence the constraint would serve to ensure that a particular group of triples were either all represented or none were.

An inference rule interpretation is perhaps more useful however and the model adopts this approach. In particular, types can be explicitly defined by such rules. For example a type secretary can be defined in the sentence syntax:

```
secretary = employee : <has job> job : secretary
```

Such a sentence is transformed to triple form as:

```
(DB <has secretary> x) <=> (DB <has employee> x)
                         & (x <has job> job : secretary)
```

Triples of the form 'DB has A B' are equivalent to triples 'B is a A', that is they represent type membership. 'is a' is not used as a relationship in the model. 'DB' is a system defined entity. This form of representing type membership is adopted to enable type membership to be deduced from rules expressing 'has' relationships. As an example consider a typical rule expressing the grandfather relationship:

```
(x <has grandfather> y) <=> (x <has parent> z)
                         & (z <has father> y)
```

Rules of this form are used normally to deduce individual relationships between entities. By virtue of the method of representing type membership chosen, the same rule can be used to define a type 'grandfather'. Substituting 'DB' for 'x' the rule can be interpreted as 'y is a grandfather if z is a parent and the father of z is y'. The model need have no reference to the child x for the rule to work.

Explicitly recorded type information is in the entity table. Normal sentence operations on triples of the form 'DB has A B' are used to manipulate this information.

As has been noted in section 4.2.2 the model does not permit simple 'has' relationships for example:

```
person : Bill <has> grandfather : Jim
```

This is to facilitate the implementation of rules of the kind illustrated.

4.6 Implementation

Software has been written simulating a triple store supporting a preliminary version of the model described. The preliminary model basic interface operations do not provide for the explicit referencing of entity disambiguating relationships. In cases of ambiguous entity reference, the system presents arbitrary instances of relationships in which an entity takes part, in order that the user can indicate the required entity.

Rules as described have been implemented using a backward chaining depth first search approach. Forward chaining is used to the extent that a rule selected for use in the 'only if' direction is used to generate all satisfying triples which are stored in a 'temporary' triple store. The rule is tagged to prevent further use in the 'only if' direction. Query algorithms access both 'temporary' and 'real' triple stores. Recursively defined rules are not implemented as yet. Rules are tagged during a query to prevent their recursive use.

4.7 A relational interface

It is stressed that it is not envisaged that the model operations described should normally be available at a user interface. The model is a target for mappings from data models.

Software has been written to examine the capability of the model to support a relational view of data. At present this is based on the preliminary model referred to. Both the transformation of relations to triples and the output of relations from underlying triples have been implemented. The ability to manipulate relations so output has not yet been implemented.

As with any embedded model, the structure of the model constrains the structure of relations that can be supported. The aim in the design of the model presented has been to limit unnatural restrictions.

Fig 5.

R

*A1	*A2	A3	A4	A5
V11	V12	V13	V14	V15
V21	V22	V23	V24	V25
.	.	.	.	.
.	.	.	.	.

Consider a general relation as illustrated in figure 5. The default assumption is that attributes define 'has' relationships from the entities of the type named by the relation. The identifying relationships of those entities are indicated by attributes prefixed '*'. Hence such a relation is transformed to triples by normal model interface 'add' operations on sentences of the form:

```
R : [<has A1> A1 : V11][<has A2> A2 : V12]
                              <has A3> A3 : V13
R : [<has A1> A1 : V11][<has A2> A2 : V12]
                              <has A4> A4 : V14
                     .
R : [<has A1> A1 : V21][<has A2> A2 : V22]
                              <has A3> A3 : V23
R : [<has A1> A1 : V21][<has A2> A2 : V22]
                              <has A4> A4 : V24
                    etc.
```

Interfaces to triple based database   169

Considering the relations of figure 1, identifying attributes must be prefixed '*' to enable correct conversion to triples. The identifying attributes are 'supplier' and 'part' in the case of the relation 'order' and 'name' in the cases of 'employee' and 'manager'. Taking 'order' as an example, the relation is transformed to triples by the adding of sentences of the form:

```
order : [<has supplier> supplier : Jim]
        [<has part> part : bolt]
                <has quantity> quantity : 43
                    etc.
```

Owing to the treatment of the 'has name' relationship in the model, both 'employee' and 'manager' relations can be transformed without inconsistency resulting between the treatment of managers and names of managers.

Output of relations is the reverse process following the specification of a relation name and attributes by a user. Identifying attributes do not need to be distinguished.

Although not yet implemented, it is intended to use the underlying simple sentences to generate an English like description of the semantics of relations on both input and output to provide some indication that the relation does indeed mean what was intended by the user.

Fig 6.

employee

*name	job	salary
Mary	secretary	6000
Bill	manager	12000
Jill	secretary	8000
Jane	manager	11000

Fig 7.

manager

*name	salary
Bill	12000
Jane	11000

secretary

*name	salary
Mary	6000
Jill	8000

The type definition facility by way of rules gives the user particular flexibility in the choice of relational format. Given rules:

```
secretary = employee : <has job> job : secretary
manager   = employee : <has job> job : manager
```

Relations in figure 6 and 7 are equivalent in the sense that 'employee' can be used to input information to the triple store whereupon relations 'secretary' and 'manager' can be generated or vice-versa. This generation of output relations does not involve algebraic manipulation of 'base' relations. Whilst 'secretary' and 'manager' can be easily derived in terms of traditional select and project operators on relation 'employee', the reverse is not the case.

Kent [12] has considered the explicit definition of relation transformation operations to generate such 'equivalent' relational views to be used as a database design aid.

5.   Ongoing Work

At present software already written is being converted to support the triple model presented. The relational interface software is being developed to support attributes specifying non 'has' relationships and selection conditions on relation names.

The need for the model to support rules and constraints has been stressed. The user models that can be mapped to the embedded model depend on the capability to represent the user model implicit and explicit constraints. A suitable core of such constraints, their interaction with rules and other data and their implementation, are the subject of further work.

Entities in the model are assumed to be uniquely identifiable by names and relationships. This is not always the case in real life. It may not be possible to definitely state whether 'Jim owns a red car' and 'Bill stole a red car' refer to the same car entity. The model is being extended to handle such 'imprecise' data.

6.   Conclusions

This paper has discussed the considerations involved in constructing interfaces to triple stores. A number of approaches to this problem have been examined. A model has been described which has been designed specifically to enable the construction of flexible interfaces to triple stores.

Triple stores are seen as potentially being a basis for the construction of interfaces providing flexibility not currently obtainable with present typically record-based database implementations. In particular, the use of inference rules and constraints should provide a powerful inferential capability. The need for care in choosing the model which triples embed has been stressed to ensure that the potential for such interfaces is not unnecessarily restricted by the model chosen. A particular model has been presented as a step in this direction.

Acknowledgements

The author gratefully acknowledges helpful discussions with Professor P J H King and other members of the Computer Science department at Birkbeck College. This work is supported by an SERC grant.

References
[1] J R Abrial, Data semantics, in Data Base Management, J W Klimbie and K L Koffeman (eds), North Holland, 1974
[2] ANSI/X3/SPARC, Study Group on Data Base Management Systems, Interim report 75-02-08, in ACM SIGMOD Newsletter, FDT, Vol 7, No 2, 1975
[3] M Azmoodeh and S H Lavington, A scheme for representing information and its implications for storage technology, University of Manchester Department of Computer Science Internal Report IFS/2/82, 1982
[4] T Crowe, R G Johnson and D Hainline, Query validation: reverse translation and the connection and selection trap, Proceedings of BNCOD1, Cambridge, 1981
[5] R A Frost, Binary-relational storage structures, Computer Journal, Vol 25, No 3, pp 358–367, 1982
[6] R A Frost and S Whittaker, A step towards the automatic maintenance of the semantic integrity of databases, Computer Journal, Vol 26, No 2, pp 124–133, 1983
[7] R A Frost, Schema1: yet another conceptual schema definition language, Computer Journal, Vol 26, No 3, pp 228–234, 1983
[8] D A Giles, private communication
[9] D A Giles, B E Roberts, G C H Sharman and N Winterbottom, private communication
[10] ISO TC97/SC5/WG3, Concepts and terminology for the conceptual schema and the information base, J J van Griethuysen (ed), ISO, 1982
[11] W Kent, Limitations of record-based information models, ACM TODS, Vol 4, No 1, pp 107–132, 1979
[12] W Kent, Choices in practical data design, Proceedings of 8th VLDB, Mexico City, 1982
[13] R Kowalski, Logic for Problem Solving, North Holland, 1979
[14] S H Lavington and M Azmoodeh, IFS – a proposal for a database machine, Proceedings of BNCOD2, Bristol, 1982
[15] D R McGregor and J R Malone, The Fact database system: a system based on inferential methods, in Research and Development in Information Retrieval, C J van Rijsbergen and P W Williams (eds), Butterworth, 1981
[16] D R McGregor and J R Malone, Generic associative hardware: its impact on database systems, in Associative Methods and Data Base Engines, IEEE PG C2 (Computing Theory) Digest No 1982/53, 1982
[17] P Massey, J Longstaff and C K Lam, Inferential feedback for DBMS user interfaces, Proceedings of BNCOD2, Bristol, 1982
[18] G M Nijssen, A gross architecture for the next generation database management systems, in Modelling In Data Base Management Systems, G M Nijssen (ed), North Holland, 1976
[19] G Pelagatti, P Paolini and G Bracchi, Mapping external views to a common data model, Information Systems, Vol 3, pp 141–151, 1978
[20] D J Pullin and G C H Sharman, Virtual file access to a binary relational database, IBM Technical Disclosure Bulletin, Vol 25, No 11B, 1983

[21] G C H Sharman, Update-By-Dialogue: an interactive approach to database modification, IBM Technical Report TR.12.164, 1977
[22] D W Shipman, The functional data model and the data language DAPLEX, ACM TODS, Vol 6, No 1, pp 140–173, 1981
[23] N Winterbottom and G C H Sharman, NDB: non-programmer data base facility, IBM Technical Report TR.12.179, 1979

An Approach to Interactive Definition of Database Views

A H F Laender
School of Computing Studies and Accountancy, University of East Anglia, Norwich NR4 7TJ

An approach is presented which makes possible the definition and construction of views by users who are not familiar with the overall structure of the database. The method used is interactive 'conversation' and users are presented with a simple form oriented view of data represented by hierarchically related dataitems. The mappings required to materialize the data are automatically generated as a result of this conversation, and users may access the database by means of the 'form'. A system which has been implemented according to this approach is briefly described, and an example of a typical session using the system presented.

1. Introduction

A view is an abstract representation of a portion of a database [5, 26[sr]. It reflects the logical organization of data as seen by individual users and applications. Thus, supporting views is very important in order to provide flexibility of use. Views contribute to data independence and data protection, and simplify the user interface by allowing users tc ignore data which are of no interest to them [4, 6, 26].

Many current database systems provide some kind of view mechanism. Existing facilities, however, are not yet sufficiently general to support a user interface as proposed by the ANSI/SPARC framework [1, 3, 4, 24]. In addition, they are often not suitable for non-technical end users, as a complete knowledge of the database structure is usually required when defining a view.

In this paper, we present an approach which makes possible the definition and construction of views by users who are not familiar with the overall conceptual structure of the database. The method used is interactive 'conversation' and the user's view of data is a 'form' represented by hierarchically related dataitems. The mappings required to materialize the data are automatically generated as a result of this conversation, and users may access the database by means of the 'form'.

The remainder of the paper is organized as follows. Section 2 introduces the form concept used as the modelling mechanism for specifying a view. The definition of these form oriented views is discussed in section 3. Section 4 briefly describes a view definition system which has been implemented according to the approach and presents an example. Section 5 concludes the paper. The database used as example throughout the paper is described in the appendix. It concerns classical gramophone records, and contains information about records, works, composers, conductors, soloists, orchestras and performances.

2. The Form Concept

Several form oriented facilities have been proposed and implemented over the past years [7, 15, 16, 18, 19, 21, 25]. The concept of form as a data modelling mechanism, however, was introduced by Shu and her colleagues [9, 21].

We see a form as a named collection of hierarchically related dataitems defined by a pair $F=(I,D)$, where I is the set of identifying dataitems and D is the set of detailing dataitems. It consists of a set of form occurrences (or instances) and its logical structure is represented by a hierarchy definition tree. Intuitively, a form may be thought of as a file of records containing nested repeating groups [15]. Fig 1 presents an example of a form $F=(\{WORK\#\},\{TITLE,NAME,REC\#,YEAR\})$ defined from the gramophone record database.

Fig 1. Example of a form

```
WORK
   WORK#:     56
   TITLE:    TRAGIC OVERTURE, OP.81
   COMPOSER
      NAME:    BRAHMS
   RECORD
      REC#:    SDD284
      YEAR:    1962
   RECORD
      REC#:    50537
      YEARDATE:  1966
```

(a) A form occurrence

```
              WORK
         -------------------
         ! WORK# ! TITLE !
         -------------------
                 !
                 !
      ---------------------------------
      !                               !
  COMPOSER !                    RECORD   !
  ------------------            --------------------
  !   NAME       !              ! REC# ! YEAR !
  ------------------            --------------------
```

(b) The hierarchy definition tree

Interactive definition of database views 175

As considered here, a form is actually an abstraction of a display form (ie a conventional paper form) whose layout is designed to please human users. This abstraction is a 'mental model' meant to represent the internal format of a form, which externally may be presented with different layouts [15, 25]. Therefore, when we talk about a form occurrence, we refer to a form entry representing a hierarchical record whose dataitem values are associated with their identifier.

3. Definition of Form Oriented Views

The definition of a form oriented view in our approach is divided into two steps. First, the user specifies the sets I of identifying dataitems and D of detailing dataitems which compose the view. Then, the mappings required to materialize the data according to a hierarchy definition tree are generated and validated in terms of the logical structure of the database, which is described by an Abstracted Conceptual Schema (ACS). The ACS has been proposed as a target logical schema in a multi-model environment [20, 23]. Its constructs are free of any semantic colouration, which makes it quite appropriate for the role played here.

Fig 2 illustrates pictorially the view definition framework. The user specifies the sets I and D of dataitems through a user interface which checks them with the ACS. The sets I and D are then passed to a view validator which, interacting with the user, generates the mappings in terms of the logical connections defined by the ACS. The process terminates when all the mappings have been generated and successfully validated, or when it fails to do so.

Before describing the process of validation in more details we have to introduce the major constructs of the Abstracted Conceptual Schema.

3.1 *The abstracted conceptual schema*

The basic construct in the ACS is the element. The element exists only in concept and its purpose is to carry what one might call indirect data functions [23]. Associated with an element is a number of properties,

Fig 2. The view definition framework

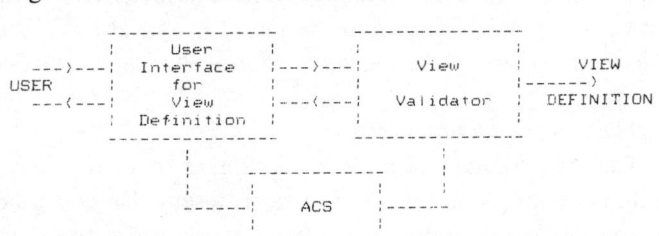

each property corresponding to a function which maps the element onto a specific dataitem value. Thus the dataitem is the basic unit of recorded data. An element set is a collection of all elements which have associated with them the same set of properties (function/dataitem combinations).

A particular property or set of properties which associates its dataitem values with one and only one element of a set is said to be the element set identifier. Names are associated with dataitems, functions and element sets, and as a property may be associated only once with an element the function/dataitem names must be unique throughout the database [20, 23].

An element set is clearly the target for representing an 'entity type'. In the example described in the appendix the element set WORK is one of such types. Its identifier is the property IS–IDENTIFIED–BY/WORK#.

In the ACS, integrity constraints are expressed by means of value sets. A value set is defined by specifying an element set and one or more properties, and is the set of (tuples of) dataitem values taken as the properties are applied to each element of the set. To define a value set constraint we write a statement of the form

V1 <operator> V2,

where V1 and V2 are pre-defined value sets. The basic value set operators are the set oriented operators 'is-equal-to', 'is-disjoint-from', 'is-contained-in' and 'contains-all'. Value sets may be operated on to derive new ones, so that more complex constraints may be expressed [20]. In the example of the appendix, the value set constraint 'WORK–COMPOSER–NOS .is-contained-in. COMPOSER–NOS' enforces that a work's composer must be one of those already existing in the database.

To capture the notions of 'role' [2] and 'generalization' [22], an element set may be defined as located in another one, inheriting so all its properties. For example, in the gramophone record database the element set COMPOSER is located in the element set PERSON. Thus, all properties associated with PERSON are automatically associated with COMPOSER.

The ACS constructs defined above are those which are relevant to this work and correspond basically to the initial proposal described in [23]. Several extentions have been suggested recently and are discussed in [20].

3.2 The view validation process

The ACS semantics have been defined in such a way that the relationships existing among the entities represented by the element sets must be expressed by compatible properties, ie properties defined over common dataitems. Moreover, the logical connections resulting from this mechanism must always involve identifiers [20]. In other words, only 'entity joins' [10] are defined by an ACS.

The set of all possible connections defined by an ACS is expressed by a graph called the ACS connection graph. It is by searching this graph that the view validator finds all possible connections among the specified dataitems and reports them back to the user in order to validate the structure of the view.

3.2.1 The ACS connection graph

The ACS connection graph is a multigraph [8] G whose nodes denote element sets and edges denote logical connections among the element sets. An element set E_i is said to be logically connected to an element set E_j if and only if:

(a) there is a set P_i of properties of E_i which is compatible to a set P_j of properties of E_j;
(b) either P_i is an identifier of E_i or P_j is an identifier of E_j or both, and
(c) $P_i \neq P_j$.

A logical connection between two element sets E_i and E_j is defined by a connection condition expressed by the formula $E_i(p_{i1},p_{i2},....,p_{in}) = E_j(p_{j1},p_{j2},....,p_{jn})$, where p_i is a property of E_i and p_j a property of E_j. 'WORK(WAS–COMPOSED–BY/PERS♯) = COMPOSER(IS– IDENTIFIED–BY/PERS♯)' is the connection condition which defines the logical connection between the element sets WORK and COMPOSER in the gramophone record database example.

In the ACS, we distinguish between three types of logical connections depending on whether there is a corresponding value set constraint defined or not. A logical connection is said to be a strong connection if there is a value set connection defined for it other than a disjoint one. On the other hand, a logical connection is said to be a weak connection if there is no value set constraint defined for it, and an empty connection if a disjoint constraint has been defined.

3.2.2 The algorithm of validation

Fig 3 presents the view validation algorithm. The basic idea of the algorithm is to search the ACS connection graph trying to relate the dataitems according to a hierarchy definition tree. It is based on a variant of the breadth-first search method, called ordered-search [17], and uses an evaluation function to order the search, ie the expantion of the nodes

Fig 3. The view validation algorithm

ALGORITHM:

begin
1. OPEN <== NIL;
2. initialise T with a dummy root r;
3. construct the set Q of primary element sets;
4. **for** each element set q in Q **do** e
   begin
5.   create a new node i of T and connect it to r;
6.   **for** each dataitem d in I **do** relate d to i;
7.   OPEN <== i
   end
8. n <== OPEN;
9. **while** n $\neq$ NIL and D $\neq \phi$ **do**
   begin
10.   **for** each dataitem d in D **do**
    begin
11.   **if** d is associated with the element set corresponding to n **then**
          begin
12.   report back to the user using P(n);
13.   **if** confirmed **then**
14.   relate d to n and delete it from D;
          end
    end
15.   construct the set S of element sets logically connected to the element set corresponding to n;
16.   **for** each element set s in S **do**
17.   **if** s is not in P(n) **then**
          begin
18.   create a new node i and connect it to n;
19.   OPEN <== i
          end
20.   n <== OPEN
    end
21. **if** D $= \phi$ **then**
22.   prune T
    else
23.   report failure
end

(see steps 8 and 20). The final output of the algorithm is a tree T, called the view definition tree, which is derived from the ACS connection graph and defines the mappings involved.

Although a discussion of the evaluation function is beyond the scope of this paper, it is worth mentioning that it has been defined in order to expand first those nodes which are associated with as many as possible dataitems in D, determine functional relationships, and are strongly connected to one which has already been considered [12].

INPUT: A form definition F=(I,D) and an ACS connection graph G.

OUTPUT: A view definition tree T.

NOTES: OPEN is a list which stores the nodes not yet expanded; P(n) is a function which defines for any node n of T its path to the root; n <== OPEN selects a node from OPEN according to the evaluation function.

3.2.3 The confirmation dialogues

During the search of the ACS connection graph, the connections found for the dataitems have to be reported to the user (see step 12 of the algorithm), so that he/she can confirm those which semantically correspond to his/her view. This interaction is carried out by the view validator through a number of confirmation dialogues. Each dialogue describes a specific dataitem connection and is composed of very simple natural language sentences generated from the ACS according to pre-defined patterns [12].

For the purpose of generating the sentences, a naming convention is applied when defining the ACS. This convention, derived from a simple data model, is meant to bring the necessary semantic information into the ACS and name the element sets and their properties (function/dataitem combinations) to match the sentence patterns properly. Basically, the element sets are named by singular nouns describing the corresponding 'entity types', the functions by verbal expressions describing the functional mappings, and the dataitems by mnemonics or singular nouns describing the meaning of the underlying values.

An example of a confirmation dialogue corresponding to the form of fig 1 is:

```
BY REC# DO YOU MEAN
THERE EXISTS A PERFORMANCE THAT IS ON THE RECORD THAT IS
IDENTIFIED BY REC#.
THE PERFORMANCE IS OF THE WORK THAT IS IDENTIFIED BY WORK# AND IS
CALLED TITLE.
PLEASE ANSWER Y(YES) OR N(NO).
>Y
```

4. A View Definition System

A system called DAVID (DAtabase VIew Definer) has been implemented according to the approach described in this paper. DAVID is an interactive database end user facility which allows not only the definition, but also the manipulation of form oriented views. DAVID has been implemented in FORTRAN on top of the relational database system RAPPORT [13, 14] and is running on a VAX–11 computer system under VMS.

Below is part of a typical view definition session using DAVID (all user inputs are preceded by '>'). The example considered is again of the form $F = (\{WORK\#\}, \{TITLE, NAME, REC\#, YEAR\})$ described in fig 1. The manipulation facilities provided by the system are not discussed here and are described elsewhere [11, 12]. They allow, however, the selection and scanning of 'form occurrences' in a way which is similar to the manipulation of conventional paper forms in a 'sequential filing cabinet'.

```
SPECIFY YOUR VIEW. ENTER DATAITEMS ON REQUEST BY TYPING  THEM  IN
SEQUENCE AND SEPARATED BY COMMA OR BLANK  SPACES.  TERMINATE  THE
SEQUENCE BY A SEMICOLON. TYPE "?' IF YOU NEED THE LIST OF DEFINED
DATAITEMS.

ENTER IDENTIFYING DATAITEMS.
>WORK#;

ENTER DETAILING DATAITEMS.
>TITLE,NAME,REC#,YEAR;

IS THE SPECIFICATION OF YOUR VIEW CORRECT? (Y/N)
>Y

BY TITLE DO YOU MEAN
THE WORK THAT IS IDENTIFIED BY WORK# IS CALLED TITLE.
PLEASE ANSWER Y(YES) OR N(NO).
>Y

BY YEAR DO YOU MEAN
THE WORK THAT IS IDENTIFIED BY WORK# AND IS CALLED TITLE WAS
PUBLISHED IN YEAR.
PLEASE ANSWER Y(YES) OR N(NO).
>N

BY NAME DO YOU MEAN
THE WORK THAT IS IDENTIFIED BY WORK# AND IS CALLED TITLE WAS
COMPOSED BY THE COMPOSER THAT IS CALLED NAME.
PLEASE ANSWER Y(YES) OR N(NO).
>Y

BY YEAR DO YOU MEAN
THE COMPOSER THAT IS CALLED NAME DIED IN YEAR.
PLEASE ANSWER Y(YES) OR N(NO).
>N

BY YEAR DO YOU MEAN
THE COMPOSER THAT IS CALLED NAME WAS BORN IN YEAR.
PLEASE ANSWER Y(YES) OR N(NO).
>N

BY REC# DO YOU MEAN
THERE EXISTS A PERFORMANCE THAT IS ON THE RECORD THAT IS
IDENTIFIED BY REC#.
THE PERFORMANCE IS OF THE WORK THAT IS IDENTIFIED BY WORK# AND IS
CALLED TITLE.
PLEASE ANSWER Y(YES) OR N(NO).
>Y
```

```
BY YEAR DO YOU MEAN
THE RECORD THAT IS IDENTIFIED BY REC# WAS ISSUED IN YEAR.
PLEASE ANSWER Y(YES) OR N(NO).
>Y

VIEW VALIDATION SUCCEEDED. YOU HAVE DEFINED THE FOLLOWING VIEW:

WORK
    WORK#:
    TITLE:
    COMPOSER
        NAME:
    RECORD
        REC#:
        YEAR:
```

In this example, seven dialogues were necessary to validate the view. This was due to the fact that the dataitem YEAR participates in several different properties in the gramophone record database. It should be noted, however, that the dialogues were always kept within a 'context' established previously by some confirmation from the user. Note also, that the dataitem NAME was automatically associated with COMPOSER as a result of the location mechanism of the ACS.

5. Conclusions

The approach presented in this paper is aimed to provide non-technical end users with a simple framework for the definition and manipulation of database views. The user's view of data is an 'abstract form' represented by hierarchically related dataitems. The definition and construction of such views are carried out interactively. The user specify a view only in terms of a set of dataitems and no formal knowledge of the database structure is required.

A prototype view definition system has been implemented according to this approach and is now operational. Although it has not yet been used in a practical environment, initial experimental results have been encouraging. A number of extensions are being considered, especially concerning the manipulation of form occurrences and help facilities for supporting the user [12].

This work has also provided several ideas for refining and consolidating the ACS, some of which have already been incorporated [20]. It should be mentioned, however, that 'naming' represents some problems when using the ACS directly to support end user interfaces.

Aknowledgements

The author would like to thank his supervisor, Prof P M Stocker, for constant support and advice, and his colleagues Charles Akinyokun, Marcos Borges and Odd Risnes for valuable comments on a previous version of this paper. Financial support from the Brazilian Ministry of

Education Agency CAPES is also gratefully acknowledged. This work was carried out while the author was on study leave from the Departamento de Ciencia da Computacao, Universidade Federal de Minas Gerais, Brazil.

References

[1] ANSI/X3/SPARC Study Group on Data Base Management Systems Interim Report, FDT Bulletin of ACM SIGMOD, Vol 7, No 2, 1975
[2] C W Bachman and M Daya, The role concept in data models, Proc Int Conf on Very Large Data Bases, Tokyo, Japan, 1977, pp 464–476
[3] E K Clemons, Design of a prototype ANSI/SPARC three-schema data base system, AFIPS Conference Proceedings, Vol 48, AFIPS Press, Montvale, NJ, 1979, pp 689–696
[4] E K Clemons, Design of an external schema facility to define and process recursive structures, ACM Trans on Database Systems, Vol 6, No 2, pp 295–311, 1981
[5] C J Date, An Introduction to Database Systems, 3rd edition, Addison-Wesley, Reading, Mass, 1981
[6] U Dayal and P A Bernstein, On the correct translation of update operations on relational views, ACM Trans on Database Systems, Vol 7, No 3, pp 381–416, 1982
[7] M Hammer et al, A very high level programming language for data processing applications, Communications of the ACM, Vol 20, No 11, pp 832–841, 1977
[8] F Harary, Graph Theory, Addison-Wesley, Reading, Mass, 1972
[9] B C Housel and N C Shu, A high-level data manipulation language for hierarchical data structures, IBM Res Rep RJ1756, IBM Res Lab, San Jose, Calif, 1976
[10] W Kent, The entity join, Proc Int Conf on Very Large Data Bases, Rio de Janeiro, Brazil, 1979, pp 232–238
[11] A H F Laender and P M Stocker, An interactive database end user facility for the definition and manipulation of forms, BCS/ACM Symp on Research and Development in Information Retrieval, Cambridge, 1984
[12] A H F Laender, A framework for the definition and manipulation of database views by end users, PhD Thesis in preparation, School of Computing Studies and Accountancy, University of East Anglia
[13] LOGICA LTD, RAPPORT-3 Fortran User Manual, London, 1982
[14] LOGICA LTD, RAPPORT-3 Interactive Query Language User Manual, London, 1982
[15] D Luo and S B Yao, Form operation by example – A language for office information processing, Proc ACM SIGMOD Int Conf on Management of Data, Ann Arbor, Michigan, 1981, pp 212–223
[16] F J Maryansky and C S Roush, Definition of database transactions by the casual user, AFIPS Conference Proceedings, Vol 49, AFIPS Press, Montvale, NJ, 1980, pp 293–300
[17] N J Nillson, Problem-Solving Methods in Artificial Inteligence, McGraw-Hill, New York, 1971

[18] R Purvy et al, The design of Star's records processing: Data processing for the noncomputer professional, ACM Trans on Office Information Systems, Vol 1, No 1, pp 3–24, 1983

[19] L A Rowe and K A Shoens, A form application development system, Proc ACM SIGMOD International Conference on Management of Data, Orlando, Florida, 1982, pp. 28–38

[20] A B Saha, A set oriented abstract conceptual schema based on logic, private communication

[21] N C Shu et al, Specification of forms processing and business procedures for office automation, IEEE Trans on Software Engineering, Vol SE–8, No 5, 499–512, 1982

[22] J M Smith and D C P Smith, Database abstractions: aggregation and generalization, ACM Trans on Database Systems, Vol 2, No 2, pp 105–177, 1977

[23] P M Stocker and R N Cantie, A target logical schema: the ACS, Proc Int Conf on Very Large Data Bases, Florence, Italy, 1983, pp 309–310

[24] D Tsichritzis and A Klug (ed), The ANSI/X3/SPARC DBMS framework report of the study group on database management systems, Information Systems, Vol 3, No 3, pp 173–191, 1978

[25] D Tsichritzis, Form management, Communications of the ACM, Vol 25, No 7, pp 453–478, 1982

[26] J D Ullman, Principles of Database Systems, Pitman, London, 1980

Appendix Example of an ACS: The gramophone record database

```
schema: GRAMOPHONE;

   dataitem:
      PERS# of INTEGER,
      NAME of CHARACTER,
      COUNTRY of CHARACTER,
      YEAR of CHARACTER,
      INSTRUMENT of CHARACTER,
      WORK# of INTEGER,
      TITLE of CHARACTER,
      FORM of CHARACTER,
      REC# of INTEGER,
      ORC# of INTEGER,
      PERF# of INTEGER,
      TRACK# of INTEGER;

   element-set: PERSON;
      property:
         IS-IDENTIFIED-BY/PERS#,
         IS-CALLED/NAME;
      identifier:
         IS-IDENTIFIED-BY/PERS#;
    end: PERSON;

   element-set: COMPOSER;
      property:
         WAS-BORN-IN/COUNTRY,
         WAS-BORN-IN/YEAR,
         DIED-IN/YEAR;
      located-in:
         PERSON by IS-IDENTIFIED-BY/PERS#;
      value-set:
         COMPOSER-NOS = {IS-IDENTIFIED-BY/PERS#};
   end: COMPOSER;

   element-set: SOLOIST;
      property:
         PLAYS/INSTRUMENT;
      located-in:
         PERSON by IS-IDENTIFIED-BY/PERS#;
      value-set:
         SOLOIST-NOS = {IS-IDENTIFIED-BY/PERS#};
   end: SOLOIST;

   element-set: CONDUCTOR;
      located-in:
         PERSON by IS-IDENTIFIED-BY/PERS#;
      value-set:
         CONDUCTOR-NOS = {IS-IDENTIFIED-BY/PERS#};
   end: CONDUCTOR;

   element-set: WORK;
      property:
         IS-IDENTIFIED-BY/WORK#,
         IS-CALLED/TITLE,
         IS-OF/FORM,
         WAS-PUBLISHED-IN/YEAR,
         WAS-COMPOSED-BY/PERS#;
      identifier:
         IS-IDENTIFIED-BY/WORK#;
      value-set:
         WORK-NOS = {IS-IDENTIFIED-BY/WORK#},
         WORK-COMPOSER-NOS = {WAS-COMPOSED-BY/PERS#};
      constraint:
         WORK-COMPOSER-NOS .is-containded-in. COMPOSER-NOS;
   end: WORK;
```

```
element-set: RECORD;
   property:
      IS-IDENTIFIED-BY/REC#,
      WAS-ISSUED-IN/YEAR;
   identifier:
      IS-IDENTIFIED-BY/REC#;
   value-set:
      RECORD-NOS = {IS-IDENTIFIED-BY/REC#};
end: RECORD;

element-set: ORCHESTRA;
   property:
      IS-IDENTIFIED-BY/ORC#,
      IS-CALLED/NAME;
   identifier:
      IS-IDENTIFIED-BY/ORC#;
   value-set:
      ORCHESTRA-NOS = {IS-IDENTIFIED-BY/ORC#};
end: ORCHESTRA;

element-set: PERFORMANCE;
   property:
      IS-IDENTIFIED-BY/PERF#,
      IS-OF/WORK#,
      IS-ON/REC#,
      IS-LOCATED-ON/TRACK#,
      IS-CONDUCTED-BY/PERS#,
      IS-PERFORMED-BY/ORC#;
   identifier:
      IS-IDENTIFIED-BY/PERF#,
      (IS-ON/REC#,IS-LOCATED-ON/TRACK#);
   value-set:
      PERFORMANCE-NOS = {IS-IDENTIFIED-BY/PERF#},
      PERFORMANCE-WORK-NOS = {IS-OF/WORK#},
      PERFORMANCE-RECORD-NOS = {IS-ON/REC#},
      PERFORMANCE-CONDUCTOR-NOS = {IS-CONDUCTED-BY/PERS#},
      PERFORMANCE-ORCHESTRA-NOS = {IS-PERFORMED-BY/ORC#},
      PERFORMANCE-CONDUCTORS =
           {(IS-IDENTIFIED-BY/PERF#,IS-CONDUCTED-BY/PERS#)};
   constraint:
      PERFORMANCE-WORK-NOS .is-contained-in. WORK-NOS,
      PERFORMANCE-RECORD-NOS .is-contained-in. RECORD-NOS,
      PERFORMANCE-CONDUCTOR-NOS.is-contained-in.CONDUCTOR-NOS,
      PERFORMANCE-ORCHESTRA-NOS.is-contained-in.ORCHESTRA-NOS;
end: PERFORMANCE;

element-set: SOLO;
   property:
      IS-PART-OF/PERF#,
      IS-PLAYED-BY/PERS#;
   identifier:
      (IS-PART-OF/PERF#,IS-PLAYED-BY/PERS#);
   value-set:
      SOLO-PERFORMANCE-NOS = {IS-PART-OF/PERF#},
      SOLO-SOLOIST-NOS = {IS-PLAYED-BY/PERS#},
      PERFORMANCE-SOLOISTS =
           {(IS-PART-OF/PERF#,IS-PLAYED-BY/PERS#)};
   constraint:
      SOLO-PERFORMANCE-NOS .is-contained-in. PERFORMANCE-NOS,
      SOLO-SOLOIST-NOS .is-contained-in. SOLOIST-NOS,
      PERFORMANCE-SOLOISTS .is-disjoint-from.
                                 PERFORMANCE-CONDUCTORS;
end: SOLO;

end: GRAMOPHONE;
```

A Design for an Implementation of a Runtime System to Support Dynamic Incremental Foreground Reorganisation of a Network Database System

A. L. Zorner
SERC Research Assistant, Sheffield City Polytechnic, Pond Street, Sheffield S1 1WB (DBAWG member)

All physical aspects of data description and the processes of reorganisation should be separate from the logical view of a database. Since the ANSC NDL [1] has taken as its base document the CODASYL DDL [2] it seems feasible to assume that some form of DSDL might be standardised.

The CODASYL DSDL [2] forms the base document of a current project into an implementation to study the feasibility of dynamic incremental foreground reorganisation. This paper describes the problems encountered in designing a runtime system which supports the DSDL specified in the CODASYL JOD 1981.

1. The DSDL – A Brief History

The schema Data Description Language (DDL) defined in the 1969 and 1971 Database Task Group (DBTG) reports [1] contained clauses addressing some aspects of storage and device representation of a database. Some examples were; Location Mode, Actual/Virtual items, Set Mode, Indexes. These representations were by no means complete. A feeling was developing that it would be desirable to separate the logical and physical aspects of data description. Therefore, over the period 1975–81, the Data Description Language Committee (DDLC) and the Database Administration Working Group (DBAWG) removed from the schema DDL those clauses associated with the representation of data and data structures on physical storage. The original reports referred to these ideas as a Device Media Control Language (DMCL). When inconsistencies were found in this DMCL and the logical, physical total separation achieved, the resultant language specification was renamed the Data Storage Description Language (DSDL).

2. The Codasyl Network DBMS Architecture

2.1 The conceptual framework

Using the Data Manipulation Language (DML) commands the run unit can request data from the DBMS. The call is analysed and supplemented with data from the subschema, schema and storage schema and specific data obtained from the User Work Area (UWA). Using this information I/0 routines acquire records from the database which are placed in the system buffers, and are then converted to subschema type records via the mapping information and placed in the UWA. Any communication or failed requests etc are passed to the communications locations.

2.2 *The DML*

The Data Manipulation Language is usually encased in a host language and is therefore language dependent, for example COBOL and FORTRAN. The verbs provided by the DML can be viewed as commands to the DBMS. The most important are the action commands: FIND and GET (or FETCH), STORE, MODIFY, ERASE and COMMIT. The unit of transfer is usually a subschema record but may only be one or more data items.

FIND and FETCH both use the record selection expressions to specify the record type and sometimes more specifically the next or prior record of its type. Further clarification as to which actual record is required is also found in the DDL set selection clause when searching via a set. This often forces a complete traverse over records and sets. Records are always stored subject to the criteria in the set selection clause.

A SET type is specified in the Set Entry of the schema, it may be owned by a record type or by the system (singular set), and may have one or more record types as its members. A record type may also be owner and member of the same set type, but a record occurrence may not be owner of more than one occurrence of the same set type nor may it participate as a member of more than one set occurrence of the same type.

Insertion of a record into a set may be automatic (when the record is stored) or manual (connected into the set by the DML command CONNECT). The retention of records in a set may be: fixed – (a record can no longer exist in the database unless it is a member of that set); mandatory – (it must be a member of that set type for it to exist); or optional – (the record may be removed from that set type and no longer connected into any set occurrence of that set type).

The order in which the records of a set are held is specified by the order clause where sorted order may affect the methods of storage in the set.

2.3 The schema/subschema

The subschema provides the program application view of the database. It is a subset of the overall schema view which needs to take account of all data which may be held in the future not just that which is currently required.

The schema DDL is used to describe a Database, and may be shared by many programs written in many languages. This description is in terms of the names and characteristics of the Data Items, Data Aggregates, records and sets included in the database and the relationships that exist and must be maintained between occurrences of those elements in the database.

2.4 The DSDL – as defined by DBAWG

A data storage description language defines how data described in a schema may be organised in terms of an operating system and device independent storage environment.

A storage schema is created by the Database Administrator (DBA) and is simply designed to affect the performance of an application program and not to alter its results.

The language description is in terms of storage records, storage areas, sets and indexes. Schema records are mapped onto one or more storage records which are logically placed within storage areas. Schema set membership and set order require the storage schema Set Entry to support the required logical links by physical pointers and links.

A storage area may be mapped onto whatever type of physical storage device the implementor wishes. The name given to the area could be encoded to indicate the type of device. An area is subdivided logically into pages which are declared in an area definition to be of a specific size and extent. Consequently the size required for buffers can be adjusted to the page size or multiples thereof enabling efficient transfer/overflow tradeoffs.

A schema record may have multiple representations defined in the storage schema of which only one will be utilised for a particular record occurrence. Each mapping, whether conditional or unconditional, may be either one to one (which is the default) or one to many. For example,

```
MAPPING FOR person
  IF persontype = male THEN
    STORAGE RECORDS ARE fullname, persondetails,
      mmeasurements
  ELSE STORAGE RECORDS ARE fullname, persondetails,
    fmeasurements
```

MAPPING FOR house
  IF housetype = 'TERRACE' THEN
    STORAGE RECORDS ARE terracehouse, neighbours
  IF housetype = 'SEMI' THEN
    STORAGE RECORDS ARE semidethouse, neighbours
  ELSE STORAGE RECORD IS dethouse

Certain information is used to define and maintain storage records.

- (a) Links must be defined to link this record to other Storage records within the mapping list, to ensure that there are sufficient links to support the schema record.
- (b) Space is reserved for those set pointers which are defined with ALLOCATION is DYNAMIC (in the Set Entry).
- (c) The placement criteria is defined (may be conditional). With relative page numbers specifying density and area allocation.
- (d) The storage criterion for data may be collective or per data item, for example a specification for an aggregate may be for the whole aggregate or each part depending on the level at which it is specified.

If a data item should be required in two different formats for different purposes then it could be replicated with different storage formats for this purpose.

Example storage record entries to support the schema record 'PERSON' could be:

STORAGE RECORD NAME IS fullname
  LINK TO persondetails IS DIRECT
  DENSITY IS ONE RECORD PER 10 PAGES
  PLACEMENT IS
    CALC nameproc USING surname, forename(1)
  WITHIN names
  01 surname
    ALIGNMENT IS 2 WORDS
    FORMAT CHARACTER
    SIZE IS 40 CHARACTERS
  01 forenames
    02 forename
      SIZE IS 20 CHARACTERS

STORAGE RECORD persondetails

```
    LINK TO fullname
    LINK TO fmeasurements, mmeasurements IS INDIRECT
      IF sex = 'MALE' THEN
      PLACEMENT
        CLUSTERED VIA SET males
        WITHIN persondetails
    ELSE
      PLACEMENT
        CLUSTERED VIA SET females
    DATA ALL
```

A set entry must be defined to support each set in the schema. Sufficient pointers must be defined for the set to completely link the schema records in order to support the schema defined set order.

The definition of a set will define which pointers will be in which storage records such that:

(a) Only one storage record per list of storage records in the mapping will be defined as being the destination of all set pointers for that set
(b) At least one storage record per list of storage records in the mapping will be defined as having a pointer of some type
(c) Allocation of these pointers may be static or dynamic
(d) Depending on whether there is a storage key index defined for the storage record or not then the destination record for that schema record will either be pointed to indirectly or directly

The set may be supported by a chain of pointers or indexed or both. The set of 'males' is a singular chained set and 'nameset' is indexed. To find the seventh member of the set 'males' involves following the chain through each destination record findin g a pointer record for the next member and thus following it to the seventh member. If the index method was used the seventh item in the index gives the seventh record. Thus the storage schema can be finely tuned to the requirements of its users as shown below.

```
SET males
  MEMBER RECORD person
  STORAGE RECORD name
    DESTINATION DIRECT POINTERS
    POINTER FOR NEXT TENANT
```

SET ownerofhome
  OWNER
    STORAGE RECORD fullname
      DESTINATION OF DIRECT POINTERS
    STORAGE RECORD fullname, persondetails
      POINTER FOR INDEX nameindex
  MEMBER RECORD house
    STORAGE RECORD terracehouse
      DESTINATION OF INDIRECT POINTERS
      POINTER FOR INDEX nameindex
    STORAGE RECORD semidethouse, dethouse
      DESTINATION OF DIRECT POINTERS
      POINTER FOR INDEX nameindex

There are three types of indexes as specified by the USED clause: a STORAGE KEY index, a RECORD KEY index and a SET index.

A STORAGE KEY index must be specified for each storage record which is pointed to indirectly. It may either be seen as a storage key plus a direct address or simply the address where the storage key is the index name plus its position in the index.

A RECORD INDEX may be defined either to support a schema defined record key or as a key to help in any access of the schema record, particularly where some order needs to be maintained but is not visible in the schema. An index which is defined to support a set may have member record types which are supported in one of three ways:

(a) A key phrase specifies a list of identifiers to use as a key
(b) The key phrase does not have an associated list so it must support the set sort key and sorted order as defined in the schema
(c) There is no key phrase and therefore no identifiers in the key, the index consists only of the address. This choice seems obvious for schema order not sorted.

The type of pointer for a set index is dependent on the destination storage record type (often dependent on the mapping used).

INDEX nameindex
  PLACEMENT IS NEAR OWNER
  USED FOR SET ownerofhome
    LINK TO OWNER

INDEX personind
  USED FOR RECORD person

    ORDER KEY ASCENDING surname, forname(1)
    POINTER IS DIRECT TO fullname
    WITHIN personaldetails FROM PAGE 41 THRU 60

INDEX terrhstkey
    USED FOR STORAGE KEY terracehouse
    WITHIN housetypes

INDEX femstkey
    USED FOR STORAGE KEY fmeasurements
    WITHIN personaldetails FROM PAGE 1 THRU 20

A change to a storage schema is termed a 'reorganisation', which is the ability to alter the physical structure or access support mechanisms of the database, usually for performance reasons, without affecting the logical structure or associated application program. The separation of logical and physical description by schema and storage schema provides the required environment to support both static and dynamic reorganisation.

A complete reorganisation may be defined and run as a background utility or alternatively reorganisation may proceed incrementally with individual record occurrences being reorganised whenever they are accessed in some way. The former is known as background reorganisation, the latter as incremental reorganisation.

Both methods require a particular version of a storage schema to contain more than one description of the same storage schema object. The requirements are controlled by the process of version control. Version control implies that each catagory of object (sets, indexes, mappings and storage records) must have an associated version number which is the same as the version number of the storage schema in which it was defined. A single sequence of version numbers relates to successive versions of the storage schema, a new version implying some change to be performed by the reorganisation process.

The example storage schema objects are given a version number of one. Let us assume that the DBA wishes to make some alterations for efficiency reasons. For example, for efficiency reasons a new mapping for house, which highlights a new type of house, the bungalow. It is also decided that fullname will need to be more accessible therefore it is given a storage key index and thus becomes indirect as far as pointers to it are concerned.

The objects to be included in the new storage schema version 2 are:

all previous definitions from version 1 plus

MAPPING VERSION 2 FOR house
    IF housetype = 'TERRACE' THEN

　　　　STORAGE RECORDS ARE terracehouse, neighbours
　　IF housetype = 'SEMI' THEN
　　　　STORAGE RECORDS ARE semidethouse, neighbours
　　IF housetype = 'BUNGALOW' THEN
　　　　STORAGE RECORDS ARE bunghouse, neighbours
　　ELSE STORAGE RECORD IS dethouse

STORAGE RECORD bunghouse VERSION 2
　LINK TO neighbours IS INDIRECT
　PLACEMENT IS
　　CALC USING noofrooms
　WITHIN housetypes
　01 houseinfo
　　02 DATA ALL

STORAGE RECORD persondetails VERSION 2.
　LINK TO fullname IS INDIRECT
etc

Although 'neighbours' is not explicitly stated it is necessary to produce a version to complete the links required.

STORAGE RECORD neighbours VERSION 2
　LINK TO terracehouse, semidethouse, bunghouse
　PLACEMENT etc(same as for version 1)

To fulfill rules of pointers for sets 'ownerofhome' must also have a new version.
SET ownerofhome VERSION 2
　OWNER
　　STORAGE RECORD fullname
　　　DESTINATION OF INDIRECT POINTERS
　　　　:
　　　　:
　MEMBER RECORD house
　　　:
　　　:
　　STORAGE RECORD semidethouse, dethouse, bunghouse
　　　:

The rules for reorganisation of an index state that no alteration is allowed to the USED clause. Since the pointer phrase is part of the used clause then for 'personind' we cannot change the pointer to fullname to be

INDIRECT. That is, the pointer is forced to remain direct. A new index type has to be created for 'fullname' to be indirect, but the old index cannot be removed.

This method of version control, where a version number is stored with each storage record, group of set pointers and index, enables the dynamic update of these objects when reference is made to the storage schema tables. Not all objects can be incrementally reorganised. For example areas, indexes (USED FOR RECORD) and storage key indexes all have to be implemented when the new storage schema is incorporated into the system.

The levels of reorganisation may be seen as:

Mapping
Storage Record : Organisation,Placement,Pointers
Areas
Sets : Linkage
Index : Placement, Contents

Mapping: A new version of a mapping could imply that :

(a) the schema record is to be mapped under changed mapping conditions
(b) as in (a) but new storage records have been defined to fulfil a new mapping picture

The effect of a change in the environment conditions may require that the types of storage record required in the mapping will be different. These may be the old ones or new ones as in (b).

Thus it can be seen that the most likely effect of a new mapping is that one or more storage records must also be reorganised.

Storage Records: An alteration to the organisation within a storage record may imply an item added or simply that the storage representation of the item is changed or moved.

The placement of records can be altered subtly within the current area or drastically to another area altogether. Its method of placement can be changed to any one of CALC, CLUSTERED or SEQUENTIAL.

The link pointers in a storage record are mainly affected during the mapping phase.

Area: Changing an area is forced only by the creation of a new area definition and the removal of the old one. All storage records and indexes in this area will also require reorganisation.

Set: Set reorganisation cannot affect what types of schema records are members or owners, but it can affect the access paths. Pointer types can be changed from, say, First and Next to Last and Prior. The destination record can be a different record or chain linkage may be replaced by an index to support the order of the set.

If one set tenant is reorganised this will probably lead to the reorganisation of any constituents which require reorganisation; this may then cascade into other sets, hence cascading reorganisation.

Index: Indexes have a limited reorganisation capability in that only their placement may be changed. The change from direct to indirect pointers or vice versa has however been allowed in this design.

3. The Network Database Language (NDL) Development and Effects

The NDL is the proposed American National Standard Committee (ANSC) Network Database Draft Standard [2], as devised by the ANSC X3H2 subgroup using the CODASYL 1981 DDL JOD [3] as their base document.

3.1 *Common NDL : DDL concepts*

Based upon the CODASYL network design the overall database concepts have changed slightly providing a stricter, more modular approach for the application programmer. This may provide access control and a further tool for transaction control.

Prior to its publication, the DBAWG removed from the 1981 DDL JOD, the base document for the standard, all references to storage and physical device structures and control mechanisms.

Providing the same concepts, apart from one or two constructs, the NDL requires underlying logical to physical mapping, either by implementation controls or by using some form of data storage mapping, such as that provided by the DSDL.

3.2 *NDL : DDL differences*

The NDL is based upon the DDL and therefore differences may affect the supporting DSDL. The following are some of the more important differences:

excluded
for records : schema record key; conditional data items; source and result; data check clause on items; null; level numbers;
for sets : set selection

included
for sets : a structural set clause.

Of these, only the removal of set selection, schema record key, and level numbers remove any real functionality from the DSDL.

The removal of set selection implies that the application programmer must provide the routes through the network. For a STORE on a record, for example, all the set occurrences into which the automatic member has to be inserted must be the current ones of the associated set types. An implementation of the Database Management System (DBMS), using the DDL guidelines, must perform the positioning of the set occurrences required, obtaining the item values for the set selection clause from the application work area.

The key phrase for a schema record defined in the DDL allowed the DSDL to provide indexes upon a record type, supporting next and prior searches on the record type. A duplicates restriction could also be placed on a record type for this key. A similar result can be achieved in the NDL by declaring a record type, as the only member type in a system-owned set, with sorted order on an equivalent set key.

The removal of the level numbers implies that all items are now on the same level, removing the data aggregate facility from the schema.

The DBAWG are currently working on a DSDL which supports the NDL.

4. The DSDL Compiler

The first aim of this project was to implement a DSDL 'compiler'.

The DSDL compiler was produced in five phases: lexical analysis, syntax anlysis, semantic analysis, table generation and version analysis. The first three of these form a machine-independent module since the only outside reference is the schema tables in semantic analysis.

The compiler has been designed so that the schema table access routines can easily be re-written to accommodate any form of object schema table, thus keeping these phases DBMS independent.

The last two phases are type dependent in that, if the storage schema is stored as code, then a different software machine must be implemented from that required by a table driven machine.

These last two phases may be machine independent as they are in this implementation, but it is forseen that certain implementations would be machine dependent, especially where reference to database files is allowed within table generation.

4.1 Lexical and syntax analysis

Lexical and syntax analysis are basic for most language compilers and as such require little explanation, other than to say that the mode of communication between them is a file of tokens. These tokens are made up of reserved word symbols, identifier tree tokens and literals. A compacted stream of those symbols is passed to semantic analysis since many of the reserved words in the DSDL are no longer required.

During the development of the syntax graphs syntax inaccuracies were found, upon which the DBAWG have acted to correct the syntax published in the 1981 JOD [3].

4.2 Semantic analysis

The rules required for semantic analysis, found as syntax rules in the DSDL JOD, are encoded into the bodies of procedures at appropriate points, using the syntax graphs as placement tools. For rules which require further information before completion, the information currently determined must be stored in temporary tables to be accessed later.

Rules which reference schema information require access to the schema tables, the design of which must be known prior to the creation of the semantic analysis schema table access routines. Furthermore, any alteration to the DDL which does not affect the information required can be mirrored by these schema table access routines.

Areas have no associated version numbers and as such are always checked. Only current version numbered entries are semantically checked, but information is kept on the youngest of all the entries for each object.

Testing tables mirroring the mapping of schema record to storage records are required to check that enough links are defined to completely link the storage records for all mappings.

The semantics of the conditional expressions, which include arithmetic expressions, requires the matching of the operand types and for this two stacks are provided.

4.3 Table generation

From the input stream of tokens a set of tables is produced, redefined as a large array, which mimic the overall structure of the language. Names of objects which are specified other than where defined are replaced by direct pointers to those definitions within the storage schema. That is the whole table is cross referenced using integer indexes. The size of a data item, if known, is also filled in, together with its offset in the record. The removal of the source/result and data aggregate facilities from records implies that size and offset calculations are simplified. The output from table generation is used by the DBMS to access the data from the physical storage.

4.4 Version analysis

This phase incorporates all syntax rules for reorganisation found in the DSDL Appendix, and is fundamental to ensuring the correctness of the new storage schema version. All entries with prior version numbers to the current one must be checked to ensure that they appeared in that exact context in the prior version of the storage schema tables. Some entries are not allowed to alter their function at all, for example, a new version of an index must have the same USED clause as in the prior version. The implication of this is that when a storage record is given a storage key index then not all pointers will necessarily point to the index, specificaly those of a set index. These pointers have an original type of direct or indirect either implicitly or explicitly stated which cannot be changed except by the creation of a new index with a new name. This produces superfluous indexes and there are no facilities provided to dispose of the old ones.

The overall effect of version analysis is to ensure that a new version of a storage schema and its immediate predecessor form a consistent increment according to the reorganisation rules.

5. The Experimental Run-Time System

There are various considerations to be taken into account when designing a Run-Time system of this type. The basic considerations common to all such systems are:-

how the DML, DDL, and DSDL are to be supported;
the types of page layout and access mechanisms;
reorganisation aspects

The aim of the experimental run-time system is to perceive the effect that dynamic incremental reorganisation has on the performance of a Network Database System. To this end we have to monitor the effect that the DML commands have in a reorganisation environment. The Codasyl documentation gives an outline of the performance architecture of such a system. Using this as a guideline we have endeavoured to design a system which can be easily used and modified. It is not forseen that the system will be used in any but a research environment. The design does not incorporate all the DML, NDL/DDL, DSDL facilities, nor can we produce (as yet) a multi-user system. It is hoped that, should shared file access ever become available, the modification required would not be insurmountable.

5.1 Supporting the DML, DDL and associated DSDL

The DML verb is used as the basis to formulate the system response. That is to follow the DML rules which call upon the DDL and DSDL table information, these rules form the basis of the system.

The application passes to the system details of the DML verb it requires to execute, together with a record containing information to support this request. (See Figure 1). The system processes this request, converting it to a request for information from the DDL and the DSDL tables. The system uses this information to send an appropriate request to the GET PAGE routine, to obtain the required page from storage. This may have been via other pages, say an index page in the index buffers or other records in a set. When the storage record has been found, other requests may be required to fulfil the needs of the verb.

If the request was initiated by the FIND then we have to make a decision as to whether all the storage records supporting the schema record must be brought in, or just one. This may depend on the subschema requirements. The method adopted has been to validate the whole schema record via accesses to the links in the prefixes to obtain all the storage records. The links can be found uniquely by reference to the version number in the storage record and then investigation of the storage record type of that version will specify how many and to which records that record is linked. A GET or FETCH processes the page(s) obtaining a view of the record as the application sees it. This is achieved by reserving the same mapped space as is required by the STORE command for the storage records. The integers of the data on the page are copied into this Work Area where the data is then compacted to form the schema record. It is hoped that this simple form of memory management will allow for investigation into whether reorganisation is affecting storage record manipulation. If the initial request had been a STORE, then an entirely different set of instructions and information would be required. Particularly required is the information about the set selection requirements for each set of which this record is an automatic member.

It has been decided however that although we were initially going to support the DDL that some of the structures ommited from the NDL would also not be included in this system. These are the set selection clause, and the data aggregate facility (only arrays of one data item type are allowed). The reasons for the change were:-

(a) for simplicity, the set selection clause will degrade the system to the detriment of reorganisation
(b) an MSc student is currently undertaking a project to produce a compiler for the NDL
(c) an NDL compatable DDL will enhance the production of a complete system

The DDL and DSDL information is stored as tables, output from their table generation phases, where all object names have been removed into a form of data dictionary. This data dictionary is required to have a static index facility which has unique references, fast retrieval and update

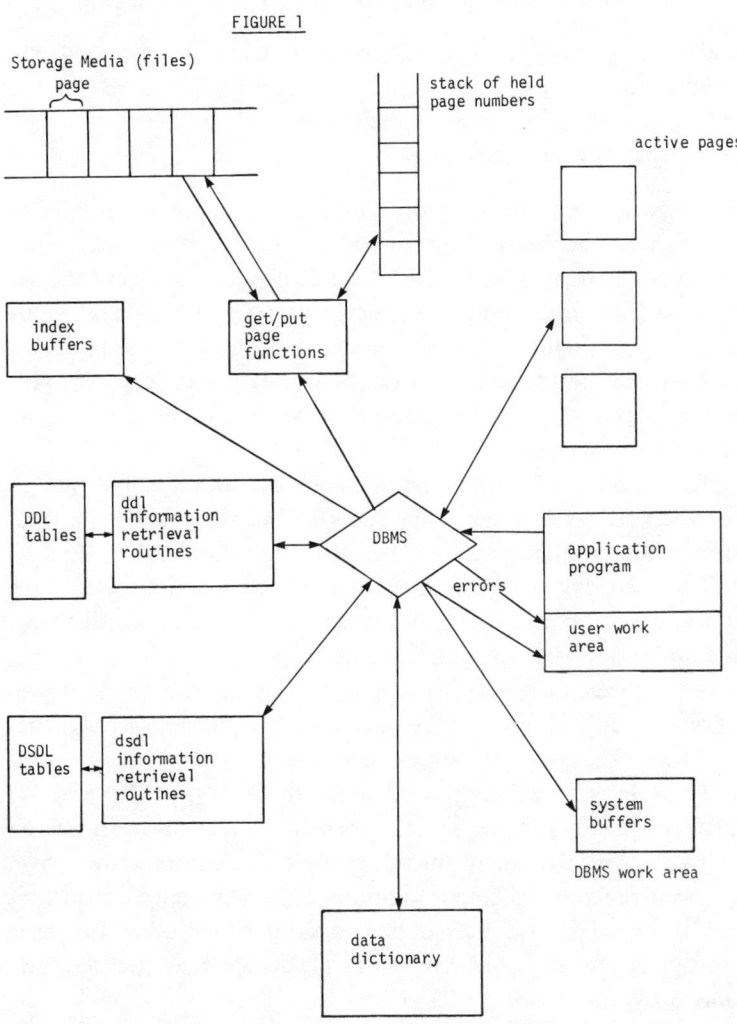

FIGURE 1

facilities, and therefore the binary tree structure was chosen. A more complex structure of the b-tree would require a tree plus an index, not the easiest system to control.[5]

Various routines are required to access the information stored in the DSDL and DDL tables; these are modular in design in that any procedure which directly accesses a table does not access more than one table type. This environment allows the environment of the DSDL table to be changed easily so that the system will not be altered should the method of storage of the object DSDL be changed.

5.2 Factors affecting DSDL implementation

The facilities required to support a DSDL include

areas : in this case stored as different files, which are subdivided into pages.
storage records: one or more make-up a schema record
indexes: of the types already mentioned
temporary run unit structures

Reorganisation is not developed as a unit of its own but interwoven with the ordinary accesses of the system.

The areas named in the DSDL refer directly to files of the same name, for ease of manipulation, where device type is controlled by separate device mapping procedures. It has been decided that all page layouts should be of fixed size and based upon the layout of the IDMS page [4]. This was done so that the resulting run-time system could be compared to an existing product.

The storage key index is created such that order is first with one integer for the address of the storage record. The storage key itself is made up from the storage key name token and the offset in the index.

The record keys are binary trees for supporting order ascending or descending or hashed key indexes, where the index holds the key value and the address of the storage record.

Set indexes must support any sort of order thus the most flexible type of index would seem to be the the linked list. The index holds the key value and the address of the storage record.

To differentiate between pointers to the OWNER and NEXT and PRIOR pointers in the set, the former have their addresses negated. In this way, we solve the problem of where a schema record is owner of one set occurrence and member of another set occurrence of the same set type. Addresses which are indirect have a value which takes 4 bytes (1 byte for storage key index name, 3 bytes for offset) whereas one that is direct takes only 3 bytes.

Simple structures need to be defined to gather together relevant information for processes such as the creating of the storage records required to map a schema record during a STORE.

Since the access of records is based around the verbs CONNECT, DISCONNECT, ERASE, FIND, GET, MODIFY and STORE, the main problems are how to support reorganisation and which of these processes trigger the reorganisation process and how the system can avoid a cascade of reorganisation.

If we were to reorganise only when a record must be 'written to' a page, as in STORE, MODIFY and ERASE then we could enclose the routines in the 'put' routines. This would imply that under certain conditions 'put's' would have to enable 'get's', where access to other affected records occurs. If a record is not required for modification, but it is required on a fast device, then this process will not cope without forced modifications.

Reorganisation must be triggered by any type of access to the record, but perhaps only to a certain degree. If the record is merely part of an access path to another record, then there is the option that it should not be reorganised.

One possible solution which involves the use of the FIND command as the initiating force, is that the execution of this would cause all storage record, mapping and affected set reorganisations to be invoked. If the mapping included new storage records which do not involve a change to the destination clause or pointer types required for the set, then that schema record can be reorganised without invoking a set reorganisation. Otherwise the other tenants of the set are involved:-

(i) if the destination record changes then the set pointers to it must be changed to point to the new destination record.
(ii) the set pointers must be able to support the order of the set which they cannot do if the pointer type chain changes for one record occurrence only.

The change to the pointers in the rest of the set need not imply that each member record type need be checked for reorganisation unless new storage records are necessary thus avoiding a cascade of reorganistion through the sets.

The higher the number of record and set types which participate in a reorganisation, past versions or present, that have not yet been included then the greater the possibility of deadlock. The processes of deadlock may not work under these conditions. The methods for controlling this cascade are either by prevention, ie not allowing so many changes to be active together, or else by restricting the changes to the immediate set occurrence.

Index reorganisation if not of the static kind, such as for record or storage key, is initiated whenever a new version exists during the use of an index or creation of a new access path.

A changed index description for storage key and schema record key indexes must be updated as soon as the new version of the storage schema is used. Since the indexes are placed in a separate area, this should not affect the availability of the database. Each set index occurrence is created during an access to that particular set occurrence. Entries into the indexes have to be made during the operation of the system.

For storage key indexes, the storage record type needs to be flagged, so that when routes pass through that record, the pointer may be changed to point to the index and the address of the record stored in the index. If this point is from an index which is used for 'record' then the rules state that type must not be changed. There are no obvious rules governing the change for set indexes, from direct to indirect or vice versa. Since a direct address can take the same space and is easily distinguishable from an indirect address, then it has been decided to allow this change. To disallow this would restrict the movement of records pointed to by initially direct pointers.

From the division of reorganisation into the categories previously mentioned, we can see that procedures are required to determine which processes will be performed, depending on which units of reorganisation are active.

5.3 Supporting the NDL – the perceived modifications

A DSDL which supports the NDL requires little modification at the system level. Only the paths for reorganisation may need to be changed. In particular, the routines for set selection have been removed and therefore there is no traversing of sets by the system; this job has to be done by the application programmer. Since data aggregates, source and result data items are not provided for, the size of records is assured.

Thus the problem of reorganisation is simplified by the NDL, albeit somewhat obtrusively.

6. Conclusion

This paper has shown how a DBMS which takes into account reorganisation can be constructed. It has highlighted some of the problems which occur when reorganisation is incorporated into a DBMS.

The system which has been described has added complexity due to the fact that both background and foreground incremental reorganisation can be undertaken, although only the latter has been described.

Acknowledgements

The author gratefully acknowledges the support given by the SERC, which enabled this work to be undertaken.

References
[1] CODASYL DBTG REPORT 1969 and DDL Journal of Development 1971 Canadian Federal Government 1969, 1971
[2] A Proposed Network Database Language NSC (X3H2-83-121) American National Standards Committee 1983
[3] Codasyl Data Description Language Committee JOD and DSDL and COBOL Committee JOD Secretariat of the Canadian Government EDP 1981
[4] CULLINANE CORP. IDMS. APPENDIX C: Space Management 1978
[5] Jenson & Wirth Algorithms + Data Structures = Programs Section 4.5

An Architecture and Language Syntax for Distributed Databases for the Network Model

British Computer Society / CODASYL Data Base Administration Working Group (DBAWG)
13 Mansfield Street, London W1M 0BP

A previous paper [1] discussed the development of an abstract syntax for distributed databases. This paper describes the use of that abstract syntax to develop a language which can be used to define distributed databases(DDB).

The architecture employed enables previously existing centralised databases to be federated into a single distributed database. An Availability Schema defines the data available to a node of the DDB. This is identical to the proposed Network Database Language [2]. A Geographic Schema describes the location and placement of data at different nodes. The Geographic Schema also enables records to be constructed from parts of one or more other records and specifies the conditions under which the constructed view can be updated. Finally each node is instantiated by means of references to an availability and geographic schema type, together with some Export Schema definitions. An Export Schema defines the conditions under which data can be exported from one node to another.

An example is included to demonstrate the flexibility of the language.

1. Introduction

When a new language is being developed it is necessary to be aware of the overall environment in which the language is going to operate. The resultant language then has a well defined function within that complete architecture. [1] described the architecture within which distributed database (DDB) could operate and then went on to develop an abstract notation which could be used to describe such DDB's. Since then the architecture has been slightly modified and the notation altered to account for these modifications and also to encompass further fuctionality to that reported previously. The notation has then been used as the basis for developing a language syntax which conforms to the norm for such database languages. The language has been influenced by the development of a proposed Network Database Language (NDL) standard

[2]. In subsequent sections we shall briefly describe the final architecture into which the language fits and the updated version of the notation which was used to develop the language. The relationship between the language specification and the notation will be discussed by means of examples together with the influences which conditioned the style of the language. Finally, an example of a complete DDB specification will be presented which uses the language elements previously discussed.

2.   The Definition of the Architectural Components

When the architecture was developed it was purposely decided to ensure that no assumptions were made about the relationship between the nodes which formed the DDB. That is, there is no master-slave relationship. We also wished to ensure that each node could operate independently of any other node when it was making an access to local data. Thus all information necessary to access local data can be stored at the local node. Further, each node should have the necessary information to initiate the access to remote data, even though all the necessary information for the actual data access will be maintained at the remote node. The architecture therefore supports fully separated independent nodes, however, an implementation may use a central node if it so wishes. We now present the definition of each of the architectural components.

(a) A **distributed database** (DDB) is a database which is supported by two or more nodes. Each **node** of a DDB is defined to have the necessary database, communications and operating systems software as in a non-distributed database. Further, each node usually, but not necessarily, supports user programs. A DDB may include data which is private (see also export schema) to a particular node. The combination of private and distributed data enables a node to provide an environment which can support many varying requirements. Therefore, in a DDB not all the data needs to be capable of being distributed to all other nodes because that data may have no relevance at other nodes. Each node is given a **name** which uniquely identifies the node within the DDB (see also geographic schema). A node is specific to one DDB. A particular unit of processing capability may support one or more nodes from one or more DDB's.

(b) A **distributed database management system** (DDBMS) provides the facilities of DBMS except that due account is taken of the fact that the database is distributed. The DDBMS therefore has

to be able to control the transportation of data between nodes of a DDB.
(c) An **availability schema** of a DDB describes all the data available to user programs executing at a node. There is only one availability schema at a node. Not all the data at a node is necessarily available to other nodes. However, this private data is combined with the shared data to form the availability schema for that node. If, for a number of nodes, the available data is identical then those nodes may use copies of the same availability schema.
(d) A **geographic schema** describes the location of all data objects which comprise the data available to, or stored at that node. The geographic schema is given a **name** which uniquely identifies the geographic schema within the DDB. The name by association is also the name by which the node could be referenced due to the 1:1 correspondence between node and geographic schema. The geographic schema describes in an unambiguous way, by means of rules, how data may be stored either upon the local node or remote node(s) or both. Such rules may contain conditions written in terms of data items defined within the record to be stored. The geographic schema also defines the record and set types which may be retrieved from other nodes. The geographic schema has the ability to indicate that the data may be replicated or partitioned.
(e) An **export schema** at a node gives rules which define the conditions under which data records, data items, sets and indexes which are described in the geographic schema at that node may be transported between that node and another node. The rules may contain conditions defined by data item values which are contained within the record to be exported and the allowable data manipulation functions. The **private data** at a node comprises that data which is described in the availability schema but which does not appear in any export schema at that node. At any node which exports data to other nodes there must be an export schema which relates the exporting node to each of the importing nodes. The export schema also provides naming conventions between the exporting and importing nodes.
(f) A **constructor mechanism** is part of the geographic schema, which specifies how data objects described by the availability schema or referred to by any export schema can be constructed from other data identified by the geographic schema at that node.

The constructor mechanism can be used in two ways, namely incoming and outgoing. In the incoming mode data is collected from one or more remote nodes together with data at the local node (though not necessarily). The total data, which may comprise complete records or just parts of records, is then formed into the format specified in the availability schema or one or more of the export schemas. (This implies that a node is able to pass data to another node where the transported data is itself imported data, the so called problem of data pass through). In the outgoing mode data from a single node is collected together to structure data into a form required by another node, and as such is used only in the export schemas of a node. The outgoing mode is particularly useful when a federated database is constructed. In this situation data can be structured in such a way so as to enable easy transference of data between nodes in a standard format. Typically this will be used to deal with the case of data which is recorded at every node but in different record structures. It is also possible to define data which is not made specifically available to the availability schema at the node. Such data is incorporated by the incoming constructor mechanism.

The export schema provides 'global' access control for the transferrence of data between geographic schemas. At any node which exports data to one or more nodes there must be an export schema which relates the exporting node to each of the importing nodes. The export schema provides global access control only.

The DSDL statements defining the storage schema are written against the geographic schema. The DSDL will merely specify the storage of data at a node. Such a storage schema is provided by the Data Storage Description Language (DSDL) contained in the CODASYL DDL Journal of Development [3]. Sub-schemas are written against the availability schema.

The definition of a DDB assumes that each node is going to be geographically distinct. In fact this may not be the case as computer systems may have the multiprocessing capacity which enables them to support several nodes possibly sharing the same DBMS software. Each node will, however, be distinct having different availability and geographic schemas. Where several nodes fundamentally carry out the same task except that they are geographically distinct then copies of the same availability and geographic schemas can be used except for the name associated with each instance. Each instance is distinguished by the name given to the node and hence the geographic schema. For ease of implementation the name of the geographic schema can be subscripted to allow instances to be separated.

There are essentially two ways in which DDB can be created, either they arise as a result of several autonomous databases being joined together or they are created as a DDB. This can be likened to the bottom-up and top-down methods respectively. The bottom-up approach equates to the concept of federated databases. That is, currently existing databases are joined together to form a distributed database. The top-down approach equates to the design and implementation of a database which since its conception was intended to be distributed. In both cases, however, the structure that has been proposed in this paper is capable of supporting the design. However, in any DDB it is going to be necessary to maintain information about the data which is available for sharing by nodes. Such design control aspects are considered to be the province of a data dictionary system rather than the specifications required in order that a DDB can operate successfully. The architecture is summarised in Fig 1.

3. The Abstract Notation

Using the preceding architectural components as a basis it was possible to develop an abstract syntax which specified the nature of the language needed to support the geographic and export schema elements of the complete architecture. We assumed that the language necessary to support the availability schema would already exist.

The syntax of the notation is specified using syntax graphs augmented by supplementary rules as necessary. It is hoped that the notation is

Fig 1. The interaction of architectural components

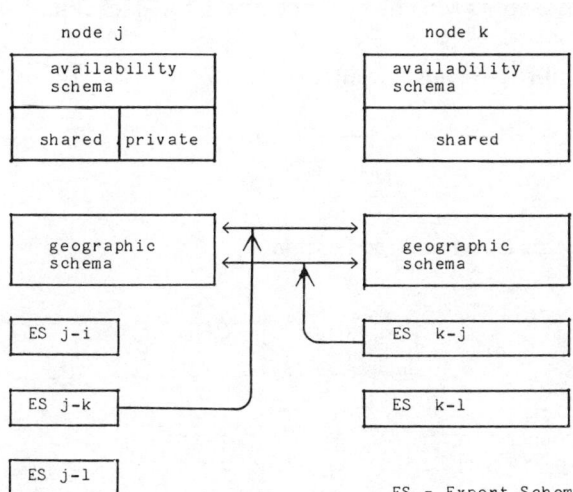

sufficiently accessible so that it can be used as a design tool when creating DDB as shown in [1].

The following symbols are used in the syntax graphs and their associated verbalisation is given to aid understanding.

(a) **Identifiers**

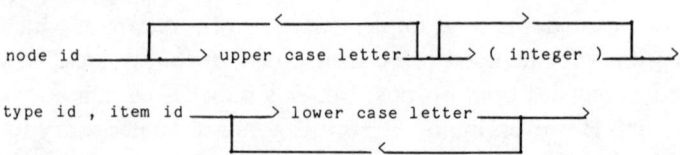

A node-id gives a name to a node of a distributed database. If the integer is specified it implies that the node-id is subscripted so as to differentiate between different occurrences of the same node-id within the same distributed database. A type-id gives a name to a record, set or index declaration. An item-id gives the name of a data item and is used in conditions within the export and geographic schemas. An item-id is also used within the constructor mechanism.

(b) **Schema Identification** The **availability schema** for a node of a distributed database is identified by the node-id subscripted by A.

The **geographic schema** is identified by the node-id subscripted by G.

At each node of a particular distributed database there must be one geographic schema and one availability schema.

(c) **Availability Schema Specification**

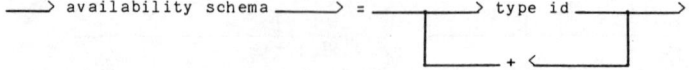

(d) **Geographic Schema Specification**

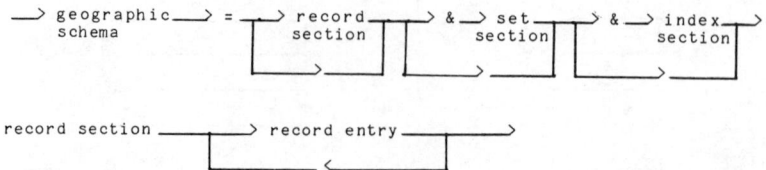

Distributed databases for the network model 213

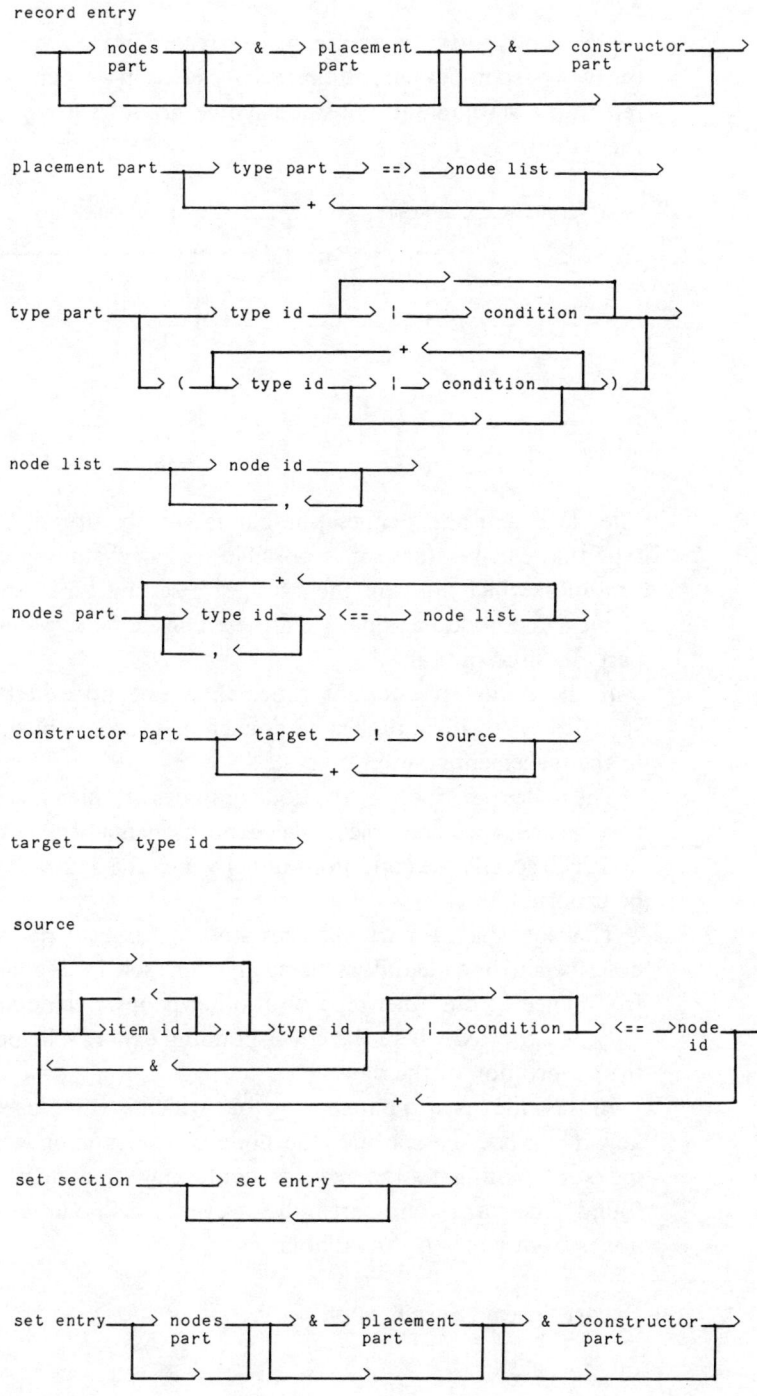

NOTE

In the record entry, type-id refers to a record in the syntax graphs for type part, nodes part and target; whereas in a set entry type-id refers to a set name in the same syntax graphs when applied to the set entry.

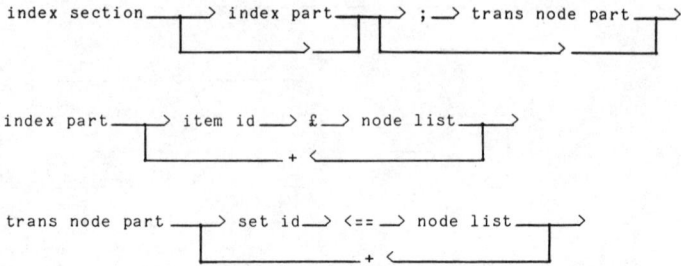

The placement part defines where data is to be stored. For each type that can be stored it is possible to specify the appropriate condition which controls the storage. If several types are stored at the same node or nodes then these can be factored using the parenthesised option.

If the node list contains more than one node-id then the specified type will be replicated at each node so specified, subject to the placement clause.

The nodes part specifies the node or nodes at which it is possible to locate the specified object. The export schema of the exporting node will specify the conditions under which the data will actually be exported.

The constructor part specifies how a target type which is described in the availabilty schema or export schema is constructed from objects from other records at other nodes. Such objects will only be exported where the corresponding export schema allows the exportation of the data.

In the index part the item-id is that which is being used as the key. The node list specifies the node or nodes upon which the indexes pointing to the records containing that item may be found. The trans-node part indicates the trans-node set and the nodes from which it is available.

(e) **Export Schema Specification**

Distributed databases for the network model 215

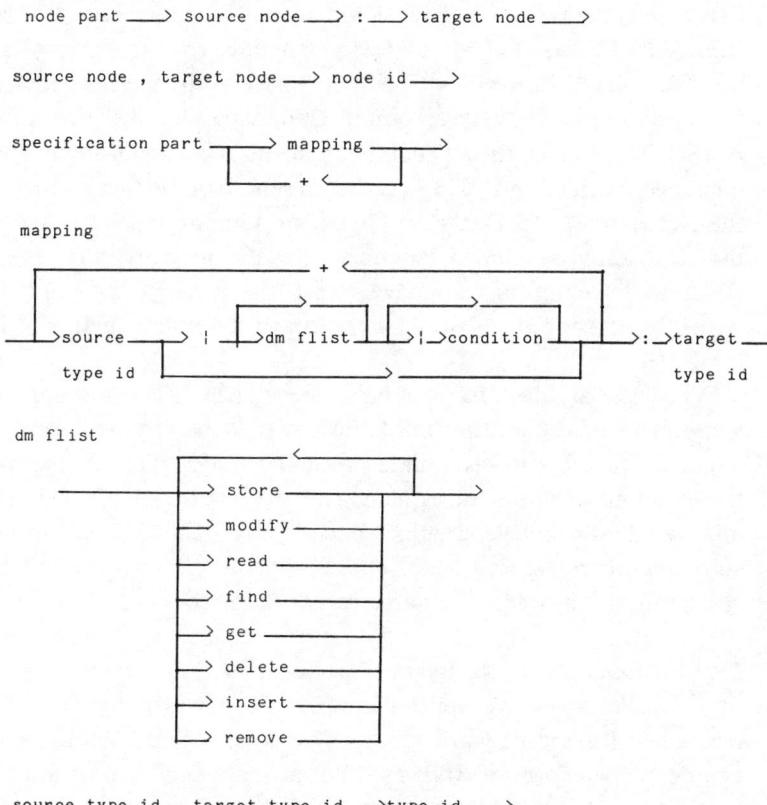

The source node identifies the exporting node and the target node identifies the importing node. There must be one export schema specification at the source node for each node which could be a target node.

The source type-id specifies the data which is to be transported between nodes together with any necessary conditions. The target type-id specifies the imported data and need not be the same name as the source. It is also possible to specify the data manipulation function(s) for which exportation is allowed.

The source type-id may be a constructed item in the geographic schema.

4. Factors Affecting the Development of Language Syntax

During the period that the architecture and notation were being developed the American National Standards Committee X3H2 (ANSC) were also developing standards for Network and Relational model database systems [2]. These will soon be made available for general public comment. It was decided that any language syntax developed should interface directly with these ANSC proposals. Further, the method used for specifying the language syntax should be identical to that used by ANSC. To this end, the Availability Schema is defined using the definition language specified by ANSC. At the present, work is further forward with the Network Model Database Definition Language (NDL) and we have therefore only developed languages for the network model. Once the Relational Definition Language (RDL) is developed we anticipate no difficulty in using the abstract notation to develop a relational interface for DDB.

When the architecture was being developed it became apparent that some form of declaration mechanism would be required from which it would be possible to instantiate particular nodes. This can be likened to 'type' definitions and subsequent 'var' declarations in Pascal. Therefore all availability and geographic schemas are defined as a type which is subsequently referenced when a node is defined. Thus the same definition can be used repeatedly, by name rather than redefinition.

5. Examples of the Syntax Specification

We now give some examples of the syntax which has been developed for the network model. The style is that used by ANSC and is an extended form of BNF as follows:- ... means zero or more repeats, | means or, { } means group sequences, [ ] means an optional element. The complete syntax is given in [10].

The first example shows the structure of a distributed database definition.

<distributed database definition> ::=
  <schema type declaration>...<ddb node definition>...

<schema type declaration> ::=
  DECLARE { <availability schema type> | <geographic schema type> }

<ddb node definition> ::=
  <geographic schema reference> [<availability schema reference>]
  [<export schema definition>...] [<storage schema>]

<availability schema reference> ::=
  SCHEMA TYPE <schema name>

```
<geographic schema reference> ::=
    GEOGRAPHIC SCHEMA TYPE <node name> INSTANCE <instance number>

<geographic schema type> ::=
    GEOGRAPHIC SCHEMA <node name>
    { <record residence definition> | <set residence definition> |
      <index residence definition> }...
```

The availability schema is declared using NDL which contains the element <schema name>.

We now look at the record residence definition in more detail.

```
<record residence definition> ::=
    RECORD <record name>
    { { <record existence clause> [ <record placement clause> ] }
    | <record constructor clause> | <record definition clause> }
```

Where the existence clause defines the nodes upon which occurrences of a record type may exist. The placement clause specifies the conditions, if any, under which an occurrence of a record type is stored at a particular node. The definition clause specifies a record which is stored locally but which is not made explicitly available in the associated availability schema; such a record is used in a constructor mechanism. We shall now look at the constructor clause in more detail as it will be used in the complete example in the next section.

```
<record constructor clause> ::=
    CONSTRUCTED BY { MATCHING | EXTENDING | COMBINING
    | PROJECTING }
    <contents part>

<contents part> ::=
    <field specifier> [ { , <field specifier> } WHEN <condition> ]

<field specifier> ::=
    [ [ ALL EXCEPT ] <data identifier>... OF ] <record name>

<condition> ::=
    <data identifier> = <data identifier>
    [ { AND <data identifier> = <data identifier> } ... ]
```

By inspection it can be seen that this syntax follows very closely the abstract notation given above.

The options MATCHING etc enable the nature of the constructed record to be determined in conjunction with the condition. Records with the MATCHING option can be fully updated whereas other options allow only partial or no updating.

6. An Example System: The Inland Revenue

This example gives the complete definition of a DDB to support the Inland Revenue when they wish to access details from employee records. It is assumed that the Inland Revenue circulate the format that they require the information to be presented in.

All firms, organisations and businesses maintain records of the salary details of their employees. These records necessarily contain information about the tax which has been paid by an employee. The Inland Revenue require to check this information against the information provided by the employee on his tax return to the Inland Revenue. Assuming that a firm's salary records are kept on a computer database then the Inland Revenue require access to the employer's computer system to extract the information required. Obviously the employer will wish to ensure that the Inland Revenue only gain access to the appropriate data.

From the point of view of the Inland Revenue a large distributed database has been formed by federating all the databases of the individual organisations and the Inland Revenue database. The Inland Revenue will circulate to all organisations the format of the data they require and its contents. Each organisation will then have to collect the appropriate data from its records to the form required by the Inland Revenue. It is

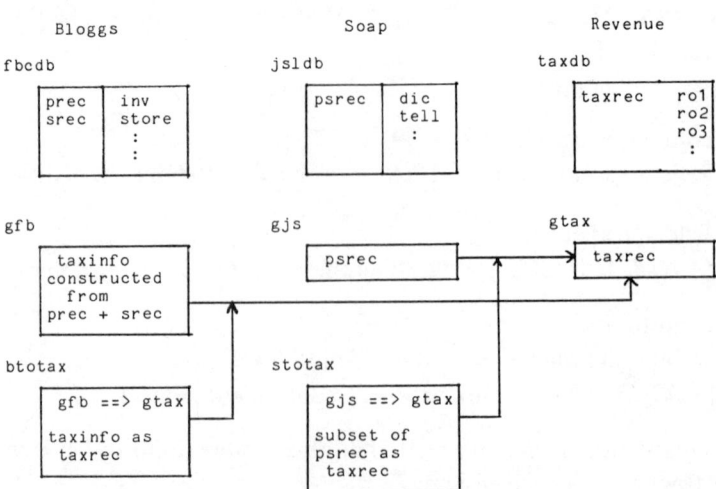

Fig 2. Structure of the Inland Revenue System

inevitable that the appropriate data will be held in different record structures in each of the organisations.

In this example two organisations are shown, each forming a node of the distributed database. Fred Bloggs and Co maintain two records which between them contain the data required by the Inland Revenue. The record 'prec' contains personal details of all employees and 'salrec' contains the salary and tax data. Fred Bloggs is therefore going to have to combine the data from two records to provide the required tax record.

Joe Soap Ltd, however, maintain a single record 'psrec' which is a superset of the data required by the Inland Revenue.

The structure of the tax distributed database is given in Fig 2.

6.1   *Schema Declaration for Bloggs*
       DECLARE SCHEMA fbcdb

RECORD prec
  UNIQUE emp-number
    emp-number CHARACTER 10
    name CHARACTER 20
    address CHARACTER 40
    age FIXED 2
    phone CHARACTER 10
    :
    :

RECORD srec
  UNIQUE pay-number
    pay-number CHARACTER 10
    salary FLOAT 6
    taxcode FIXED 4
    tax-ref-code CHARACTER 10
    taxable-pay FLOAT 6
    tax-deducted FLOAT 6
    pensionable-pay FLOAT 6
    pension-deducted FLOAT 6

RECORD inv
    :
    :

RECORD store
    :
    :
:
:

DECLARE GEOGRAPHIC SCHEMA gfb

RECORD prec EXISTS LOCALLY PLACEMENT LOCALLY

RECORD srec EXISTS LOCALLY PLACEMENT LOCALLY

RECORD taxinfo
CONSTRUCTED BY MATCHING
name OF prec ,
ALL EXCEPT pensionable-pay , pension-deducted OF srec
WHEN emp-number OF prec = pay-number OF srec

RECORD inv EXISTS LOCALLY PLACEMENT LOCALLY

RECORD store EXISTS LOCALLY PLACEMENT LOCALLY

⋮
⋮

6.2   *Schema Declarations for Soap*
      DECLARE SCHEMA jsldb

RECORD psrec
  UNIQUE clock-number
    clock-number CHARACTER 6
    name CHARACTER 15
    address CHARACTER 35
    wage-per-week FLOAT 5
    total-wage FLOAT 6
    tax-code FIXED 4
    tax-reference CHARACTER 10
    taxable-pay FLOAT 6
    tax-paid FLOAT 6
    supperan-paid FLOAT 6
    ⋮
    ⋮

RECORD dic
  ⋮
  ⋮

RECORD tell
  ⋮
  ⋮

⋮
⋮

DECLARE GEOGRAPHIC SCHEMA gjs

   RECORD psrec EXISTS LOCALLY PLACEMENT LOCALLY

   RECORD dic EXISTS LOCALLY PLACEMENT LOCALLY

   RECORD tell EXISTS LOCALLY PLACEMENT LOCALLY

   :
   :

6.3   *Schema Declarations for Revenue*
       DECLARE SCHEMA taxdb

   RECORD taxrec
       works-number CHARACTER 20
       name CHARACTER 30
       reference-code CHARACTER 10
       tax-code FIXED 4
       total-pay FLOAT 7
       taxable-Pay FLOAT 7
       tax-paid FLOAT 6

   RECORD ro1
      :
      :

   RECORD ro2
      :
      :

   RECORD ro3
      :
      :

:
:

DECLARE GEOGRAPHIC SCHEMA gtax

   RECORD taxrec EXISTS ALL

   RECORD ro1 EXISTS LOCALLY PLACEMENT LOCALLY

   RECORD ro2 EXISTS LOCALLY PLACEMENT LOCALLY

   RECORD ro3 EXISTS LOCALLY PLACEMENT LOCALLY

6.4 Instantiation of the Distributed Database

GEOGRAPHIC SCHEMA TYPE gfb INSTANCE 1
SCHEMA TYPE fbcdb
EXPORT SCHEMA btotax FROM gfb TO gtax
  RECORD taxrec FROM taxinfo
    DATA
      name AS name
      pay-number AS works-number
      tax-code AS tax-code
      salary AS total-pay
      tax-ref-code AS reference-code
      taxable-pay AS taxable-pay
      tax-deducted AS tax-paid
    FOR GET

GEOGRAPHIC SCHEMA TYPE gjs INSTANCE 1
SCHEMA TYPE jsldb
EXPORT SCHEMA stotax FROM gjs TO gtax
  RECORD taxrec FROM psrec
    DATA
      name AS name
      clock-number AS works-number
      tax-code AS tax-code
      total-wage AS total-pay
      tax-reference AS reference-code
      taxable-pay AS taxable-pay
      tax-paid AS tax-paid
    FOR GET

GEOGRAPHIC SCHEMA TYPE gtax INSTANCE 1
SCHEMA TYPE taxdb

7. Relationship to other Distributed Database Systems

Much work has been undertaken in the area of DDB, a review of which is given in [4]. In particular, there has been much development in the area of relational DDB, which is typified by SDD–1 [5,8] and R* [6,7,8]. There has not been a corresponding for network systems as yet.

SDD–1 does not maintain a global schema but does contain directories from which a global schema could be constructed. It is therefore similar to the approach given in this paper whereby the geographic schema can be equated to the directory. However, SDD–1 contains no capability for defining private data.

R* is much closer to our approach in that each nodal database is independent and makes its own bilateral arrangement for data sharing. This is achieved in our architecture by the export schema. Similarly in R* each node maintains its own information concerning distribution.

Perhaps the closest architecture to that described in this paper is propounded by Mcleod [9] which originally justified the concept of federated databases. However, we have gone further in this architecture in that we have allowed private data and defined a mechanism which enables constructed views (synonymously relational views) to be updated, albeit under tightly controlled conditions. These conditions were derivable due to the uniqueness constraints in the network model for databases.

8. Summary

This paper has shown how, by considering the architectural requirements of distributed database systems it has been possible to define the architecture and a notation to describe such databases. Then, by using the notation it was shown how a complete language could be developed for a particular environment, in this case the Network Model. Finally an example was presented which demonstrated the flexibility of the complete architecture.

Acknowledgments

This paper has been written jointly by seventeen authors. They are all members of the British Computer Society / CODASYL Data Base Working Group (DBAWG). The specific authors are H H Alexander (International Computers Ltd), T Beetstra (Philips BV), D Bell (Aberdeen University), S J Cannan (John Brown E & C Ltd), E G Dee (DMW (UK) Ltd), P Doyle (CACI Inc International), G Fitzgerald (Aston University), C French (International Computers Ltd), J 0 Jefferys (John Hoskins and Co Ltd), J M Kerridge (Sheffield City Polytechnic), W R Pilgrim (Sperry Corporation), D Rabone (John Brown 0 S Ltd), F G Ras (Database Consultants Europe BV), M Reilly (Software Sciences Ltd), H M Robinson (The Open University), G M Stacey (University of Edinburgh), and A J Weatherhead (Scicon Ltd).

References

[1] Fitzgerald G et al, A Reference Model and Abstract Syntax for Distributed Databases, BNCOD–2 1982.
[2] ANSC (X3H2–83–151), A Proposed Network Database Language, American National Standards Institute 1983.
[3] CODASYL DDL Journal of Development 1981, Canadian Federal Government 1981.

[4] Draffan I W and Poole F (eds), Distributed Data Bases, Cambridge University Press 1980.
[5] Rothnie J B et al, Introduction to a System for Distributed Databases (SDD-1), ACM ToDS vol 5, no 1, March 1980.
[6] Williams R et al, R*: An Overview of the Architecture, IBM Research Report RJ3325, December 1981.
[7] Lindsay B G and Selinger P G, Site Autonomy Issues in R*: A Distributed Database Management System, IBM Research Report RJ 2927 September 1980.
[8] Date C J, An Introduction to Database Systems, Vol 2, Chapter 7, Addison Wesley, 1983.
[9] Mcleod D and Heimbigner D, A Federated Architecture for Database Systems, Proc Nat Comp Conf 1980.
[10] Alexander H H et al, An Architecture and Syntax for Distributed Databases, Computers and Standards, to be published March 1984.

The Proteus Distributed Database System

M.P.Atkinson[1], J.B.Bocca[2], T.J.Elsey[3], N.J.Fiddian[4],
M.Flower[2], P.M.D.Gray[5], W.A.Gray,[4], P.Hepp[1],
R.G.Johnson[6], W.Milne[3], M.Norrie[1], A.O.Omololu[4],
E.A.Oxborrow[7], M.J.R.Shave[8], A.M.Smith[5], P.M.Stocker[3] and
J.Walker[3]

The authors represent the main researchers on the Proteus project, and their affiliations while working on the project were the universities of Edinburgh[1], Bristol[2], East Anglia[3], Cardiff[4], Aberdeen[5], London (Birkbeck College)[6], Kent[7], Liverpool[8]. This paper was prepared by E.A. Oxborrow from contributions by N.J. Fiddian, P.M.D. Gray, M. Flower, R.G. Johnson, E.A. Oxborrow, M.J.R. Shave, and P.M. Stocker.

Proteus is a heterogeneous distributed database system which has been designed and developed as a result of a collaborative research project involving a number of British universities.

The initial version of the Proteus system consists of a central switch node, and various query and data nodes. Database distribution is transparent to the user of the Proteus system. Queries are expressed in the query language supported by the DBMS at the user's node. These are then translated into an internal network query language by reference to an internal network schema, before being passed to the switch node for decomposition and distribution to the data nodes in the network. Responses and other messages are also passed around the network using a common internal format.

The network languages and network schema are central to the Proteus system. They provide the means by which different database management systems may coexist together and communicate with each other, in a manner which is transparent to the user. Both the network schema and network query language are based on the relational approach, but with significant extensions to provide the necessary support in a distributed data base environment.

This paper gives an overview of the initial version of the Proteus system.

1. Introduction

The Proteus distributed database system has been developed as a result of an SERC-funded project involving a number of British universities. The main objective of the project has been to assess the problems of heterogeneity in distributed database systems and investigate ways in which they may be solved. These problems arise as a result of attempting to integrate a number of existing database systems, which run on different hardware at widely separated sites. A further objective of the project has been to provide an environment to support doctoral research programmes in this area.

An initial version of the Proteus system has now been developed which permits queries expressed in various external (local) languages to be processed at sites which support various different local DBMSs. The degrees of heterogeneity and geographical distribution entailed are illustrated in Figure 1, which shows the universities involved in the project and the local database systems and query languages which are currently supported.

An important feature of the Proteus system is the transparency of database distribution as far as the end-user is concerned; the distributed database environment appears to the user to be virtually identical to his local database environment. This is made possible by the use of common internal formats for the transmission of messages (queries, responses, etc) across the network. Central components of the Proteus system are therefore the network schema and network languages.

Other major distributed database projects include SDD–1, SIRIUS, Multibase, Distributed INGRES, R*, POREL and PRECI [12, 13, 15, 16, 18, 24, 25, 26]. Most of these are homogeneous, supporting the relational data model, and as such they are not concerned with the problems associated with different languages and data models at different sites in the network. Two of the heterogeneous systems are Multibase [12, 18] and SIRIUS–DELTA [13]. The important difference between Proteus and Multibase is that whereas all Multibase users use a common query language, DAPLEX, with a global schema defined using the Functional Data Model, Proteus users use the query language available at their own local site and view the database in terms of the locally-supported data models; the Proteus network query language and schema are purely internal. The Proteus query language is similar in concept to the 'pivot' language of the SIRIUS–DELTA system; both are designed to cater for database systems supporting different languages at different sites.

This paper gives an overview of the initial version of the Proteus system.

In section 2, the overall system architecture is described. The internal network schema and network languages are considered in sections 3 and 4, while in sections 5 to 7 various aspects of the implementation of the Proteus system are discussed.

2. System Architecture

The initial version of the Proteus system has a star network structure with a switch node at the centre of the star, and query and data nodes at the tips. An individual site may participate in the distributed system as a query node, a data node, or both. The relationships between the three types of node in the processing of a query, together with the software modules involved, are illustrated in Figure 2.

Fig 1. Participant Sites in the Proteus System

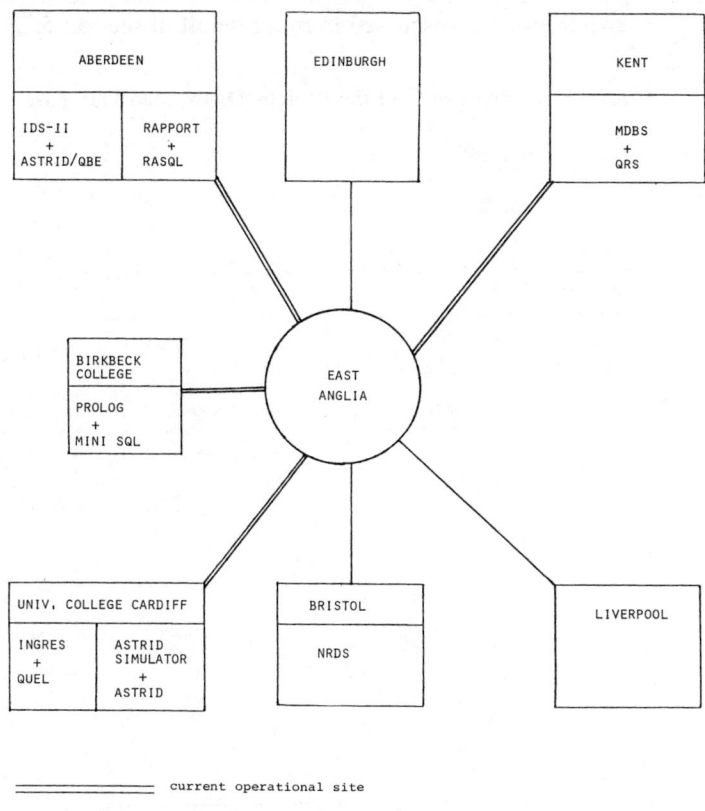

====== current operational site

────── current participant site

Note: Transmission of messages between sites is by means of standard JNT networking facilities over PSS/SERCNET

A query submitted to the system is expressed in the external query language used at the query node. This query is then translated into the internal Network Query Language (NQL). The philosophy behind the NQL is discussed in section 4 and an example is provided of a network query message and the associated network response message. The translation of the query to NQL requires reference to be made to the network schema, a copy of which is held at each site. There is currently no mechanism for processing schema updates comparable with that of R* [25], although the Network Transfer Language (NTL) has the power to transmit a schema to nodes in the network.

The switch node software coordinates and controls query distribution and response collection. Once a query has been received by this node it is decomposed as necessary and derived queries are distributed to relevant data nodes; when responses are received from the data nodes these are composed into a single response which is returned to the originating query node. The switch node is discussed in more detail in section 5.

Fig 2. Query Processing in the Proteus Distributed Database System

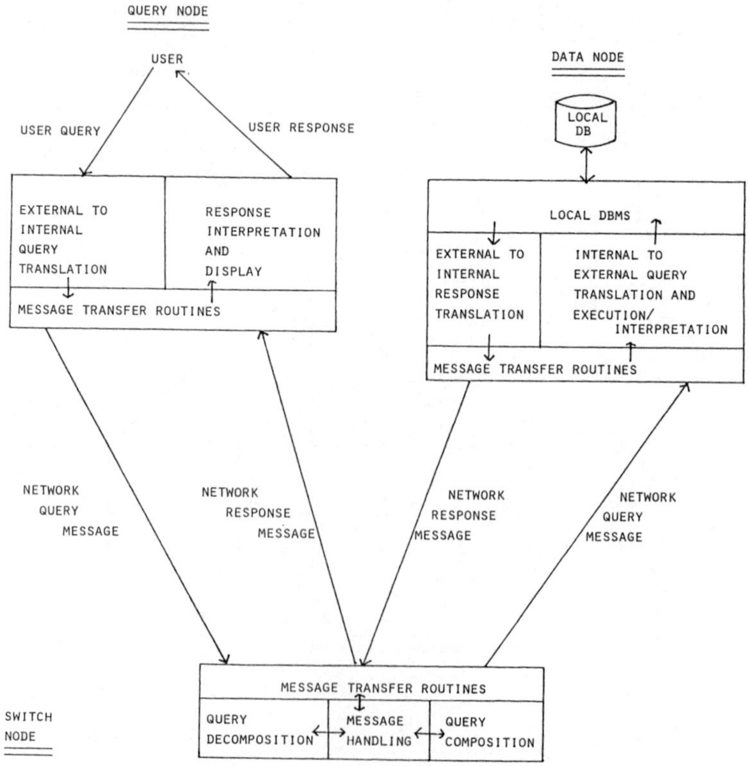

When the data node receives a query expressed in the internal NQL, it translates it to the external query language supported by the DBMS at that node, and passes it to the DBMS for execution (or alternatively interprets the query instead). The response to the query is then translated into the internal Network Response Language (NRL) format for passing back to the switch node.

Queries, responses, etc are preceded by identification headers before being transmitted to another node in the network. The headers are part of the NTL, which provides for various types of message. Mail, query, response and error messages are the four types currently implemented at most of the Proteus sites. The Message Transfer Routines [5] include routines to attach headers to queries, etc ready for transmission, and also to separate headers from queries, etc when messages are received from another node.

The Proteus system architecture has enabled us to develop the system incrementally. At the start of the project much time was devoted to the definition of the network languages, but once this was complete individual sites were able to develop their own software independently. It was envisaged that some sites would progress faster than others, hence a minimal subset of the NQL was defined for the initial version of the system to ensure that each operational site could at least process a common class of queries. A very simple switch node (without query decomposition and response composition modules) was developed initially to enable testing to take place between query and data nodes at an early stage of development. The NTL provides for messages to be addressed to a single site on the network, and the simple switch node was designed to route messages to a specified site, without any intermediate processing taking place. The full switch node (cf Figure 2) is now operational.

3. The Network Schema Language

From the previous section it is apparent that there must be a network schema, but it is, perhaps, not immediately apparent that it fulfils a weaker role than a conceptual schema. The role of a conceptual schema is two-fold. First, viewed from the outside by a person it provides a logical model for the data and places it in a structure (entity-relationship for example) which connects it to real-world semantics. It attaches meaning to the data and turns it into information for people.

Viewed from the interior of the network, data has no meaning; it is merely a set of binary patterns which must obey certain rules. These rules are summarised as functional relationships and constraints. It is the role of the conceptual schema module of a DBMS to take the user model (with appropriate interaction and services) and convert it to a compact and appropriate logical representation of the functionalities and constraints [19].

In a heterogeneous system the conceptual schema module (and associated language) may be different at each site. The only requirement for the Proteus network is that the output, the specification of functionalities and constraints, shall be in a standard format and shall contain the same content (metadata) for every site.

There is an issue, too broad to consider here, of how one obtains a global view consistent with the local views of the nodes. Once this has been done, however, it is most desirable if the conceptual schema at each site can be generated on the basis of the network standard description of the functionalities and constraints.

In the Proteus project, the network schema – the Abstracted Conceptual Schema (ACS) [20, 22] – is used to record functionalities and constraints. This specifies that the data proper will be placed in relations (which captures some of the required functionalities) and also uses relations to store the metadata which records the remaining functionalities and constraints.

The fact that the ACS may be expressed as relations means that information concerning the functionalities and constraints on the data can be transmitted to each site as normal data using the NTL. Routines to convert an ACS schema to a conceptual view (for example, an ADAPLEX schema) are available. It is likely, of course, that cosmetic action on the resulting names, and local service routines will be necessary before this schema is 'user friendly' at a particular nodal site.

In the initial phase of the Proteus project, the global ACS schema has been compiled by means of human co-operation between sites, but is now complete for a particular database application. Again, neither the switching node nor the other nodes are currently capable of enforcing the constraints that are specified. At present the ACS structure serves as a convenient mechanism by which to specify a relational database and its basic semantics. As time goes on the implementations may allow the system to become much more powerful semantically than is usual in a relational system.

4. The Network Query Language (NQL) and Transfer Language (NTL)

Two main criteria were borne in mind for the design of the NQL. Firstly, it had to be capable of representing a wide variety of queries in different source languages in a single common form, which could be implemented on a wide variety of data nodes. Secondly it had to be capable of compression into a concise form to reduce transmission costs.

The basic language operations were chosen to be those of relational algebra. This was an obvious choice since the ACS is based on relations and since this forms a common base to the relational systems in use and to Codasyl databases via the ASTRID translator [8]. However ASTRID has extensions to Codd's original algebra, particularly the Group-By Operator and arbitrary procedures for computation both of selection criteria and derived results. Thus the language had to be capable of representing pieces of code to operate on data items. This enables us to ship functions to a data source so that we may reduce the amount of data that has to be transmitted across the network back to the originating site.

4.1 The stack-based language

This led to the choice of a stack-based language, rather like a generalisation of Pascal P-Code. We were guided in this by the knowledge that P-Code had proved itself as a concise universal intermediate code, capable of being implemented straightforwardly on a wide range of computers and even used as a target language for other compilers.

A language like P-Code is easily extended to relations by allowing it to push and pull relation-descriptors on the stack. Individual operation codes can take the function-name/data-item-name pairs used in the ACS, or lists of such names, as parameters. In fact it has been extended one stage further to allow it to compute objects of compound type whose components, which may include several relation descriptors, have been pushed on the stack. An instance of an ACS schema can be represented in this way.

The NQL, then, is based on relational algebra with extensions. The main extensions are the ability to use procedures as predicates and the ability to compute new properties (function-name/data-item-name pairs). For convenience, procedure calls and parameter passing are represented by means of a stack, but this does not alter the underlying relational nature of the NQL and the ACS schema on which it operates.

4.2 An example using NQL and NTL

The general form of a query is a set of instructions to a hypothetical machine. One can either interpret them directly, or else use them to reconstruct the query as a tree structure. The instructions consist of one-address and zero-address instructions. Each instruction is denoted by a word which is intended to be mnemonic, followed optionally by one parameter. The instruction also has a type; initially this is one of: boolean, string, integer, floating (real), or relation (ACS element set); normally these are indicated by the initial letter (cf rvar, rload, rjoin, sprop, sload, bor, etc in the example). A fuller description of the language is given in [21], and a detailed manual is available [2].

The example at the end of this section shows how the query and response are embedded in the NTL. The query is transmitted with a query header, while the results are transmitted with a response header, plus an exact repeat of the query header for identification purposes. The headers contain such information as the source site and originating site of the message (Network and Aberdeen in the query message), a unique sequence number for each message for coordination purposes (67 for the original query from Aberdeen), the destination site (Kent in the query message), and other information. The response (in NRL format) contains both the actual query results and data description information (in square brackets) which includes the ACS function names and data item names. The subset of the schema applicable to the example is provided for information, and follows the example response.

It is beyond the scope of this paper to discuss the example query in detail, but it will be explained in outline. The line with the label × ans introduces a temporary relation variable called 'ans'. The block of NQL instructions labelled × start represents the main part of the query, ie the operations on relations. In this example the relation 'degree–course' is first loaded onto the stack, and a selection expression is carried out on it as indicated by the instructions at label × s1. The relation 'offers' is then loaded onto the stack, and the selected tuples from 'degree–course' are joined with it on the join list elements specified at the label × j2. 'Department' is then loaded onto the stack, and this is joined with the result of the previous join using the join list elements at × j3. Then 'university–poly' is loaded, and this is joined with the result of the previous join using the join list elements at × j4. Next the required elements are projected using the project list at × p, and the result is stored in the temporary relation 'ans'. Finally the result of the query is specified as being the list of objects at the label × res (in this example just the temporary relation 'ans').

Another example, showing the progress of a query as it passes from a query node, through the switch node, to a data node, and back again can be found in [6].

Proteus distributed database system 233

Example

```
Query: Retrieve the university name, department name, and degree title
       for departments which offer either ucca code "3130" or
       "3131" (Computing Science)
```

Network query message: (comments are enclosed in !)

```
Q KENT MDBS NETWORK PROTEUS 3 ABERDEEN ASTRID 67 1 840319 143000 MULTIPLEXER *
$ans     rvar                         !declare result variable 'ans'!
$start   rload    degree_course       !main part of query!
         rselect  s1
         rload    offers
         rjoin    j2
         rload    department
         rjoin    j3
         rload    university_poly
         rjoin    j4
         rproj    p
         rput     ans
         cresult  res
$res     rget     ans                  !result list!
         end

$s1      proc     ">b"                 !selection procedure!
         sprop    has ucca_code
         sload    "3130"
         seq
         sprop    has ucca_code
         sload    "3131"
         seq
         bor
         bresult

$j2      pairhd   has ucode            !join list!
         pairtl   has ucode
         pairhd   has dg_code
         pairtl   has dg_code
         end

$j3      pairhd   has ucode            !join list!
         pairtl   has ucode
         pairhd   has dept_code
         pairtl   has dept_code
         end

$j4      pairhd   has ucode            !join list!
         pairtl   has ucode
         end

$p       elem     has uname            !project list!
         elem     has dname
         elem     has dtitle
         end
```

Network response message:

```
R NETWORK PROTEUS KENT MDBS 62 ABERDEEN ASTRID 67 1 840319 154500 PROTEUS *
Q KENT MDBS NETWORK PROTEUS 3 ABERDEEN ASTRID 67 1 840319 143000 MULTIPLEXER *
[C R ans]
[R ans 3 2 2 S S S /has has has /uname dname dtitle]

"University of Kent" "Computing Laboratory" "Computer Science" /
"University of Kent" "Electronics" "Computer Science" /
*
```

Subset of Schema applicable to the Example

Schema diagram:

```
------------------     has      ------------    offers    ----------------
|university_poly|------------>|department|<------------>|degree_course|
------------------              ------------              ----------------
```

Corresponding ACS Components:

Element Set Names: university_poly, department, degree_course, offers

Function Names: has, situated_at, is_within, headed_by

Data Item Names: ucode, dg_code, uname, dtitle, address, tel_no, dname, fac_sch_name, degree_type, dept_code, pcode, ucca_code

Element Set Associations:

Element Set Names	Function Names	Data Item Names
university_poly	has	ucode
university_poly	has	uname
university_poly	situated_at	address
university_poly	has	tel_no
department	has	ucode
department	has	dept_code
department	has	dname
department	headed_by	pcode
department	is_within	fac_sch_name
degree_course	has	ucode
degree_course	has	dg_code
degree_course	has	dtitle
degree_course	has	degree_type
degree_course	has	ucca_code
offers	has	ucode
offers	has	dept_code
offers	has	dg_code

5. The Switch Node

5.1 Role

It is the switch node which controls the handling of a query incoming to the network. The role of the node is to create the semblance that all the data required is present at the switch node, so that data location is opaque to the user and is irrelevant to the reply to the query.

The switch node (which is a composite structure) has the following tasks:

(i) it must transform the incoming query into a number of operations (expressed in NQL) which must be performed at each site holding data relevant to the query;

(ii) it must control the despatch of the transactions and the resultant data flows;

(iii) it must have available to it, somewhere in the network, a processing node to which it may schedule tasks concerned with the combination of data extracted from the nodes.

The only such processing node in the network at present is East Anglia.

5.2 Implementation

The node at East Anglia is currently a compound of three separable nodes. The implementation is such that the current communication between these nodes is in terms of NQL and simulates NTL. Thus at some later date other nodes on the network could play a similar role. The three component nodes are described briefly below, and are illustrated in Figure 3.

5.2.1 Message handler

This module receives the incoming query and directs it to the Query Decomposer (QD) node. It receives from the QD node a 'script', which contains the information necessary to monitor and initiate (when appropriate) all subsequent data flows and NQL flows.

5.2.2 Query decomposer

This takes the incoming query and generates a strategy for its solution. This strategy comprises NQL scripts for the sites involved and for the Query Composer, and the script to the Message Handler. It contains the algorithm which attempts to satisfy the chosen optimisation condition (fastest response, least line traffic, etc, whichever is chosen). The project has a phased implementation of algorithms, starting from the simple.

5.2.3 Query composer

This node assembles the final data response, a process which normally requires additional relational operations on the data. It holds no data (but does hold metadata). It must necessarily have the facility to perform data description dynamically (since its data is not the base relations of the database). East Anglia Query Composer is the only node which currently has such a facility.

6. The Query Nodes

The local query languages at the sites which currently act as query nodes include ASTRID, QBE, QUEL (INGRES), QRS (MDBS), and a mini version of SQL. Implementation aspects concerning these nodes are described briefly below. A RASQL (RAPPORT) node is also currently being implemented.

6.1 ASTRID and QBE

The ASTRID query language (ASTRID R.A.) is a full relational algebra which includes the set difference operation for formulating quantified queries, along with the extend and group-by operations [7],

236   M. P. Atkinson et al.

which define derived fields; all these facilities are supported by NQL. A translator has been written for queries in Query-By-Example (QBE), into ASTRID R.A., which shows the generality of the language. The queries in QBE are formed interactively by filling templates on a screen and allow complex selection and join conditions along with extend and group-by operations.

The translation path from ASTRID R.A. to Proteus NQL text goes via an 'NQL tree', which is linearised into NQL text, as shown in Figure 4A. The NQL tree is a key intermediate data structure, and it is also used when

Fig 3. The Operation of the Switch Node

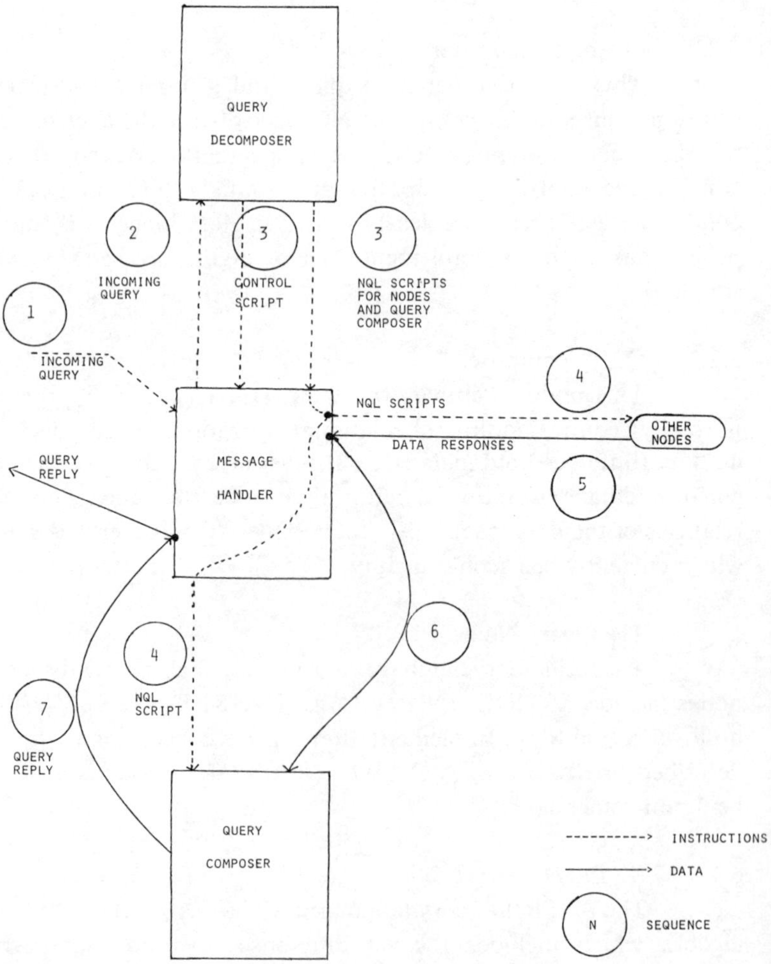

Proteus distributed database system 237

answering queries (Section 7.1). It contains relational algebra operators at the nodes and stored relations at the tips. The tree is defined as a Pascal data structure and portable routines have been produced to enable other sites to use it in their translators [17].

Fig 4. The ASTRID/QBE query node and IDS–II data node

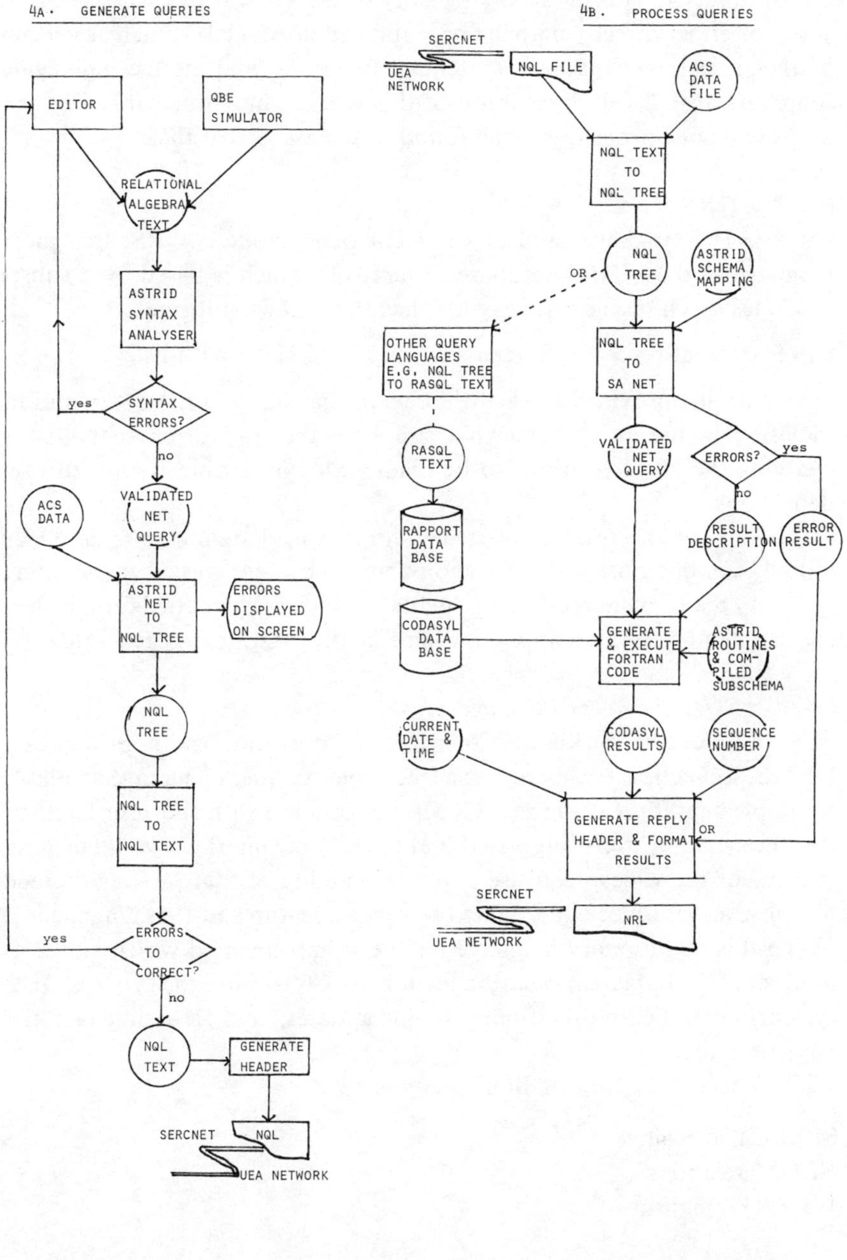

6.2 QUEL

An INGRES QUEL [23] query node for Proteus has been developed on top of a replicated ASTRID query node at Cardiff by implementing a preprocessor from QUEL to ASTRID relational algebra. This has been constructed using the LEX and YACC translator-writing tools of UNIX [11]. The implementation supports virtually all of the QUEL query language, excluding only those few features which cannot easily be either directly mapped or simulated in ASTRID, such as certain mathematical and pattern matching functions and nested aggregate function calls. A full description of this work, which was carried out as an MSc degree project, may be found in the associated thesis [1].

6.3 QRS

The language used at the Kent query node is QRS, the query language of the MDBS database system [14], which is based on a subset of Codasyl. The basic query syntax has the following format:

LIST <target list> FOR <expression> THRU <path list>

The path list provides a list of the sets participating in the query and its inclusion in the query somewhat simplifies the translation to NQL by enabling the NQL relations to be readily identified from the MDBS set definitions.

QRS queries are first converted to an intermediate coded form which initially contains only MDBS components; by reference to a mapping directory the relevant ACS components are added. This coded form is then used to identify NQL components and finally NQL text is generated.

6.4 *SQL-like query language*

Since the Birkbeck College node does not use a proprietary DBMS, see section 7.3, there was a free choice of query language available for implementation at the site. General experience with end-user facilities and the syntax of NQL suggested that a relational interface would be best. In view of the widespread use and acceptability of SQL, it was decided to utilise an interface embodying the general features of that language [3, 4]. To this end a query language has been implemented which supports a subset of the data manipulation facilities of SQL. Since the Proteus DDB system does not currently support online updates, no SQL update facilities have been included.

The basic structure of a SQL query is:

SELECT attributes
FROM relations
WHERE conditons

The 'attributes' identify the fields to be retrieved, and the 'relations' indicate the relations from which the attributes are to be obtained. The 'conditions' are optional, but if included can be either a simple test or another SELECT expression which can be used as a selector for the outer SELECT expression.

This has been found to provide a very wide range of query facilities and can be readily extended in the light of experience.

7. The Data Nodes

The data nodes receive queries in NQL and convert them to queries in the local DBMS language. These are then submitted to the local DBMS and results are formed into a network response message (or network error message if an error has occurred).

A university database has been set up at each of the data nodes. This contains information about departments, staff, degree courses, lecture courses, and other information. This database was chosen because the data is readily available at all sites and interesting relationships can be constructed.

The database systems which are currently connected to the Proteus system are IDS–II, MDBS, and PROLOG. A Proteus link to a separate local network of relational database systems, NRDS, is also under development and nearing completion. These nodes are briefly discussed below. In addition, INGRES and Rapport nodes are being developed.

7.1 Codasyl (IDS–II or IDMS)

The ASTRID System [8, 9] answers queries from a full relational algebra against a Codasyl database by generating and executing Fortran code that makes efficient use of Codasyl sets. The system has been interfaced to Proteus as shown in Figure 4B. Since NQL is a stack language it is first converted into a 'NQL tree' structure. This is done by executing the NQL code, and producing pointers to portions of tree which describe the desired results in terms of the operations required to produce them. Next it is converted into an equivalent net structure (SA net), as though it had been produced by parsing an ASTRID R.A. expression; it is then executed as a normal ASTRID query. Extra information is produced by the NQLtree to SA net translator (see Figure 4B), which is used to provide column name and type information to send with the results. If errors are detected then an error message is sent instead. Alternatively, the NQL tree may be used to generate a dialect of SQL for querying Rapport databases instead of Codasyl.

Three main problems were found in developing the system; (i) the ACS relations had to include the primitive data type of a function for use in

Fortran (real, integer, boolean or string) as well as its abstract type; (ii) temporary property descriptors had to be invented for those columns in temporary relations which were not described in the ACS; (iii) the NQL language had to be extended to store and output multiple result relations. The ASTRID system has the potential to handle multiple results, but the extension to do this is not complete.

7.2   MDBS

The database system at the Kent data node is MDBS (Micro Data Base System) [14]. It is running on a Vector 2800 micro under CP/M. A major problem encountered in the development of the translation software on the micro has been the limitation on program size. This led to an early decision to map directly from NQL text to QRS (the MDBS query language), bypassing the NQL tree (referred to in section 7.1 and illustrated in Figure 4).

An intermediate code form is generated as in the QRS to NQL translation (see section 6.3). The NQL text is used to create the skeleton code, and the MDBS components are added by reference to the mapping directory. At the same time data description information for the response is generated. QRS text is then generated from the coded form and an MDBS command (startup) file is created containing the query (or queries). The command file is passed to MDBS which processes the queries and creates a result file. The result file is combined with data description information generated earlier to form the network response in NRL format.

Only the minimal subset of NQL has so far been implemented, but this is sufficient to enable a range of queries, including composite queries, to be processed.

7.3   Prolog

The BIDS (Birkbeck Intelligent Database System) project is concerned with applying a number of expert systems techniques to the storage and retrieval of data from databases [10]. The basic data structure used is the 'triple', which is used to store simple facts, for example,

(John, studies, Computing)

All the data held in a database can be reduced to this simple form. In addition, metadata can be stored in this form, for example,

(student, studies, subject)

Having reduced both data and metadata to a common format it is now possible to use a common language to manipulate and access the data. By adding logical statements about the data and metadata, it is possible to include validation and similar rules in the database. To carry out data manipulation and retrieval on the database, it is necessary to use reasoning techniques. The decision was made, therefore, to implement the BIDS system in Prolog.

The Birkbeck node is a simple example of a BIDS database. It uses a Pascal program to convert NQL statements into Prolog assertions which can be added to the Prolog program holding the triples before it is executed. Development work on the BIDS database is continuing, using the experience gained from the Proteus project.

7.4 *NRDS – a homogeneous network of relational database systems*

To extend the topology of the PROTEUS distribution, another research group at Bristol has designed and implemented a local Network of Relational Database Systems (NRDS). The specific aims of NRDS are twofold; firstly, to support the shared use of resources amongst its local community, ie to integrate the data and processing power of a number of different relational DBMS in a local network and, secondly, to act as a gateway to other database networks, in particular the Proteus network. Since it is dealing solely with relational systems, the internal query language (IQL) of NRDS is simpler than the NQL of Proteus, but it must be emphasised that the relational systems involved in NRDS (INGRES and MRDS) have very different characteristics. The most important point is that Proteus users outside the NRDS subsystem see just a single node. Their requests for data are automatically distributed (if necessary) within NRDS and forwarded to INGRES or MRDS, as appropriate. Conversely responses from these systems are co-ordinated within NRDS and a single reply forwarded to the controlling node of the wider Proteus network.

The NRDS system involves three types of logical units. These are:

LQG The Local Query Generator, which receives queries in the local query language, such as QUEL, translates them into an internal query language form (IQL), and calls the central node.

DSC The Distributed System Controller, which receives queries in IQL form, decomposes them with reference to the NRDS global schema, and passes on the decomposed queries to appropriate nodes for processing. In due course it accepts replies from these nodes, co-ordinates them, and returns a single response to the LQG, unless some abnormal condition has been detected during processing of the query – eg an error condition.

LQP The Local Query Processor, which receives IQL queries from the DSC, translates them into its local query language, and thereby accesses its local database. The data which is retrieved is returned to the DSC.

Many LQGs and LQPs may be connected to one DSC but it should be noted that these three processing units are logical components of the NRDS. Physically they may well be sharing one processor, or alternatively each of them may be running on a processor of its own.

Information about the distribution of all data used by NRDS is, like the data itself, held in relational form. This meta database is stored as part of the DSC and is used by a suite of routines which carry out the decomposition of queries automatically.

8. Conclusion

It can be seen from the previous sections that the Proteus system is a truly heterogeneous distributeatabase system. Four different types of DBMSs are involved, running on different hardware and under different operating systems, but communicating by means of a single language and a common global schema.

It was the aim of the project primarily to show that this was possible, and in addition to propose that this is an appropriate level for international standardisation and to provide targets for discussion (NTL, NQL and ACS). Although the project has been primarily concerned with distributed databases, the advantages which have been gained by creating the possibility of accessing foreign, remote database systems using their own local query languages should not be overlooked, since that must be a major objective of standardisation. Equally important, the global schema may be regarded as a convenient, compact form in which a foreign schema may be exported to the local site to support the query language.

The success of the project owes much to the availability of the common ('blue book') file protocol on both the PTT packet network (PSS) and the private universities and research network (SERCNET, now renamed JANET). The network protocol sits happily on top of the file transfer protocol. It duplicates some data which exists in the packets as metadata, and this might ultimately be removed, when easy access is available to the packet metadata via high-level languages at the user (as distinct from the system) level. It is our view that the existing communications systems are adequate to support a distributed database system of the type described, but not adequate, at present, for one in which concurrency control requires a great number of locking messages. However, our troubles with the present system (and they are not trivial) are primarily due to system availability, system changes and addressing changes in the universities, not the network itself.

The original reason for the choice of a 'star' network through a single node was that protocol standardisation with a single site was more easily organised than with an n x n free-for-all. That proved to be true and site-to-site queries which bypass the central node are now effective. From the aspect of the global distribution system, the central node is essential. It was soon realised that the inability of most database systems to support temporary relations and dynamic changes of schema, made it extremely difficult to use the nodes as relational processors rather than relational retrievers. Thus, at present, only the central node software, which was specially produced, can be used for the 'result de-multiplexing' phase. In particular, a query decomposition algorithm based on virtual joins is not currently feasible.

Finally, it was realised that, although it is desirable to invent as few temporary names as possible, the distribution system does require them, and the purely applicative stack-based language was modified to allow the naming and storage of relations. This allowed the switch node to communicate between its modules in precisely the same way as the nodal network, and hence freed the modules themselves for distribution at an appropriate stage.

The Proteus software architecture has so far provided the flexibility needed for development of the system in parallel at the different sites involved, and we anticipate that it should also provide the flexibility for future development.

Acknowledgements

The work at each of the sites has been supported by SERC grants as follows: Aberdeen (GR/B/69081 & GR/C/63120), Birkbeck College, London (GR/C/86457), Bristol (GR/B/65687), Cardiff (GR/B/75198), East Anglia (GR/B/7268.5), and Kent (GR/B/74290). In addition, thanks are due to Amita K. Patel, for the implementation of the initial version of the Birkbeck query interface.

References

[1] K Alwan, Translation between high level database query languages, MSc Thesis, Department of Computing Mathematics, University College Cardiff, 1984, (to be submitted).

[2] M P Atkinson, P M D Gray and P E Hepp, Message Formats for Inter-Site Communications (Version 4), Proteus Working Paper E2, Research Report, Dept of Computer Science, Edinburgh University, July 1983.

[3] D D Chamberlin, A Summary of User Experience with the SQL Data Language, IBM Research Report RJ2767, 1980.

[4] D D Chamberlin et al, Sequel2 : A Unified Approach to Data Definition, Manipulation and Control, IBM Research Report RJ1798, 1976.

[5] N J Fiddian, W A Gray and A O Omololu, NTL Pascal Message Routines, Proteus Working Paper C2, Research Report, Department of Computing Mathematics, University College Cardiff, June 1983.

[6] N J Fiddian, W A Gray, A O Omololu, P M D Gray, A M Smith, E A Oxborrow, P M Stocker, T J Elsey and J Walker, First PROTEUS Queries Successfully Transmitted, (submitted to the IUCC Bulletin).

[7] P M D Gray, The GROUP–BY Operation in Relational Algebra, in Proc British National Conf on Databases BNCOD–1, S M Deen and P Hammersley (eds), Pentech Press July 1981, pp 84–98.

[8] P M D Gray, The ASTRID System for Access to Codasyl DataBases, IUCC Bulletin, No 4, pp 70–76, 1982.

[9] P M D Gray and D S Moffat, Manipulating Descriptions of Programs for Database Access, Proc ; ¡CAI–83 Karlsruhe, A Bundy (ed), Kaufmann USA, 1983.

[10] R G Johnson, Integrating Data and Metadata to Enhance the User Interface, Research Report RGJ/01/83, Birkbeck College, London University.

[11] S C Johnson and M E Lesk, UNIX Time-Sharing System: Language Development Tools, Bell System Technical Journal, Vol 57, No 6.2, pp 2155–2175, 1978.

[12] T Landers and R L Rosenberg, An Overview of Multibase, in Distributed Databases, H J Schneider (ed), North-Holland 1982.

[13] W Litwin et al, SIRIUS Systems for Distributed Data Management, in Distributed Databases, H J Schneider (ed), North-Holland 1982.

[14] MDBS, MDBS I Users Manual, MDBS.
QRS Query System/Report Writer Manual, Micro Data Base Systems Inc, 1981.

[15] E J Neuhold and H Biller, POREL: A Distributed Data Base on an Inhomogeneous Computer Network, Proceedings of the Conference on VLDB, 1977.

[16] J B Rothnie et al, Introduction to a System for Distributed Databases (SDD–1), ACM TODS, Vol 5, No 1, pp 1–17, 1980.

[17] A M Smith and P M D Gray, Portable Software for PROTEUS, Proteus Working Paper A4, Research Report, Department of Computer Science, Aberdeen University, Oct 1983.

[18] J M Smith et al, MULTIBASE – Integrating Heterogeneous Distributed Database Systems, AFIPS National Computer Conference 50, pp 487–499, 1981.

[19] P M Stocker, Canonical Schemata, Canonical Queries and Standardisation, in Database, Infotech State of the Art Report, Series 9, No 8, Pergamon Infotech 1981.

[20] P M Stocker and R Cantie, A Target Logical Schema: The ACS, UEA School of Computing Studies and Accountancy, Report No CSA/5/DBG/1, 1983 (more detailed than 22).

[21] P M Stocker, M P Atkinson, P M D Gray, W A Gray, R G Johnson, M J R

Shave and E A Oxborrow, PROTEUS: A Search for Standard Components in an Inhomogeneous Distributed Database System, in Databases: Role and Structure, P M Stocker (ed), Cambridge Univ Press (to be published 1984).

[22] P M Stocker and R Cantie, A Target Logical Schema: The ACS, 9th International Conference on Very Large Data Bases, Florence, October 1983.

[23] M Stonebraker et al, The Design and Implementation of INGRES, ACM TODS Vol 1, No 3, pp 189–222, 1976.

[24] M Stonebraker and E Neuhold, A Distributed Data Base Version of INGRES, Proc 2nd Berkeley Workshop on Distributed Data Management and Computer Networks, pp 19–36, May 1977.

[25] R Williams et al, R*: An Overview of the Architecture, in Improving Database Usability and Responsiveness, P Scheuermann (ed), pp 1–27, Academic Press 1982.

[26] S M Deen et al, PRECI* Project and its Data Communications Links, in EUTECO European Teleinformatics Conference, T Kalin (ed), pp 359–368, North-Holland 1983.

The Design and Implementation of an Analyst/Programmer Training Scheme for a large IMS DB/DC User

A. J. Wakefield
Department of Computer Studies and Mathematics, Bristol Polytechnic, Coldharbour Lane, Frenchay, Bristol BS16 1QY

Based on experiences of the past five years the paper describes the structure and teaching methods of a training course developed and run by Bristol Polytechnic, specifically to meet the requirements of a local IMS/VS user. The course structure has been designed to accommodate graduates in Computer Science and other disciplines and, using blocks of taught material backed up by in company placements, train them to be able to take permanent positions as analysts or programmers on completion of the course. The five taught modules are described, together with the objectives set for each module. The case studies, used in the database training module to provide the trainees with experience of using the companies message handling packages and to expose them to the scale and type of problem they are likely to encounter in data analysis studies, are described in some detail. The paper ends with a discussion of the conclusions drawn from the operation of the course in respect to the use of certain systems and programming methods such as JSP and Data Analysis.

1. Introduction

Organisations implementing large database/data communications systems are faced with a requirement for a number of trained staff familiar with complex software products. Recruitment of experienced analysts and programmers can prove expensive and hard to achieve. One method of meeting this requirement is to design a 'bespoke' training course covering the particular areas the company specialises in. One such course has been in operation at Bristol Polytechnic for the past five years.

Section one of this paper considers reasons for establishing the course originally and the requirements for the scheme are outlined in section two. A description of the course content, teaching methods and case studies is provided in section three and the lessons that have been learned through running the course are shown in section four.

2. Course background

One of the interesting areas of growth in the development of large on-line systems in the past ten years has occurred in the creation of complex Materials Requirement Planning systems within manufacturing organisations. In line with most commercial companies these organisations had, by the begining of the sixties, achieved a reasonably high degree of mechanisation of their accounting systems and commenced the design and implementation of production control systems. These systems rapidly grew in complexity.

The sorting and merging of files, which hitherto had proved effective in creating management reports often described as Integrated Management Information Systems [1] soon proved inadequate to meet the widely varying activities in the manufacturing areas and the introduction of database techniques was a natural method of overcoming these deficiencies and eliminating data redundancy.

In the past ten to fifteen years these users have in consequence invested a substantial number of man years in the development of their systems and derived considerable benefit from their successful operation.

Providing the necessary level of trained, experienced staff to support the maintenance and development of these systems has often posed management with severe problems.

Organisations experiencing this problem are often faced with three problems which conspire to exaggerate the rate of staff turnover above the already high market norm.

(a) Medium to heavy manufacturing companies are requently found in the outskirts of the towns and cities they are based in and are often in areas which are considered unattractive or inaccessible by staff.
(b) The need to maintain parity of earnings between large work force and office based staff limits the opportunity for data processing management to implement flexible and responsive salary scales to reduce staff turnover.
(c) Large organisations are frequently forerunners in the implementation of complex software products and develop skills within their data processing staff which greatly increase their market value.

Avon, in the West of England, has seen the arrival of three major Insurance companies in the past five years in addition to the more recent developments in the field of electronics, thereby creating an increasing the demand for analysts and programmers.

3. Designing a training scheme to meet these needs

Although the scheme under consideration has been designed specifically to meet the needs of a large IMS user faced with problems similar to those above it is suggested that given the above requirements similar schemes can be mounted for organisations u sing any well established database/data communications software system. Bristol Polytechnic is presently investigating the extension of the above scheme to provide a similar facility for ICL IDMS [2] users. The basic requirements for the scheme were identified as follows:-

(a) Trainees should emerge as competent COBOL programmers on completion of the course and should be capable using the JCL and utilities employed by the organisation.
(b) The training scheme should make recruits familiar with all aspects of commercial data processing activities.
(c) The recruits should complete and test a suite of programs using company developed programming tools processing conventional files.
(d) Trainees should have a theoretical understanding of the principles of IMS physical and logical databases and be familiar with the DL/1 [3,4] code used to specifiy them. (Detailed training in Database Administration has been excluded from the course as being appropriate only to a limited number of analyst/programmers whose recruitment into DBA typically occurred after some two years of experience in other systems/programming areas.)
(e) Trainees should be thoroughly conversant with all database calls, status codes, command codes and be able to undertake programming projects with minimal assistance from senior programmers.
(f) Trainees should be able to program to access messages from message queues, insert messages to output queues and perform message switches.
(g) Trainees should be able to use generalised message handling and conversational programming packages developed by the company.
(h) Trainees should be able to use structured techniques [5] to design programs.
(i) The investigation and analysis phases of Systems analysis should have been covered and the students should have obtained some experience of documenting a systems investigation.

(j) The trainees should be capable of contributing to the work of a systems team undertaking a data analysis study.
(k) Trainees should become conversant with the standards terminology, packages and operational methods used by the company as early as possible to enable them to become engaged in productive work rapidly.
(l) Trainees should be examined by an outside body to assess their competence to work in a systems department.

4. Course structure and content

It was decided that these requirements could best be met by establishing a course structure based upon taught modules and 'in-house' blocks of practical experience. The required taught modules were established as:-

(a) Data processing and computing principles
(b) COBOL programming and program design
(c) DL/1 calls, and message processing
(d) Data modelling [6]
(e) Systems investigation and analysis
(f) Systems design and implementation

In all these areas the company employed experienced and capable staff who were technically well able to teach the material required for their specialist area but were unable to make available the time to prepare this material to meet the requirements of a training programme. Alternative methods of covering the technical material had been attempted (audio visual etc) but it had been discovered that these were only effective when supported by a tutor.

The timescale allocated for the training period amounted to approximately 18 months although it was anticipated that some productive work would be completed during this period. Table 1 details the timetable of modules and blocks that was established to meet the requirements. The objectives served by each section of the course are indicated by reference to the numbers in the right-hand column.

4.1 Data Processing and Computing Principles

The trainees are drawn from a wide and disparate range of backgrounds and it has proved necessary to preface the programming training course with a general introduction to computing and data processing.

In addition to the substantial intake of graduates drawn from all disciplines a number of trainees have been accepted from the companies existing staff and workforce. Candidates without previous computing experience are introduced to programming using BASIC and receive introductory lectures on hardware, software and data processing.

4.2   Cobol Programming and Program Design

As shown in the table above the initial stages of the course concentrate upon the development of the trainees competence to program in COBOL. A heavy investment in COBOL and IMS currently impedes the direct change to user written 'fourth generation language' systems.

Meeting the objectives of this section of the training has posed a major dilemma which has only partially been resolved. The requirments for the programming content are that participants should become competent COBOL programmers, obtain an understanding of JCL for testing and running programs and be able to write well structured programs.

The introduction of structured techniques using JSP [4] has proved difficult to combine with the need to develop the trainees familiarity with COBOL. In many cases the more rigorous demands of the structuring technique are considered by trainees to over complicate the relatively simple programs used as case studies at this stage in the training. Equally, the teaching time required to develop a reasonable level of competence in the technique seriously reduces the time available for teaching the syntax

Table 1

TAUGHT MODULE	IN-HOUSE BLOCK	DURATION (WEEKS)	OBJECT-IVES
Data Processing		1	(2)
Cobol programming		4	(1,3,8)
	JCL Program testing TSO	4	(1,3,11)
IMS Calls Message processing		3	(4,5,6,7)
Data analysis		1	(10,9)
Systems investigation and Analysis		3	(2,9)
	IMS programming experience	12	(1,3,5) (6,7)
	Systems/data analysis experience	12	(9,10)
Systems design & implementation.		3	(12)

of COBOL. Three different approaches to this aspect of the training have been attempted in the Polytechnic in this and other courses, although each has revealed disadvantages.

- The structuring technique is taught before any programming syntax.
- The technique is taught in parallel with the language.
- The technique is taught when programmers have become reasonably conversant with the language.

The approach which has proved most effective for the training scheme involves a combination of the above. Structuring is introduced at an early stage in the programming course but the students are not required to apply the technique to the initial programming exercises. Initially a 'top down' [7] approach is suggested in combination with the use of flowcharts although JSP structures are provided for exercises.

In this four week period trainees are expected to code and test a suite of batch programs accessing conventional files only. It was decided that although the course is IMS based the combination of database calls, COBOL and the design of programs comprised too large a body of knowledge to present to trainees in one block and that the IMS training should not commence until the participants were fully conversant with COBOL and program testing.

The COBOL course uses the college dual PRIME 850 system and it has been found that the continuous availablity of work stations combined with a rapid turn round on compilations more than compensates for the additional teaching time required to cover differences in the use of the IBM and PRIME COBOL compilers.

4.3 IMS Calls and Message Processing

It is at this stage of the training scheme that the database data communications training is introduced. It was found, by experience, that a lengthy and generalised introduction to the concept of database was confusing to the trainees who had only recently grasped the meaning of file processing. Introducing the database calls using a comparison of an indexed or random file access routine and describing the DL/1 call parameters required to execute a similar data retrieval operation (cf fig 1) has proved to be a more practical than the discussion of the concepts of data independence and shared access. Each call function is introduced separately and a series of call sequence exercises are used to tested the trainees ability to construct the logic required to execute queries and updates of increasing complexity. For the most part exercises are set requiring only function code, segment search arguement and status code answers and trainees are not expected to code complete programs for each query. It has been found to be essential that this aspect of the training be thoroughly understood and for that reason the first week of the module is dedicated to these topics.

The Database description (DBD) and Program Communication Block (PCB) are introduced informally as trainees become more aware of the concepts involved in the use of database. Since it is not the intention of the training scheme to prepare staff for work in database administration the construction and use of logical databases is only briefly covered at the end of the first week. The second phase of the course covers the conversion from batch processing to transaction driven systems. Although considerable emphasis is placed on the nature of programs working in this environment it is noticeable that the most common initial misconception is the assumption that values in working storage remain available to a transaction during conversational processing.

A breakdown of the technical aspects of the message processing knowledge required by the companies programmers revealed an extensive range of factual and conceptual information. Briefly it was felt necessary for the following aspects to be understood:-

- The concept of a 'transaction driven system'
- The concept of a conversation.
- The coding for message reading and inserting.
- The coding for screen formatting.
- The facilities provided by Message Formatting Services. (MFS).
- The use of message switches.
- Synchronisation of the database and the message queue.

Fig. 1

FUNCTION	STORAGE AREA	IO AREA	STATUS CHECK	SEGMENT REQUIRED
READ	filename	FD filename LABEL RECORDS etc 01 Recname.	AT END GO TO	next
GU	PCB-NAME	01 IO-AREA etc	IF PCB-STATUS	SSA
READ	filename	FD filename etc	INVALID KEY	RECORD KEY IS

In addition to the conventional calls for getting and inserting messages to the message queue a requirement existed to explain the operation of two in-company packages produced to standardise the sending and receiving of messages. Conversational programming using scratch pad areas was not favoured by the user in view of the high overhead of disc access time. The Read/Insert package made use of a terminal database to record the steps in a conversation and this concept also required explanation. Two problems have been found to conflict in attempting to cover this aspect of the training scheme. The factual information required to write even a simple DB/DC program in an IMS environment is extensive and imparting this information by lecturing or tutorials overloads the students. Secondly, the concepts embodied in on-line programming require considerable emphasis for the trainees to be able to grasp the fundamental aspects of program design and they can become 'submerged' in the detail of the above factual data.

Currently, the most successful method that has been used to cover this material has been to limit the amount of lecturing used to explain the technical aspects of message processing and to emphasise mainly the concepts mentioned above giving examples of their use in application systems.

The practical details are then covered by splitting the course into small project groups, typically comprising 3 to 4 students per group, and setting a programming case study covering these technical areas.

This case study is used to introduce a wide range of on-line program facilities and although the versions coded by the students rarely progress beyond an initial compilation the specimen version of the case study, supplied at the end of the course, is seen as a more useful reference tool than a set of notes or user manuals.

4.4 Data Analysis Training

The use of data analysis [8] techniques within organisations using both formatted and relational database software appears to have become well established. The technique provides a rigourous method of ensuring the detailed examination of the applications area and enables analysts to express conceptually the structure of the data model required by their system, without prescribing the physical structure implemented and maintained by the database administrators.

The training programme required to familiarise the analysts with the principles of data analysis and allow them to practise the use of these principles modelling data structures found in the business environment they would be likely to encounter. Text book case studies were found to concentrate upon either relatively simple models of customers, orders and stock items or upon models of colleges, hospitals, libraries and other well known institutions. In both cases the semantic of the data was already well known to the participants and the study served only to exemplify the principles of the methodology rather than develop skills in their use within a new and unfamiliar environment.

To develop these skills it was decided to design a case study based upon a live system study which provided the following features:-

- A reasonably limited model (10–15 entities) with few apparent lnks with other models within the organisation. The analysts could then look at the area as a discrete model.
- Entities and attributes which were complexly 'embedded' in the existing system documentation.
- An area which used terminology generally unfamiliar to the trainees.
- Entities and attributes which were frequently encountered in systems studies within the company.

The study chosen considers the structure of a database used to store details of estimates produced as a particular part or subassembley passes through a series of design stages before entering production. The case study is presented with a written and verbal explanation of the application area and the system requirements accompanied with the documentation (figs 2,3,4) currently in use. Working in groups of three or four the analysts are required to supply the following:-

- A conceptual schema [6] showing the entities and their relationships.
- A pseudo relational entity graph removing the many many relationships and showing concatentated keys to indicate access paths.
- Conceptual segments detailing the attributes conforming to TNF requirements belonging to the entities in (2) above.
- Screens suitable for use by functional transactions [9] capable of supporting the application area.
- A 'rationalised' transaction set suitable for prototype demonstrations for users.

The first problem the participants encounter is to establish the significance of a manufactured part and its relationship to a 'scheme'.

Fig. 2

SCHEME IPS9999	ISSUE 1	DESCRIPTION SUMMARY	PRODUCTION ESTIMATE PROFORMA DOCUMENT NUMBER PEP 1290	ITEMS COST CONTROLLED: 1, 2 and 3			
COST TYPE	RAW MATERIAL COST	B.O.F. COST	SUB-CON COST	FACILITY	STANDARD HOURS	TOTAL FACTORY COST	
TARGET COST	3 12990.68	3 .	3	NORTH WORKS	7.00	3 18187.47	
				SOUTH WORKS	2.00		
				WEST WORKS	327.00		
INITIAL ESTIMATE	3 7942.00	3	3	NORTH WORKS	7.00	3 12722.64	
				SOUTH WORKS	2.00		
				WEST WORKS	302.46		
CONFIRMED ESTIMATE	3 3820.00	3	3	NORTH WORKS	8.00	3 14198.64	
				SOUTH WORKS	3.10		
				WEST WORKS	309.96		

REMARKS: DISCS AND RINGS – CHANGE OF MAT. SPEC. OR SUPPLIER.

Fig. 3

				PRODUCTION ESTIMATE PROFORMA			
SCHEME IPS9999	ISSUE 1	DESCRIPTION RING	DOCUMENT NUMBER PEP 1290	FOR COST CONTROLLED ITEM NO. 1	SHEET 1 OF 3		
QUANTITY PER ENGINE 1	RAT CODE ZD						
COST TYPE	RAW MATERIAL COST	B.O.F. COST	SUB-CON COST	FACILITY	STANDARD HOURS	TOTAL FACTORY COST	
TARGET COST	£ 963.72	£	£	NORTH WORKS			
				SOUTH WORKS		£ 1471.56	
				WEST WORKS	26.00		
INITIAL ESTIMATE	£ 442.00	£	£	NORTH WORKS			
				SOUTH WORKS		£ 855.00	
				WEST WORKS	26.00		

REMARKS:

RAW MATERIAL TARGET ALLOCATED BY CHANGING WASPALLOY TO JETHETE. ST. HRS. BASED ON JETHETE MACHINING. SIMILAR TO OUT. DOPE-BURSTING RING. CAN FIT TO Z965-81 IF COAXED WITH HAMMER.

Fig. 4

DESIGN STAGE ESTIMATE SLIP

SCHEME IPS9999	ISSUE 1	ITEM 1	DESIGN STAGE NUMBER 1	DESIGN STAGE REFERENCE IPS9999			
	RAW MATERIAL COST	B.O.F. COST	SUB-CON COST	FACILITY	STANDARD HOURS	TOTAL FACTORY COST	
DESIGN STAGE ESTIMATE	£ 445.00	£	£	NORTH WORKS			
				SOUTH WORKS		£ 857.00	
				WEST WORKS	26.00		
ALTERNATIVE ESTIMATE 1	£ 450.00	£	£	NORTH WORKS			
				SOUTH WORKS		£ 925.00	
				WEST WORKS	30.00		
ALTERNATIVE ESTIMATE 2	£	£	£	NORTH WORKS			
				SOUTH WORKS		£	
				WEST WORKS			
ALTERNATIVE ESTIMATE 3	£	£	£	NORTH WORKS			
				SOUTH WORKS		£	
				WEST WORKS			

REMARKS: *RING SPACER REFERENCE EX WEST WKS PURCHASING DEPARTMENT, F NORTH TEL. 6199/85.*

The 'scheme', being a partial synonym for part, represents the design engineers view of an item to be produced by the company. Viewed from this perspective changes to schemes cause new issues to be produced and each issue itself consists of one or more physical items. Establishing this initial hierarchy, without direct guidance from the case study leader, forms the basis of the study and experience has shown that deriving even a simple sub-model such as this can require 6 to 8 hours study time. The second stage of the analysis requires an understanding of the stages of design which occur before a part is put into production. Briefly, the analyst must recognise that an individual item passes through a series of progressively refined design stages and that estimates are recorded for each stage together with estimates for alternative methods of production.

Finally to complete the entity graph the companies method of production, using a number of manufacturing locations or facilities, must be recognised creating cost data which is recorded by facility for issues of schemes, items within issues and alternative designs for these items at each design stage. The resulting entity graph and the 'normalised' set of relational data groups are shown in figs 5 & 6.

4.5   Systems Analysis Training

The company had for some years used the NCC Basic Systems [10] course as a means of introducing recruits to Systems Analysis and the availability of the written and oral exam provided a means of obtaining an 'outside' measure of the trainees performance. The course content required only slight modification to permit the inclusion of material specific to their method of operation and it was therefore decided to structure the Systems Analysis training in this way. To enable trainees to obtain the necessary systems experience it was decided to cover the systems training in two blocks. Commencing with the analysis and investigation aspects of the course provides a basis for the 'in-house' block when trainees are assigned for three months to systems areas. The second stage of the systems training covering design and implmentation is then undertaken at the end of their training period after they have completed placements in both systems and programmers.

5.   Conclusions

The operation of the course has provided an insight into several different aspects of database/data communications systems not only in connection with the training but also in the use of methodologies.

Fig. 5

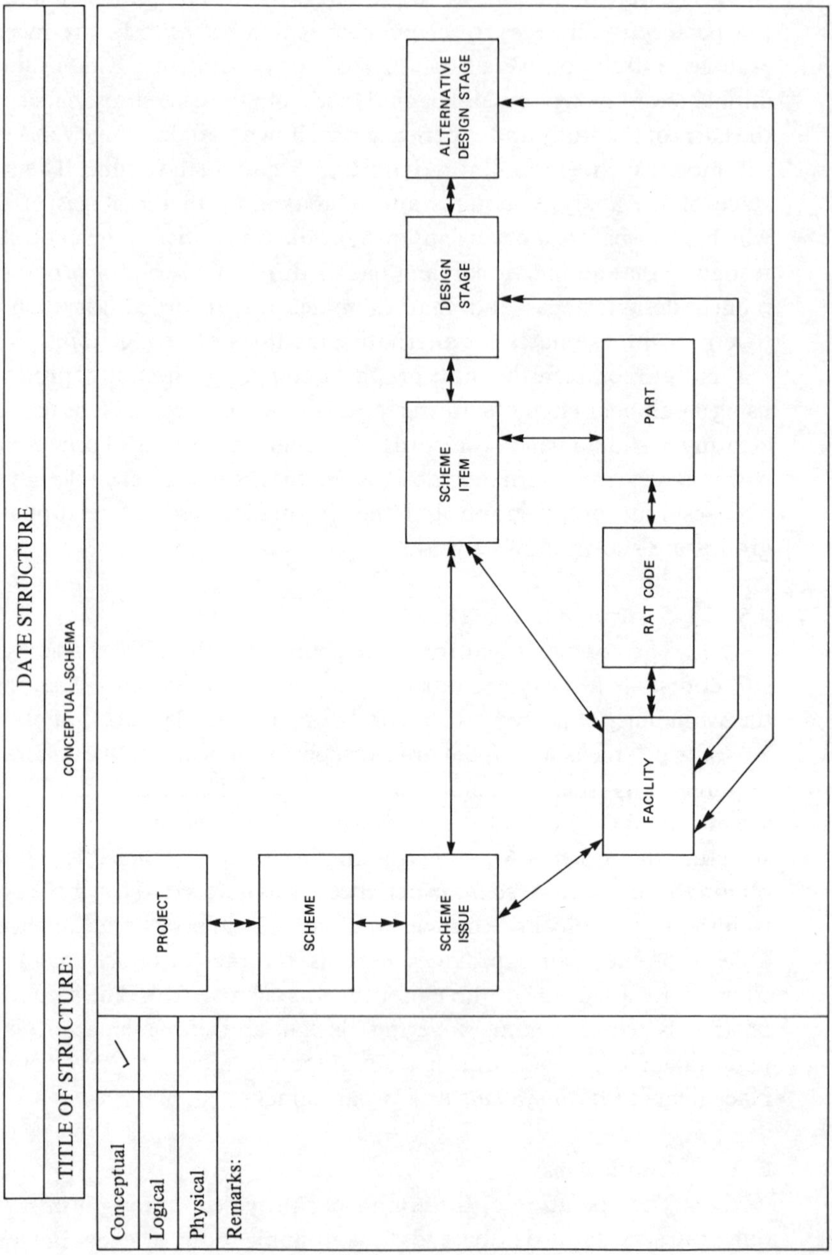

Fig. 6

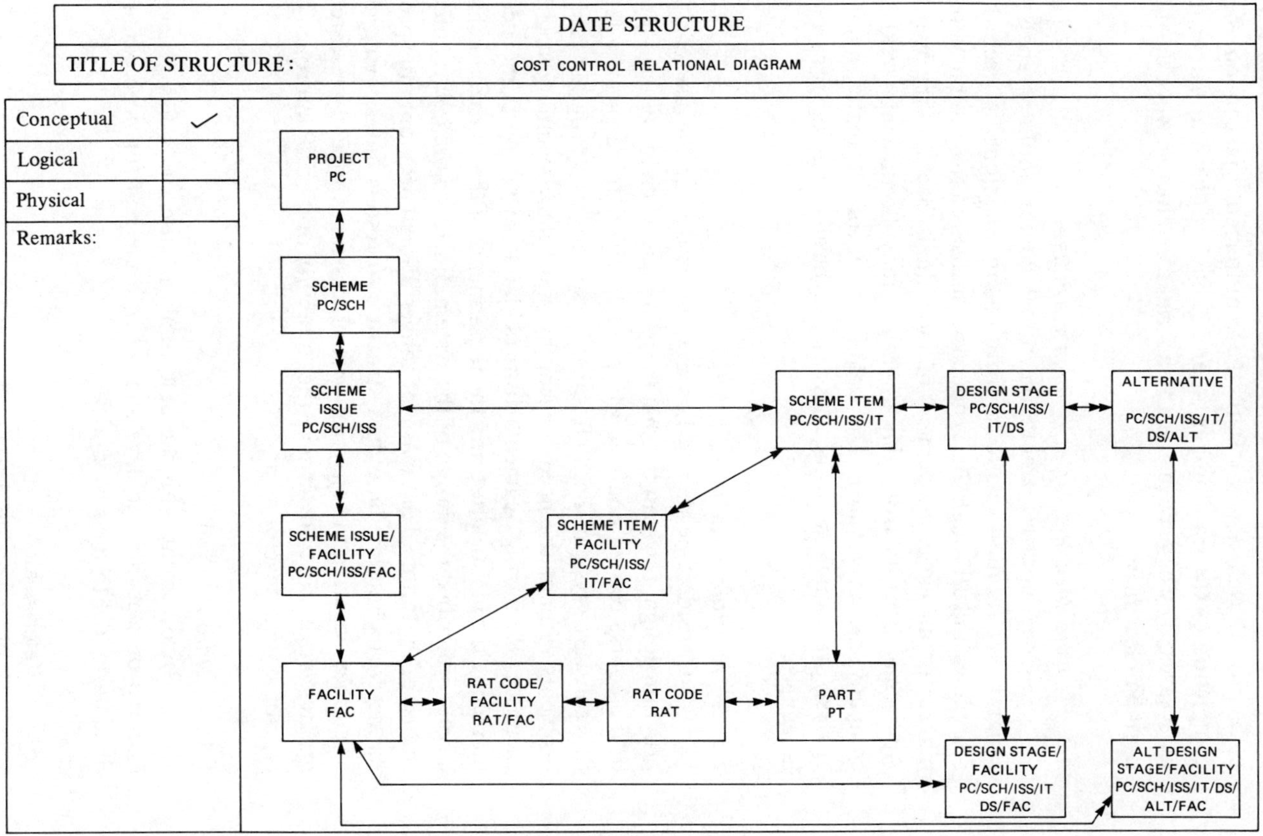

TITLE OF STRUCTURE: DATE STRUCTURE

COST CONTROL RELATIONAL DIAGRAM

Conceptual	✓
Logical	
Physical	
Remarks:	

PROJECT
PC

↔ SCHEME
PC/SCH

↔ SCHEME ISSUE
PC/SCH/ISS

↔ SCHEME ISSUE/ FACILITY
PC/SCH/ISS/FAC

↔ FACILITY
FAC

↕ RAT CODE/ FACILITY
RAT/FAC

↕ RAT CODE
RAT

↕ PART
PT

SCHEME ITEM/ FACILITY
PC/SCH/ISS/IT/FAC

SCHEME ITEM
PC/SCH/ISS/IT

DESIGN STAGE
PC/SCH/ISS/IT/DS

DESIGN STAGE/ FACILITY
PC/SCH/ISS/IT/DS/FAC

ALTERNATIVE
PC/SCH/ISS/IT/DS/ALT

ALT DESIGN STAGE/FACILITY
PC/SCH/ISS/IT/DS/ALT/FAC

5.1 Meeting the defined objectives

In general the scheme has proved successful in that the trainees have proved well able to fulfil the requirements placed on them on completion of the training period and it has also been apparent that, in most cases, they have been able to undertake productive work during their training placements.

5.2 Combined analyst/programmer training.

One objective behind the initial combination of analyst and programmer training was to improve communications between the two disciplines and although this is not easily measured the combined training makes for an easier movement of individuals between the two areas. Additional benefits from this approach may become apparent as the company moves towards the establishment of a greater number of analyst/programmers using less procedurally based programming languages.

5.3 Program Structuring

Considerable debate has been created over the use of JSP for program design. It was noted that the technique when introduced too early in the course caused confusion to most trainees. It was also noted that the software system itself frequently solved the program structure problems without the need for lengthy and time consuming structuring exercises. Retrieving segments from a database removed the need for modelling the file structure and the requirements of the transaction handler largely prescribed the design of the system. Furthermore it was noted that the use of the terminal database for conversational programming provided the necessary intermediate data structure to resolve interleaving clashes when they occurred in conversational processing. Currently research is in progress at Bristol to determine the suitability of the JSP approach to this type of system development.

5.4 Data Analysis

Involvement with the data analysis case study has generated a research project into the development of a method for proceeding from the data model to the system design.

References

[1] I Palmer, Database Systems, CACI, 1975
[2] TME: Using an IDMS Database, ICL, RP1153
[3] IMS/VS Version 2 General Information Manual, IBM

[4] C J Date, An Introduction to Database Systems, Addison-Wesley
[5] M A Jackson, Principles of Program Design, Academic Press
[6] M J Shave, Entities, Functions and Binary Relations: Steps to a Conceptual Schema, The Computer Journal Vol 24 No 1 Feb 1981
[7] M252 Computer and Computing, Open University
[8] D R Howe, Data Analysis for Database Design, Arnold, 1983
[9] A Wakefield, Functional Transaction Prototypes, Bristol Polytechnic Dept CSM, SDR0283